Education, Learning, Training

International Development Policy

Editor-in-Chief

Gilles Carbonnier (*Professor of Development Economics, the Graduate Institute, Geneva*)

Guest Editors

Michel Carton (*Emeritus Professor, the Graduate Institute, Geneva*)
Kenneth King (*Emeritus Professor, University of Edinburgh*)

VOLUME 5

The titles published in this series are listed at *brill.com/idp*

Managing Editor
Marie Thorndahl
Research and Communication Officer
Maren Schulte
Infographics and Figure Layout
y-b design www.ybdigital.com
Copyeditors
Katharine Millar, Dave Brooks, Katharine Mann Jackson
Translation
Randall Jones
Cover Photo
Marie Thorndahl
Visit International Development Policy and associated documents online
http://devpol.org and http://debate.devpol.org

Cover photo by Marie Thorndahl, Université Cheikh Anta Diop de Dakar, Senegal, 2006.

This publication has been typeset in the multilingual "Brill" typeface. With over 5,100 characters covering Latin, IPA, Greek, and Cyrillic, this typeface is especially suitable for use in the humanities. For more information, please see http://www.brill.com/brill-typeface.

ISSN 1663-9383
ISBN 978-90-04-28114-1 (hardback)
ISBN 978-90-04-28115-8 (e-book)

This book is printed on acid-free paper.

FSC
www.fsc.org
MIX
Paper from responsible sources
FSC® C109576

Printed by Printforce, the Netherlands

Education, Learning, Training

Critical Issues for Development

Edited by

Gilles Carbonnier, Michel Carton, and Kenneth King

BRILL
NIJHOFF

LEIDEN | BOSTON

Contents

Foreword

This thematic issue of *International Development Policy* appears amid post-2015, post-Education for All (EFA) debates and a plethora of conferences and research activities on education and development. While researchers and policy-makers seek to take stock of progress and setbacks, there is a revival of the 'learning crisis' discourse as millions of children are failing to learn the basics despite now being in school. Taking a broad view, this special issue draws on scholarly work and lessons learnt over the last four to five decades to unpack major shifts in international education and development policies. It assesses how key academic work and influential policy documents have shaped global discourses and local practices over time. Seeking cross-fertilisation between the fields of education and development studies, several chapters focus on critical issues that have been neglected by researchers, including technical and vocational training as well as adult education and literacy.

Many articles build on research carried out by the Network for International Policies and Cooperation in Education and Training (NORRAG). The Network is composed of researchers and policy-makers from a range of disciplinary and institutional backgrounds. It offers a multi-stakeholder North-South platform for exchange and research on international cooperation in education and training. The Network plays an active role in both education and development studies associations.[1]

This special issue thus reflects some of NORRAG's characteristics: the authors come from multiple constituencies and are involved in North-South research partnerships. Additional contributors have been brought in from outside the Network to address specific issues such as the likely impact of massive online open-access courses in Africa or knowledge and migration. Draft chapters were presented and discussed at an international workshop in Geneva in September 2013. This was followed by intense exchanges between the authors and external reviewers, including an anonymous peer review of the special issue as a whole.

---

1 In development studies, NORRAG has been associated with the European Association of Development Research and Training Institutes (EADI) since 1997 (see http://www.eadi.org/, accessed on 14 May 2014); and in education studies with the United Kingdom Forum on International Education and Training (UKFIET) since its foundation in 1991 (see http://www.norrag.org/, accessed on 14 May 2014).

The book is organised in three sections. The first sets the scene. It analyses the major issues being debated within the scholarly and policy communities in relation to learning, training and development. Bringing diverging views to the fore, the authors highlight issues around which there is contention. The second part critically examines the role and contribution of the state and selected non-state actors in shaping the design of national policies, focusing in particular on vocational education and training as well as lifelong learning with case studies from Latin America, sub-Saharan Africa and Asia. It also considers the potential for innovative evaluation based on a capability approach. The third section looks at higher education in Africa vis-à-vis the rise of China and the rapid expansion of information and communication technologies and of massive open online courses (MOOCs). It further discusses interactions between the globalisation of knowledge and migratory aspirations among West African students.

We decided to examine selected topics in the education-development nexus, considering today's competing forces of globalisation and re-nationalisation. We do not claim to cover all the relevant topics or areas of concern. Many issues obviously deserve further scrutiny, such as the impact of diverging demographic shifts in Africa and elsewhere, gender inequality, and discrimination along ethnic, religious and socio-economic lines. It is our hope that this special issue will provide all interested readers with a timely, broad-ranging and insightful volume on education and learning in the post-2015 context.

Last and not least, we thank the authors, external reviewers, anonymous referees and all the production team for their contributions. A special thank you also to Marie Thorndahl and Maren Schulte for unfailing editorial and organisational support throughout the whole process.

The Editors
Geneva and Edinburgh, May 2014

Preface

International Development Policy is a critical source of analysis of development policy and international cooperation trends and is aimed at scholars, policy-makers, development professionals, and journalists. It offers a diverse range of academic views from both industrialised countries and emerging economies.

International Development Policy is edited by the Graduate Institute of International and Development Studies, an institution of research and higher education dedicated to advancing world affairs. Located in Geneva at the heart of an international centre of multilateral governance, the Graduate Institute benefits from a rich legacy linked not only to the founding of the international system and the League of Nations in the 1920s, but also to the emergence of the developing world in the 1960s.

http://graduateinstitute.ch/publications
http://devpol.org | http://debate.devpol.org

We extend our thanks to the Swiss Agency for Development and Cooperation (SDC) for its financial support.

Schweizerische Eidgenossenschaft
Confédération suisse
Confederazione Svizzera
Confederaziun svizra

List of Figures

List of Tables

Acronyms and Abbreviations

ACCES	Acceso Con Calidad a la Educación Superior (Colombia)
ASER	Annual Status of Education Report (India)
AUF	Agence universitaire de la Francophonie
AVU	African Virtual University
BE2	Building Evidence on Education Group (UKCDS, UK Aid, ESRC, WB, and USAID)
BEN	Bangladesh Early Childhood Development Network
BNFE	Bureau of Non Formal Education
BOB	Bolivian Boliviano (currency)
BRAC	Bangladesh Rural Advancement Committee
BRICS	Brazil–Russia–India–China–South Africa
BSSC	Bolivian System of Skills Certification
CAMPE	Campaign for Popular Education (Bangladesh)
CBO	community-based organisation
CC	Confucius Classroom
CCF	Colleges Collaboration Fund (South Africa)
CEDE	Center for Digital Education at EPFL (Switzerland)
CEFET	Federal Centres of Technological Education (Brazil)
CESE	Comparative Education Society in Europe
CI	Confucius Institute
CIES	Comparative and International Education Society
CLC	community learning centre
CSO	civil society organisation
CSR	corporate social responsibility
CUE	Center for Universal Education
DAC	Development Assistance Committee
DHET	Department of Higher Education and Training (South Africa)
DFID	Department for International Development (UK)
DoE	Department of Education (South Africa)
EADI	European Association of Development Research and Training Institutes
EFA	Education for All
EFA/GMR	Education for All (EFA) / Global Monitoring Report (GMR)
EPFL	Ecole Polytechnique Fédérale de Lausanne (Switzerland)
ESRC	The Economic and Social Research Council
FDI	foreign direct investment
FET	further education and training

FIVDB	Friends in Village Development Bangladesh
FOCAC	Forum on China-Africa Cooperation
FOMO	Servicio Nacional de Formación de Mano de Obra (Bolivia)
FUN	France Université Numérique
GBP	pound sterling (currency)
GCE	Global Campaign for Education
GDP	gross domestic product
GMRs	Global Monitoring Reports
GNP	gross national product
GNRE	National Bureau of Evaporative Resources (Bolivia)
GO	governmental organisation
GOI	government of India
GPE	Global Partnership for Education
GRALE 2	Second Global Report on Adult Learning and Education
HEI	higher education institution
HIPCs	highly indebted poor countries
HRD	human resource development
ICT	information and communication technology
IDS	Institute of Development Studies (Sussex University)
IEA	International Association for the Evaluation of Educational Achievement
IIEP	International Institute of Education Planning
ILO	International Labour Organization
IMF	International Monetary Fund
ISS	International Institute of Social Studies
IT	information technology
ITU	International Telecommunication Union
JICA	Japan International Cooperation Agency (Japan)
KOICA	Korea International Cooperation Agency (South Korea)
LA	Latin America
LLL	lifelong learning
LS	learning society
LSMS	Living Standards Measurement Study
MDGs	Millennium Development Goals
MICS	Multiple Indicator Cluster Survey
MNR	Movimiento Nacionalista Revolucionario (Bolivia)
MOOCs	massive open online courses
MOOPs	massive open online programmes
MPA	Masters in Publication Administration
NCCR	National Centre of Competence in Research (Switzerland)

NEET	not in employment, education, or training
NEM	new economics of migration
NEPAD	New Partnership for Africa's Development
NESAP-ICT	New Economy Skills for Africa Program-Information and Communication Technologies
NFE	non-formal education
NGO	non-governmental organisation
NORRAG	Network for International Policies and Cooperation in Education and Training
ODA	official development assistance
OECD	Organisation for Economic Co-operation and Development
PCAST	President's Council of Advisors on Science and Technology (US)
PFM	People's Forum for MDG (Bangladesh)
PhD	Doctor of Philosophy
PIRLS	Progress in International Reading Literacy Study
PISA	Programme for International Student Assessment
PPP	purchasing power parity
PRSP	Poverty Reduction Strategy Papers
RDRS	Rangpur Dinajpur Rural Services
SABER	Systems Approach for Better Education Results
SBT	skills-based training
SDC	Swiss Agency for Development and Cooperation
SENA	National Apprenticeship Service (Colombia)
SENAC	National Service of Trade Apprenticeship (Brazil)
SENAI	National Service of Industrial Apprenticeship (Brazil)
SENAR	National Service of Rural Apprenticeship (Brazil)
SESD	Support to Education and Skills Development (Danish-funded programme in South Africa)
SINAES	National System for Higher Education Evaluation (Brazil)
SNIS	Swiss Network for International Studies
TICAD	Tokyo International Conference on African Development
TIMMS	Trends in International Mathematics and Science Study
TTE	tertiary technical education
UDAPE	Economic and Social Policy Analysis Unit (Bolivia)
UKCDS	United Kingdom Collaborative on Development Sciences
UKFIET	United Kingdom Forum for International Education and Training
UN	United Nations
UNDP	United Nations Development Programme
UNESCO	United Nations Educational, Scientific and Cultural Organization
UNFPA	United Nations Population Fund

UNICEF	United Nations International Children's Emergency Fund
UNRWA	United Nations Relief and Works Agency for Palestine Refugees in the Near East
UPC	universal primary completion
US	United States of America
USAID	United States Agency for International Development (USA)
USD	United States dollar (currency)
VET	vocational education and training
WB	World Bank
WCEFA	World Conference on Education for All
WTO	World Trade Organization
YFPB	Yacimientos Petroliferos Fiscales Bolivianos (Bolivia)

Notes on Contributors

Patrick Aebischer
has been President of EPFL, Switzerland since 1999. Trained as a doctor and neuroscientist at the universities of Geneva and Fribourg, he was previously Associate Professor of Medical Sciences at Brown University, USA.

Manzoor Ahmed
is Senior Adviser, BRAC University Institute of Educational Development, Dhaka, Bangladesh, and Chair, Bangladesh Early Childhood Development Network. Previously, he was Convenor of Education Watch Bangladesh. He has held senior positions with UNICEF and written extensively on education and development.

Fritz Brugger
holds a PhD in Development Studies from the Graduate Institute, Geneva where he carries out research into natural resources governance and CSR. Prior to returning to academia, he worked in international development cooperation in NGOs, bilateral and multilateral agencies, and business.

Nicholas Burnett
holds a PhD in Economy from the Johns Hopkins University. He is Managing Director at the Results for Development Institute (R4D) in Washington D.C. He was formerly UNESCO Assistant Director General for Education, Director of the Education for All Global Monitoring Report and a World Bank staff member and manager.

Gilles Carbonnier
is Professor of Development Economics at the Graduate Institute, Geneva; Editor-in-Chief, *International Development Policy*; and President, Centre for Education and Research in Humanitarian Action. His research focuses on international development cooperation, energy and extractive resources governance, and humanitarianism, conflict, and disaster.

Michel Carton
is Emeritus Professor at the Graduate Institute, Geneva. He holds a PhD in Education from Geneva University. He is currently Executive Director of NORRAG where his research focuses on skills development policies in

Western/Southern Africa and South East Asia. He was Deputy Director of the Graduate Institute until retiring in 2010.

Alexandra Draxler
is an education expert and consultant. Previously, she was Executive Secretary of the 'Delors Commission'. She has written widely about technology in education and development strategies, and is Associate Editor of the *International Journal of Educational Development.*

Denise Efionayi
is Deputy Director of the Swiss Forum for Migration and Population Studies at the University of Neuchâtel and is attached to the National Centre of Competence in Research (NCCR) On the Move.

Gérard Escher
is Senior Adviser at EPFL. He holds a PhD in Neuroscience from Lausanne University. Previously, he was a postdoctoral fellow at Stanford University, USA. Subsequently, he was a scientific adviser and Assistant Director to the Swiss Secretary of State for Education and Research.

Ana García de Fanelli
holds degrees in Economics from the Universidad de Buenos Aires and the Facultad Latinoamericana de Ciencias Sociales. She is a researcher at CEDES, Buenos Aires, Argentina. Previously she was a consultant for IIEP in Buenos Aires and Paris, the ILO, and CINDA.

Claudia Jacinto
has a PhD in Sociology from the University of Paris III. Currently, she is Lead Researcher at CONICET in Argentina and Project Coordinator at the Instituto de Desarrollo Económico y Social, Centro de Investigaciones Sociales. Previously, she was Regional Coordinator of the IIEP RedEtis project.

Kenneth King
is Emeritus Professor at the School of Education and the School of Social and Political Studies, University of Edinburgh. His research interests focus on the politics and history of international education, skills development, aid policy, and most recently Chinese education assistance to Africa.

Kathlen Lizárraga Zamora
has a PhD in Economics from the University of Münster, Germany. Currently she works for UNDP and is Visiting Professor at INESAD, Bolivia where she has acted as a consultant for a joint Ministry of Education—Inter-American Development Bank study on education.

Simon McGrath
is Professor of International Education and Development at the School of Education, University of Nottingham. Previously, he was Director for Human Resources Development Research at the Human Sciences Research Council of South Africa. He is co-author of UNESCO's 2014 World Report on Technical and Vocational Education and Training.

Dimitrios Noukakis
has a PhD in Chemistry from Fribourg University. Currently, he is at EPFL where he promotes inter-institutional collaboration for education in French-speaking Africa through novel e-learning platforms, such as MOOCs. Previously, he held research positions at Kodak, USA, and the Catholic University at Leuven, Belgium.

Etienne Piguet
is Professor of Mobility Geography at the University of Neuchâtel. He is Chair of the Population Geography Commission of the International Geographical Union (IGU) and Vice Chair of the Swiss Federal Commission on Migration (FCM).

Lesley Powell
is a research associate at the School of Education, University of Nottingham. Previously, she worked as a policy researcher in South Africa on further education and training and higher education, and served as Research Manager of the College Collaboration Fund.

PART 1

Education Policies and Development: Issues in the Debate

CHAPTER 1

International Education and Development: Histories, Parallels, Crossroads

Gilles Carbonnier, Michel Carton, and Kenneth King

Abstract

Education has been a priority sector when considering foreign aid allocation since the 1970s. The stated objective has been to ensure universal access to basic education, with a more recent emphasis on quality and outcomes. Aware that these goals will not be met universally, the major actors involved in the post-2015 debate are turning back to the concept of learning. In this chapter, we briefly review major scholarly work and strategic papers that have shaped the discourse and policies of international development organisations and national actors over the past four decades. We discuss how the central notions of skills, learning, and both formal and non-formal education have evolved in conjunction with ideological shifts. We examine the tensions between public and private education as well as between individualised and standardised delivery modes. We further look at (big) data and online education promises. To conclude, we question the current focus of major stakeholders on post-2015, post-EFA agendas. As several articles in this special issue underscore, national policies and local practices are largely driven by persistent political economy dynamics while the influence of 'the global agenda' tends to remain confined to the international cooperation community itself.

Authors' Note

In this chapter, the term 'education' is understood in the broader sense of education and training.

1 Introduction

The donor community has expressed a consistent concern for education since the establishment of the Development Assistance Committee of the

 | DOI 10.1163/9789004281158_002

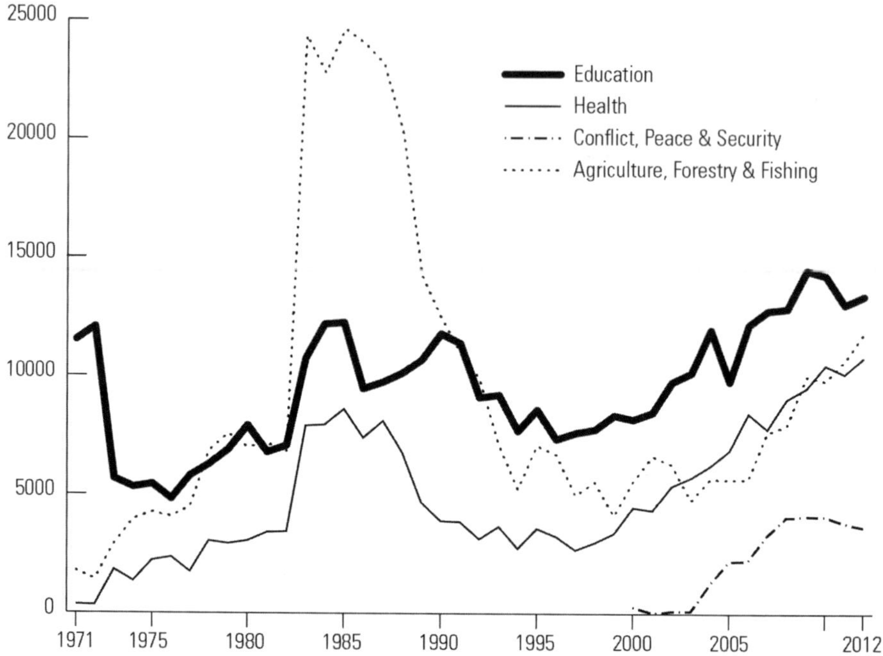

FIGURE 1.1 *Official development assistance, all DAC donors, for a selection of sectors (1971–2012—in million USD constant, 2011).*
SOURCE: OECD–DAC, CRS DATABASE (2014).

Organization for Economic Cooperation and Development (OECD/DAC) some fifty years ago. As a sector, education has received one of the highest share of official development assistance over the past four decades. It received a larger share than health, 'conflict, peace and security', and, in most years, than agriculture as well (see Figure 1.1). Interestingly, this is not the case for private development assistance: a recent study by the Brookings Institution highlights the fact that corporate giving to global health is sixteen times higher than its support to education (Winthrop et al., 2013).

The major bilateral donors in the education sector have been Germany, France, and the United Kingdom, followed by Japan and the United States. Among multilateral agencies, the largest donors include the Bretton Woods Institutions, the European Union, and the United Nations Relief and Works Agency for Palestine Refugees in the Near East (UNRWA) given its special mandate in support of Palestinian refugees (see Figure 1.2).

Despite this apparent priority given to education, the 2015 targets and goals for education respectively set, following 2000, in the Millennium Development Goals (MDGs) and the Education for All (EFA) World Forum, will not be met

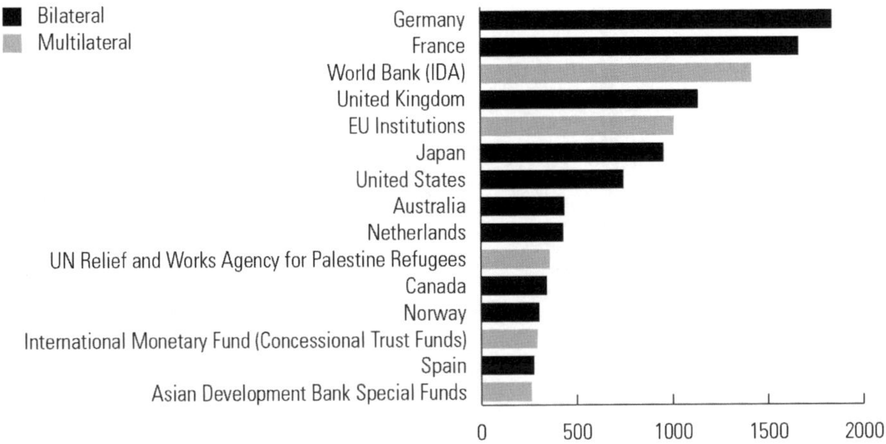

FIGURE 1.2 *Top bilateral and multilateral aid donors to education, 2011* (*in million USD*).
SOURCE: OECD–DAC, CRS DATABASE (2013).

(UNESCO, 2014). Many children, therefore, still do not enjoy access to free and compulsory primary education, an objective that was already established in the UN Declaration of Human Rights in December 1948.[1] In several countries, adult illiteracy remains far too high. Achieving these basic education goals will require much greater commitment, including increased budgetary means and more qualified teachers.

The provision of private education and vocational training has been on the rise. Several initiatives aim at strengthening public-private partnerships in the education sector, not least the UN Secretary General's Global Education First Initiative. A campaign entitled Business Backs Education—launched in partnership with UNESCO and the Global Business Coalition for Education—challenges the private sector to allocate 20 per cent of its philanthropic giving to education initiatives by 2020 with a focus on countries and groups most in need.[2] Yet, the precise role and remit of states versus those of non-state actors in the education sector remain a major bone of contention within academic and policy circles (Macpherson et al., 2014).

In relative terms, total public expenditure on education averages between 3.4 and 6 per cent of gross domestic product when looking at different regions

1 Art. 26 Universal Declaration of Human Rights, http://www.un.org/en/documents/udhr/index.shtml#a26 (accessed on 14 May 2014).

2 Global Education & Skills Forum (15–17 March 2014, Dubai), *Press release: 20.20.20 Business Backs Education*, https://educationandskillsforum.org/press-release-20-20-20-business-backs-education/#.U0ueAMeoURg (accessed on 14 April 2014).

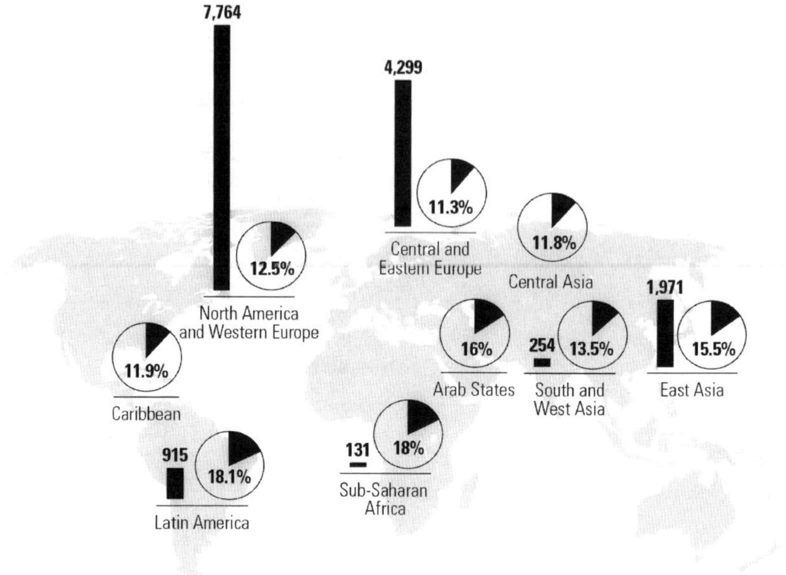

FIGURE 1.3 *Public expenditure on education and money spent per pupil, 2011 (in percentage of total public expenditures and in USD).*
Note: Total public expenditure on education as a percentage of total government expenditure and public expenditure on primary education per pupil (unit cost) at purchasing power parity (PPP) in constant 2010 USD.
SOURCE: UNESCO, STATISTICAL TABLES, *EDUCATION FOR ALL GLOBAL MONITORING REPORT*, 2013/2014.

around the globe (Figure 1.3). In absolute terms, the amount of money allocated per child in primary school varies enormously from one region to another, and school life expectancy rates[3] remain much lower in Africa compared to other regions (Figure 1.4). Poverty and inequality have a dire impact on educational attainments.

Against this background, this chapter connects two parallel histories: that of international education and that of development. These two fields have often evolved in separate silos. But those of us who have sought to contribute to both fields believe in the value of cross-fertilisation. We discuss how the meaning of key concepts in the education world has evolved, and we review the persistent tension between two opposing but complementary visions of education. We highlight parallels between policy debates raging in the 1960–80s and contemporary post-2015 discussions revolving around data, evidence, impact, and

3 Measure of how many years of education a child would receive during a life time if the school enrolment rates stay the same as today.

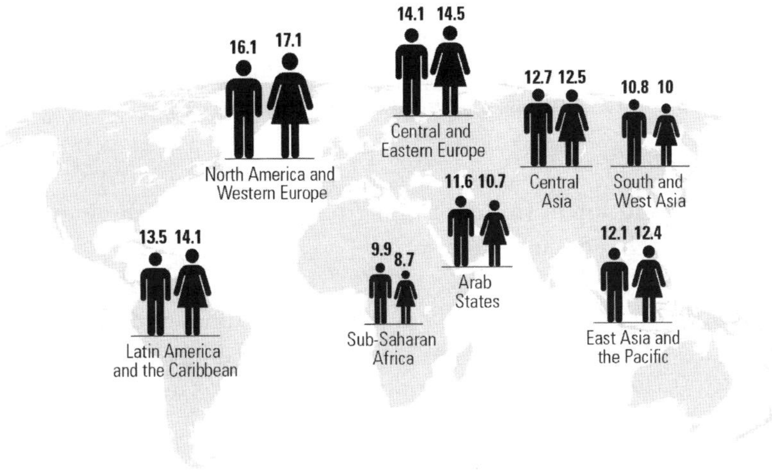

FIGURE 1.4 *School life expectancy (school year ending 2011).*
Note: Expected number of years of formal schooling from primary to tertiary education; school year ending 2011.
SOURCE: UNESCO, STATISTICAL TABLES, *EDUCATION FOR ALL GLOBAL MONITORING REPORT*, 2013/2014.

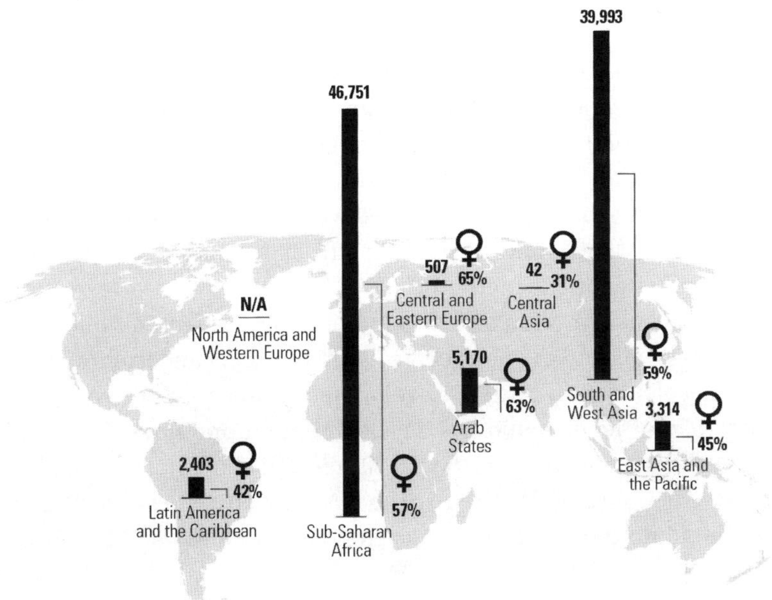

FIGURE 1.5 *Youth illiteracy (projections 2015).*
Note: Youth (15–24 years) illiterates, in thousands, and proportion of girls (projections 2015).
SOURCE: UNESCO, STATISTICAL TABLES, *EDUCATION FOR ALL GLOBAL MONITORING REPORT*, 2013/2014.

value for money. To conclude, we argue that addressing the needs of the 1.25 billion youths and adults excluded from education requires much more than mere adaptation in education discourse and grand strategies.

2 Co-Evolution of International Education and Development: Research, Policies, Buzzwords

The expansion of both international education studies and of development studies dates back to the 1950s. The Comparative and International Education Society (CIES) was founded in the United States in 1956 with the aim to 'foster cross-cultural understanding and societal development through the international and multidisciplinary study of educational ideas, systems, and practices'. The Comparative Education Society of Europe (CESE) was established five years later in London. Interestingly, the very title of those two organisations includes *comparative education*, a discipline that had developed in parts of Europe in the 19th century already (see Jullien de Paris, 1817) following the rise of nation states. Education systems were confined within national borders with a recurrent debate between proponents of universalism versus those of particularism.

As of the 1960s and 1970s, the focus of international education studies was extended beyond its Western origins to developing countries, based on an enhanced theoretical corpus embedded in comparative studies addressing cross-cultural settings in general, and developing countries in particular. In the Cold War's aftermath, this intensified with the extension of cross-national comparisons of school systems and learning achievements, and the comparative study of assessment methods.[4] This, in turn, gave rise to regional and international rankings often based on implicit value judgments about national education systems and the politico-economic systems underpinning them.

In the decolonisation context, development studies emerged as an interdisciplinary field of its own and has developed in Europe since the early 1950s. The International Institute of Social Studies (ISS) was established in 1952 in The Hague, followed by the African Institute in Geneva in 1961 (rapidly transformed into the Institute for Development Studies), and the Institute of

4 The International Association for the Evaluation of Educational Achievement (IEA), however, goes back to the late 1950s, and its first twelve-country study was carried out in 1960. This was followed by the First International Mathematics Study in 1963–67 (see http://www.iea.nl/brief_history.html, accessed on 15 April 2014).

Development Studies (IDS) at Sussex University five years later. There were very few counterpart organisations in the US.

From the outset in the 1950s and 1960s, there have been tensions between rights-based and market-based approaches, or between (neo-)liberal policies and state-driven interventions. As Draxler and Burnett discuss in the next two chapters respectively, there has long been a vivid debate between the proponents of a rights-based vision of education as a public good and the proponents of an instrumental approach whereby education should above all be geared towards responding to labour market demand and contributing to economic development. Education buzzwords have echoed the dominant development discourse over the past five decades. The focus on modernisation and economic growth in development theories has been paralleled by an emphasis on human capital accumulation; basic needs by basic formal and non-formal education; market liberalisation by private funding of post-basic education and vocational training; endogenous development by community education; structural adjustment by public divestment from higher education; the knowledge economy by science and technology education; inclusive and equitable growth by education and training for the marginalised.

More recently, the notion of capabilities has gained much traction. In an attempt to strengthen the interplay between education and human development, Sen proposed that educators, like 'developers', seek to conceive of new policies and tools that no longer take economic growth and human capital as sole references. In this issue, McGrath and Powell explore the value of the capability approach when it comes to the evaluation of vocational education and training, with a case study on South Africa. The authors suggest that the capability approach offers a critical conduit for emphasising what individuals and institutions value and seek to achieve when evaluating programmes, while it also allows economic objectives to be retained in the equation and for the role of evaluation in improving delivery and achievements.

3 Forty Years Later: Have We Come Full Circle?

In parallel to the buzzwords cited above, the meanings of key concepts have kept evolving over the past forty years, be it 'learning', 'non-formal education and training', or 'skills'. The discussion regarding learning has not progressed much, as reflected in the post-2015 literature's claims that there is now a 'learning crisis'. This is in spite of the existence of repeated declarations and action frameworks on Education for All (EFA) and on learning needs since the World Conference on Education for All in Jomtien, Thailand, in March

1990 (WCEFA, 1990; King and Palmer, 2013). The fact that 'learning for all' has recently appeared in bilateral and multilateral agencies' key strategy papers on education actually bears witness to the actual lack of effective learning or to very poor learning outcomes.[5] That is why the 2020 education strategy of the World Bank has been entitled *Learning for All* rather than *Education for All*, putting the emphasis back on educational quality and achievement (World Bank, 2011).

But, at the same time, lifelong learning—a concept dating back to the 1970s that addresses all ages via different institutions and modalities—is now more narrowly understood as learning primarily in the school sphere. Very little attention is being paid to the 1.25 billion young people and adults who have received little or no schooling or training whatsoever and remain outside the formal labour market. In this issue, Ahmed looks at precisely this point by questioning the very notions of lifelong learning and learning societies and exploring to what extent community-learning centres can serve as institutions for adult and lifelong learning, contrasting the case of Bangladesh with those of China and India. The rediscovery of 'learning' can be seen as a narrowing of focus from the world of 'education' as a holistic and social process as well as institution, to a preoccupation with what 'learning' has contributed to individual achievement at the end of the educational process.

The discovery in the early 1970s, by the research and policy communities, of existing informal and non-formal learning (which became almost anti-school in some ways) paralleled the excitement regarding the 'discovery' of the informal economic sector by Hart in Ghana in 1971, and its widespread dissemination by the World Employment Programme's mission reports of the International Labour Organization (ILO) in Sri Lanka (ILO, 1971) and Kenya (ILO, 1972). In both schooling and employment, we witnessed in the 1970s something of a retreat from the formal sectors towards a focus on basic learning and basic work (rather than salaried jobs). In contrast, the post-2015 discourse now emphasises quality in primary and lower secondary education along with decent employment.

The literature on non-formal education (NFE), a term that encompassed the diversity of structured learning outside the formal school, proliferated rapidly in the 1970s, and included the World Bank's seminal *Education Sector Working Paper* (World Bank, 1974). The plot of the academic discourse was written in

5 See DFID's *Learning For All* (DFID, 2010) and *Education Position Paper: Improving Learning, Expanding Opportunities* (DFID, 2013); USAID's *Opportunity Through Learning* (USAID, 2011); and the World Bank's *Learning For All* (World Bank, 2011).

the North while its object was the South, just like post-2015 proposals today. In the end, it did not materially alter or improve the status and position of adult, non-formal or community education in the South.

The discovery of a whole world of non-formal and informal learning beyond the confines of the formal school system took place just at the moment Illich published *Deschooling Society* (1971) and Reimer's *School is Dead* (1971). Such explorations of different alternatives to the framing of the formal school with its examination rituals were soon reinforced by Dore's writings about *The Diploma Disease* (1976). Arguably, China's Cultural Revolution, removing university entrance examinations, had encouraged some of these trends. But they were also present in the ILO World Employment Programme's mission reports mentioned above. The latter even talked about examinations being the 'root cause of the disease affecting the present functioning of the schools' (ILO, 1972, 244). It is interesting to reflect on the way that the 1970s saw the role of examinations questioned, while the post-2015 discussions regarding access versus quality have actually put assessment, learning outcomes, and examinations right back into the centre of the education agenda, reflecting a strong desire to favour evidence-driven policies based on simple, measurable indicators.

A similar case could be made for 'skills', a term associated over the last 50 years with changing assumptions about development and the role of technology. Vocational schools and training systems were borrowed from industrialised countries on the assumption that they could play a fundamental role in the modernisation of developing countries. This may have worked out successfully in a number of East and South East Asian as well as in some Latin American countries, in association with compulsory primary and secondary education and in conjunction with industrialisation policies. But in many other countries the conditions for successful 'modern' skills development were simply not present. Echoing the discovery of the informal sector by the ILO in the early 1970s, traditional apprenticeships and on-the-job training were considered alternative, complementary means for providing minimum vocational skills to apparently unemployed young people in Sub-Saharan Africa (see Carton, 1980). Forty years down the line, youth unemployment ranks even higher as a priority and the emphasis has shifted from a supply-driven, institution-based approach to skills delivery towards a demand-driven approach in tune with job market requirements.

In this issue, the chapter by Brugger and Lizzaraga calls for caution regarding such an approach. The authors show how, in the case of Bolivia—a mineral-dependent developing country—the mining sector consistently favoured the production of an unskilled, cheap labour force, which did not contribute to anticipating demand for higher skills and led to a relative neglect of vocational training. Private education and so-called demand-driven skills programmes are far from offering an adequate substitute to a proper public vocational training system. Jacinto and de Farelli also examine tertiary technical education, but with case studies on Brazil, Colombia, and Mexico. Their comparative research underscores the importance of perceptions, prestige, and employer behaviour, which vary greatly from one country to another as a result of specific institutional and policy environment factors.

4 Finding a Balance between Human Rights and Instrumental Approaches?

During the whole period under review, the design of education, training, and development policies has fluctuated with the evolving positions of individual states, the international aid community, business, and civil society. Oversimplifying, education has been envisaged along a continuum ranging from a human right to be enjoyed by everyone irrespective of the cost and the return on investment on one extreme, to a tool aimed at responding to market demand in support of economic growth on the other extreme. Likewise for the development continuum, education would serve economic growth as the sole objective pursed at one extreme or pursue the sole advancement of the social dimension of human development at the other.

The reality, of course, lies somewhere between those extremes. This is reflected in the different approaches of UNESCO, ILO and the World Bank in this respect: while UNESCO envisages a model based on the nation-state in which education is promoted and protected as a human right, the ILO position is shaped by its tripartite governance. The World Bank tends to look at every public policy area with a prime concern for economic return on investment (see Figure 1.6). In the post-2015 context, the pendulum seems to swing towards an instrumental approach to education and a highly productivist vision of vocational training. This reflects the preferences of a majority of the public and private actors that are setting the new educational norms, starting with the OECD and the World Bank. Young people themselves tend to pay increased attention to skills for life and for work, with a greater appetite for short-term vocational courses tailored to fit shifting demand on job markets.

Despite a global post-2015 discourse geared towards education in general (including the right to education), the Education for All movement—spearheaded for the past fourteen years mainly by UNESCO—suffers from low

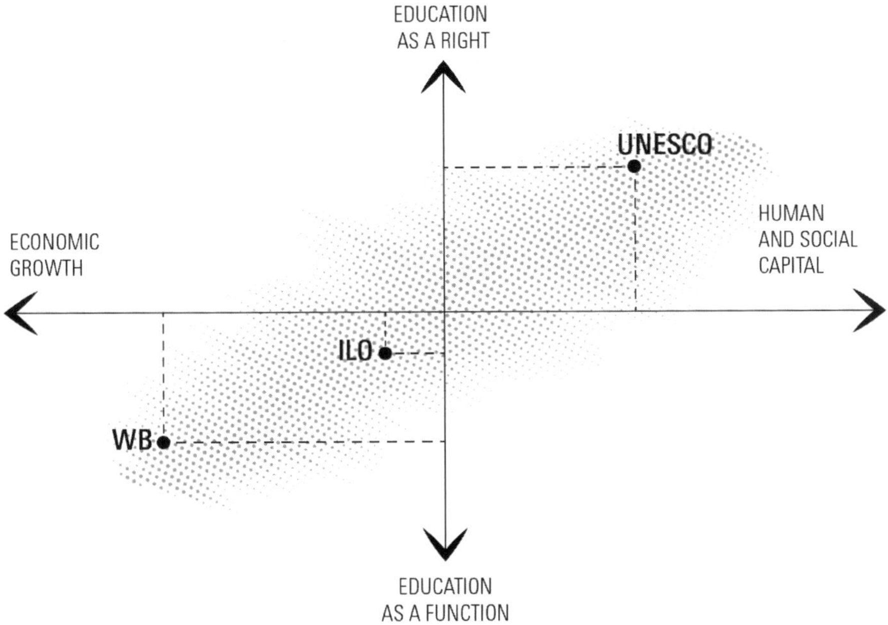

FIGURE 1.6 *The education and development continuums.*
SOURCE: AUTHORS.

visibility. In parallel, the Global Partnership for Education (GPE),[6] a successor to the Fast Track Initiative, is developing vigorously, as is UNICEF influence in the education field. This reflects the rise of what is called the global governance of education involving a variety of international public and private stakeholders. This movement started in the mid-1990s with OECD recommendations insisting on consensus building, peer review and pressure (Vinokur, 2005). In spite of being much less influential than the GPE and the OECD, the Global Campaign for Education, an international civil society global education lobby group now based in South Africa,[7] has contributed to making education more present than would otherwise be expected in the post-2015 debates,

6 The GPE develops education strategies and programmes, shares innovative solutions, finances EFA, and monitors educational results. It covers primary and secondary schooling. The partners are representatives of governments, donors, international organisations, civil society organisations/NGOs, and the private sector. The GPE is present in 60 developing countries. It has mobilised USD 3.6 billion during the last ten years.

7 http://www.campaignforeducation.org/en/ (accessed on 29 March 2014).

while their national affiliates have seized the opportunity to push education further up regional and national political agendas.

5 Standardisation vs. Individualisation

Approaches to education tend to be ever more tailored in response to individual demand rather than institutional supply, whether public or private. This shift can be attributed to the poor performance of education access policies and the low quality of basic learning outcomes in many school systems (see UNESCO, 2014). Criticism of the formal school is not new, and its portrayal as a Taylorist education industry dates back a few decades (e.g. Illich, 1971). Forty years later, such criticism originates as much from the business sphere that encourages information and communication technology (ICT) as from education NGOs' leaders in the South (e.g. BRAC founder, Hazlan Abed)[8] who tend to favour an education system guided primarily by civil society. If these two actors differ in the responses they advance, they both criticise the supply-driven approach of today's schools that does not address the individual learning requirements and creativity of pupils (see also Ahmed in this issue).

There is a tension between this call for individualisation and a strong movement towards universal outcome measurement systems such as the Learning Metrics (LMTF, 2013a; 2013b). This proposes some universal basic and soft skills for young people up to 18 years of age, or other learning outcomes measurement through international rankings supposed to reflect differentials in learning quality across countries (e.g. PISA/OECD). Individualisation and standardisation are simultaneously at work following a technocratic and apolitical trend, which some education experts and policymakers deem unhelpful to efforts to increase learning quality and better use of acquired skills.

6 Public-Private Education: An Adequate Mix?

The role of non-state actors in education differs widely for level of education, country, and tradition. The rise of private education has drawn a lot of attention with regard to so-called low-cost private schools, in particular in

8 The Bangladesh Rural Advancement Committee (BRAC) is the largest NGO in the country (and in the world) and is heavily involved in different types of education and training activities.

South Asia and parts of Sub-Saharan Africa (Macpherson et al., 2014; Burnett, Chapter 2 in this issue). In developing Asia, students attending public primary and secondary schools routinely use private, 'shadow' schooling systems after formal school hours and at weekends (Bray, 2007). This causes anxieties in the post-2015 context since many of the goals being advanced by UN agencies, civil society organisations, and think tanks emphasise the crucial responsibility of the state in providing quality basic education for all. Yet the central role of the state in educational provision is far from universal, particularly in the field of early childhood education. And in the world of skills development, there is a remarkable diversity of providers as examined in depth in several articles in the second part of this special issue, focusing on the role of diverse stakeholders in shaping education and development policies. Furthermore, some of the most admired systems of vocational training involve strong public-private partnerships where employers work with dedicated, publicly provided training schools as well as with workforce representatives. Equally, the massive systems of so-called traditional apprenticeships are essentially operating within the micro, small, and medium-sized private enterprise sector, in both rural and urban areas.

There has been concern about the commodification and liberalisation of higher education and technical training in the context of the World Trade Organization (WTO) General Agreement on Trade in Services; a phenomenon again facilitated by the development of ICTs and the individualisation of educational processes (Verger and Robertson, 2012). This is illustrated, for example, by the rapid development of franchised, private, professional training institutions and programmes (including e-learning) in the South. Such training tends to place greater emphasis on the employability and short-term productivity of individuals than on the role of training for the social integration of both individuals and marginalised groups.

Another dimension of the increasing role of non-state actors is that, while NGOs were invited to the 1990 Jomtien World Conference on Education for All as members of national delegations for the first time, the post-2015 debates see many of the well-known international NGOs promoting their own position papers. The same is true of European and North American think tanks (King and Palmer, 2013). The Brookings Institution's Center for Universal Education has for instance partnered with the UNESCO Institute of Statistics to develop a whole framework for thinking about education post-2015 including associated metrics and indicators (LMTF, 2013a; 2013b). The involvement of NGOs in post-2015 discussions may arguably be directly related to their perception that the final shape of the post-2015 agenda will have implications for their own future funding opportunities.

7 The ICT and (Big) Data Revolutions: More Access and Quality for All?

The dizzying acceleration of ICT diffusion for independent learning, a cause and consequence of the cross-border nature of education systems and of the 'services' they offer on the market, has led to increased mobility of individuals, businesses, and resources.

A prime example of this is the emergence of MOOCs (massive open online courses), which are 'massive' in the sense that they are primarily available to a potentially huge number of individual consumers who possess the necessary hardware and decide to take a course online; this is very different from the earlier 'mass' literacy campaigns of the 1960s that sought widespread social and individual impact that continues to be felt today in countries such as Cuba and Vietnam. Debates are going on in the Global South as MOOCs can be viewed as a game changer for the younger generation or can be resented as a new form of technological and cultural dependency (for the case of Sri Lanka see Liyanagunawardena et al., 2013).

The article by Escher, Noukakis, and Aebischer (Chapter 10 in this issue) provides an original account of ongoing endeavours to establish partnerships between a technological institute of higher education in the North and partners in developing countries in general, and in francophone Africa in particular. The authors note that MOOCs have taken the world of higher education by storm with the spread of tablets and smartphones, of Internet broadband penetration, and the new generation of digital natives that sees millions of students following MOOCs. This offers novel insights into the vast potential opportunities and the specific obstacles associated with North–South partnerships aimed at the delivery of MOOCs.

In tertiary education, the use of 'big data' generated by the diffusion of virtual learning platforms allows the prediction of students' learning problems by producing algorithms similar to those used by Internet providers to anticipate 'customer needs'.[9] In the USA, some people have contrasted the high change potential of big data with MOOCs: big data, not MOOCs, 'will give institutions the predictive tools they need to improve learning outcomes for individual students' (Guthrie, 2013). These two examples show that it is worth considering to what extent a partially free distribution of knowledge and information can

9 See Ferrera (2013); Van Rijmenam (2013); Warner (2013); Fletcher (2013); and Tim Harford—'Big data: are we making a big mistake?' *FT Magazine*, 28 March 2014, http://www.ft.com/cms/s/2/21a6e7d8-b479-11e3-a09a-00144feabdc0.html#axzz2yqiSuUha (accessed on 14 April 2014) for some opposing views about big data in the US.

compensate for a lack of sufficient investment in educational institutions in the South. The ICT revolution raises numerous questions regarding the future role of education policies and institutions and the role of teachers themselves (see UNESCO, 2014; devoted to Teaching and Learning), while it opens up new strands on learning theories alongside progress in neurosciences (see Piety, 2013).

8 From Discourse to Data and Evidence in International Cooperation: By Who and for Whom?

Examining the evolution of international development cooperation, and aid policies and practices in particular, provides another perspective on formal and non-formal education and vocational training. In the annex at the end of the chapter, we provide a timeline listing the major milestones in international educational research and training over the past five decades bearing witness to the production by the international aid community of many of the elements of discourse that have become common parlance in the post-2015 debates. The inter-agency commission involving UNICEF, the World Bank, UNESCO, and the United Nations Development Programme (UNDP) was behind the Education for All (EFA) and Meeting Basic Learning Needs discourses that emerged from the Jomtien World Conference on Education for All in 1990. The same inter-agency group convened the World Forum on Education for All in Dakar in April 2000, from which the six Dakar EFA Goals emerged. Meanwhile the OECD/DAC produced international development targets in 1996 (OECD–DAC, 1996), which soon turned into the Millennium Development Goals. The same actors maintain the lead in framing the post-2015 agenda. In fact, many of the 88 so-called 'national' consultations on post-2015 have actually been led or facilitated by the UNDP.

What has changed is a growing concern for evidence-based policy, encouraged by the rapid dissemination of scientific experimental methods for evaluating the impact of education policies and aid programmes (Banerjee and Duflo, 2011), ranging all the way from the big question of whether education policy should be supply- or demand-driven to the impact of specific conditional cash transfer programmes. It is also arguably the search for evidence of the impact of EFA goals and of the MDGs that has put learning outcomes back onto the agenda of the post-2015 goals and targets (King and Palmer, 2013). This is reflected in the very detailed reporting of the aid-supported EFA *Global Monitoring Reports*, as well as the *Results for Learning Reports* of the Global Partnership for Education (GPE). The requirement for evidence-based policy has spread widely and rapidly, and in some countries even independently of aid. In many developing countries, much of the evaluation work is now mundane and routinised with regular examination of enrolments, completions, and dropouts, and students' transition into the job market, including into formal or informal work. But there are other approaches (Powell and McGrath, Chapter 7 in this issue).

Yet a number of more demanding questions remain unanswered. We do not know enough about the hundreds of millions of adult illiterates nor about the 250 million young people who are either un-schooled or de-schooled. This requires urgent attention. Education systems, and universities in particular, in many developing countries have suffered from the negative impact of structural adjustment programmes. The dramatic weakness of tertiary education in many aid-dependent countries has also been in part attributed to the aid community's constant focus on basic needs and basic education since the World Conference on Education for All (WCEFA). As shown by Efionayi and Piguet in this issue, African students, for example, increasingly migrate to Western countries in order to pursue their university education. This may reflect their analysis of the quality of higher education in their own countries.

The international aid community's emphasis on evidence, results, impact, evaluation, and value for money has translated into a lively market for short-term consultancy rather than increasing research capacities in African universities. The recent launch of the Building Evidence on Education (BE2) group (UKCDS, UK Aid, ESRC, WB, and USAID), with its GBP 20 million research budget, will have to be carefully scrutinised in order to evaluate the proportions of consultancy studies and more autonomous research in its portfolio.

Skills development has also shifted from being a donor priority in the 1960–80s to being neglected, along with higher education, from the 1990s until very recently. With the financial crisis in 2008, and its impact on youth unemployment in particular, there has been renewed interest in technical and vocational education and training worldwide, including on the part of aid agencies, based on a claimed link to growth and jobs (NORRAG, 2013).

9 Post-2015 Priorities and Paradoxes

It should be acknowledged that schooling is not only part of the solution, but has too often also been part of the problem. Quality schooling is a prerequisite if the post-2015 education agenda is to ensure that the millions of children, young people, and adults who have still not benefited from effective literacy and numeracy more than 20 years after Jomtien do so in the near future. The poorest and most marginalised are not profiting from schools, either because of poor quality or fees, or both. Developing countries themselves have to adapt their education systems and curricula accordingly, mobilising the resources necessary to address challenges. Foreign aid cannot do much more than assist on the margins, but can do so more forcefully in those countries that are most aid-dependent.

Mobilising the resources necessary to address these educational challenges cannot be taken for granted. There is an annual financing gap of USD 26 billion for providing coverage of just three of the Dakar 2000 Goals (early childhood, primary education, and adult literacy) for just 46 low- and lower-middle-income countries. This can only be met by dedicated, increased, domestic financing supported by resolute political commitment and civil society involvement.[10] This is not to say that donors should not continue to aspire to, and be held accountable for, providing the required resources in the form of Official Development Assistance (ODA) transfers. But it underlines the primary responsibility of each and every state, increasingly with other stakeholders such as business, to ensure that no child, however poor, is left behind.

As discussed earlier, UN agencies and the World Bank have driven the international education agenda since the 1970s. How far has this agenda actually trickled down in ministries of education and labour? To what extent has this impacted on education and training policies and practices in low-income and lower-middle-income countries? Burnett convincingly argues that the greatest MDG and EFA impact has been on influencing donor policies (Burnett, 2012, 5). Manning's MDG review suggests that while the time-bound MDGs did have an impact on international development discourse, and selectively on donor governments, they only had a modest impact on developing countries (Manning, 2009, 39). The chapter by Brugger and Lizárraga in this issue bears witness to the fact that education policies and practices in the South are driven by domestic political dynamics including political pressure from education and other lobby groups such as parents, teachers, teachers' unions, and examination boards. Education ministries obviously cannot focus on EFA alone but must respond to the very powerful domestic pressures to expand secondary and tertiary education. There are very much weaker lobbies arguing for the expansion of adult literacy and community learning.

The influence of traditional donors on the changing global discourse regarding international education and training, and in particular on the priorities of international NGOs based in the North, has actually been much

10 For a discussion of the education financing gap in relation to the different post-2015 options, see King (2013).

less pronounced in Latin America and Asia than it has in Sub-Saharan Africa. Emerging economies have bolstered South–South cooperation as an alternative option associated with the rise of non-DAC donors (Carbonnier, 2012; NORRAG, 2010). Interestingly, this group of countries, from China to India, and from the Gulf States to Brazil, seems much less preoccupied with the discussions around the post-2015 development agenda. In some ways, they focus much more on the higher and technical education levels, and advance claims regarding mutual benefit instead of aid. Several of these so-called emerging donors have developed their own discourse and established concrete targets for educational aid. So, for example, thousands of scholarships, short-term training, and experts for Africa are offered by both India and China. In his chapter in this issue King analyses China's investment in human resource development in Africa with a focus on higher education. He identifies key differences between China's approach and that of DAC donors and interrogates the distance between China's discourse and the reality of practice in the field.

10 Conclusion

This chapter provides a brief historical perspective on the education and development nexus, focusing on the last five decades. It analyses the evolving notions of—and approaches to—schooling, non-formal education, literacy, and skills development. The diversity of education systems and approaches is examined in light of the range of stakeholders involved, looking in particular at the roles of the state, business, civil society, and international aid organisations. The chapter discusses the politics of the development—education nexus along two axes, whereby the balance has shifted towards a functional or instrumental understanding of education and training, as also reflected in the emerging global education governance architecture.

Fifty years ago, Philip Foster wrote about the 'vocational school fallacy' applied to the case of Ghana (Foster, 1965), showing the absurdity of assuming that curriculum change could alter the labour market.[11] A new version of the fallacy might be written 50 years later, perhaps termed the 'learning outcomes fallacy', to point up the dangers of the preoccupation with assessment and evaluation that is associated with the so-called 'learning crisis'.

11 'The vocational school fallacy in development planning' was first presented at a conference on Education and Economic Development in Chicago in 1963, and then published in the conference proceedings in 1965 in Anderson and Bowman (1965). See also King and Martin (2000).

There is a need to look behind the numbers, whether provided in Global Monitoring Reports (GMRs), or made available by the rapid expansion of MOOCs and the so-called big data revolution. When striving to integrate those who have so far remained excluded, we should better grasp how teachers are critically essential to the challenge of 'teaching children of the poor' (NORRAG, 2014).[12] In addition, when it comes to adult education and lifelong learning, there is a need to consider both traditional and ICT literacy, numeracy, skills, and learning through the eyes of those adults who did not have access to school and those who have decided to enter schools and training centres at a later stage. Increasing vertical and horizontal inequalities have obviously affected, and will continue to affect, the conditions under which learning and teaching develop. In this context, we still have to learn how to evaluate learning, whether in schools or in further education and training, in a way that puts learning and teaching—that is to say, students and teachers—at the very centre of our concerns.

References

Anderson, A.A. and M.J. Bowman (eds.) (1965) *Education and Economic Development* (London: Aldine Publishing).

Avalos, B. (1986) *Teaching Children of the Poor* (Ottawa: International Development Research Centre).

Banerjee, A. and E. Duflo (2011) *Poor Economics. A Radical Rethinking of the Way to Fight Global Poverty* (New York: Public Affairs).

Bray, M. (2007) *The Shadow Education System: Private Tutoring and its Implications for Planners*, Fundamentals of Educational Planning, 61 (second edition), International Institute for Educational Planning (Paris: UNESCO), http://unesdoc.unesco.org/images/0011/001184/118486e.pdf (accessed on 14 April 2014).

Burnett, N. (2012) *A Learning Goal for Education? Scoping for MDG2 Post-2015*, Report to Hewlett Foundation/Wellspring Advisors, 5 March, Washington, D.C.

Carbonnier, G. (ed.) (2012) *International Development Policy: Aid, Emerging Economies and Global Policies* (Basingstoke: Palgrave Macmillan), http://poldev.revues.org/890 (accessed on 14 April 2014).

Carton, M. (1980) *La formation dans le secteur non structuré*, Document de base du Colloque sur l'acquisition des qualifications et l'emploi dans le secteur non structuré des zones urbaines d'Afrique francophone, Ouagadougou, Programme mondial de l'emploi (Geneva: ILO).

12 See Avalos (1986) for a moving ethnographic account of this challenge.

Department for International Development (DFID) (2013) *Education Position Paper: Improving Learning, Expanding Opportunities* (London: DFID), https://www.gov.uk/government/uploads/system/uploads/attachment_data/file/225715/Education_Position_Paper_July_2013.pdf (accessed on 14 April 2014).

DFID (2010) *Learning For All: DFID's Education Strategy 2010–2015* (London: DFID), http://www.ungei.org/resources/files/educ-strat.pdf (accessed on 14 April 2014).

Dore, R. (1976) *The Diploma Disease: Education, Qualification and Development* (London: Unwin).

Ferrera, J. (2013) 'Big Data in Education', *Knewton Blog*, 18 July, http//www.knewton.com/blog/2013/07/18/ (accessed on 14 April 2014).

Fletcher, S. (2013) 'How Big Data is Taking Teachers Out of the Lecturing Room', *Scientific American*, 29 July, http://www.scientificamerican.com/article.cfm?id=how-big-data-taking-teachers-out-lecturing-business (accessed on 14 April 2014).

Foster, P. (1965) 'The vocational school fallacy in development planning' in Anderson, A.A. and M.J. Bowman (eds.) *Education and Economic Development* (Chicago: Aldine Publishing).

Guthrie, D. (2013) 'The Coming Big Data Education Revolution', *US News*, 15 August, http://www.usnews.com/opinion/articles/2013/08/15/why-big-data-not-moocs-will-revolutionize-education (accessed on 14 April 2014).

Illich, I. (1971) *Deschooling Society* (New York: Harper and Row).

International Labour Organization (ILO) (1972) *Employment, Incomes and Equality: A Strategy for Increasing Production Employment in Kenya* (Geneva: ILO), http://www.ilo.org/public/libdoc/ilo/1972/72B09_608_engl.pdf (accessed 14 April 2014).

——— (1971) *Matching Employment Opportunities and Expectations: A Programme of Action for Ceylon* (Geneva: ILO).

Jullien de Paris, M.-A. (1817) *Esquisse et vues préliminaires d'un ouvrage sur l'éducation comparée* (Paris: Colas).

King, K. (2013) *Development Assistance for Education Post-2015*, Regional Consultation Meeting of the Western European and North American States on Education in the Post-2015 Development Agenda, 5–6 December (Paris: UNESCO), http://www.unesco.org/new/fileadmin/MULTIMEDIA/HQ/ED/ED_new/pdf/K-King-ENG.pdf (accessed on 14 April 2014).

——— (1991) *Aid and Education in the Developing World: The Role of Donor Agencies in Educational Analysis* (Harlow: Longman).

King, K. and C. Martin (2000) *The Vocational School Fallacy Revisited: Education, Aspiration and Work in Ghana, 1959–2000* Occasional Paper, No 85, Centre of African Studies (Edinburgh: University of Edinburgh) http://www.cas.ed.ac.uk/__data/assets/pdf_file/0016/27322/No_085__The_Vocational_School_Fallacy_Revisited-_Education_as.pdf (accessed on 14 April 2014).

King, K. and R. Palmer (2013) *Education and Skills Post-2015: What Evidence and Whose Perspectives?*, NORRAG Working Paper No. 6, http://www.norrag.org/en/publications/working-papers.html (accessed on 14 April 2014).

Learning Metrics Task Force (LMTF) (2013a) *Towards Universal Learning: What Every Child Should Learn*, Report No. 1 (Montreal & Washington, D.C.: UIS/CUE), http://www.uis.unesco.org/Education/Documents/lmtf-rpt1-toward-univrsl-learning.pdf (accessed on 14 April 2014).

Liyanagunawardena, T.R., S.A. Williams, and A.A. Adams (2013) *The Impact and Reach of MOOCs: A Developing Countries' Perspective*, eLearning Papers, 33, pp. 1–8, http://elearningeuropa.info/en/download/file/fid/26956 (accessed on 14 April 2014).

LMTF (2013b) *Towards Universal Learning: A Global Framework for Measuring Learning*. Report No. 2 (Montreal & Washington, D.C.: UIS/CUE), http://www.uis.unesco.org/Education/Documents/towards-universal-learning-a-global-framework-for-measuring-learning-metrics-task-force-education-2013-en.pdf (accessed on 14 April 2014).

Macpherson, I., S. Robertson and G. Walford (2014) *Education, Privatisation and Social Justice: case studies from Africa, South Asia and South East Asia* (Oxford: Symposium Books Ltd).

Manning, R. (2009) *Using Indicators to Encourage Development: Lessons from the Millennium Development Goals* (Copenhagen: Danish Institute for International Studies), http://www.econstor.eu/bitstream/10419/59842/1/591898950.pdf (accessed on 14 April 2014).

NORRAG (2014) 'The Global Politics of Teaching and Learning: The Real Story of Educational Cultures and Contexts', *NORRAG News*, No. 50, http://www.norrag.org/en/publications/norrag-news.html (accessed on 12 May 2014).

——— (2013) '2012: The Year of Global Reports on TVET, Skills and Jobs', *NORRAG News*, No. 48, http://norrag.t3dev1.cross-agency.ch/en/publications/norrag-news/online-version/2012-the-year-of-global-reports-on-tvet-skills-jobs-consensus-or-diversity.html (accessed on 14 April 2014).

——— (2010) 'A Brave New World of "Emerging", "Non-DAC" Donors and their Differences from Traditional Donors', *NORRAG News*, No. 44, http://www.norrag.org/en/publications/norrag-news/online-version/a-brave-new-world-of-emerging-non-dac-donors-and-their-differences-from-traditional-donors.html (accessed on 14 April 2014).

Organisation for Economic Co-operation and Development—Development Assistance Committee (OECD–DAC) (1996) *Shaping the 21st Century: The Contribution of Development Co-operation* (Paris: OECD), http://www.oecd.org/dac/2508761.pdf (accessed on 15 April 2014).

Piety, P. (2013) *Assessing the Educational Data Movement* (New York: Teachers College Press).

Reimer, E.W. (1971) *School is Dead: Alternatives in Education* (New York: Doubleday).

UNESCO (2014) *Teaching and Learning: Achieving Quality for All*, Global Monitoring Report 2013/14 (Paris: UNESCO), http://unesdoc.unesco.org/images/0022/002256/225660e.pdf (accessed on 14 April 2014).

USAID (2011) *USAID Education Strategy 2011–2015: Opportunity through Learning* (Washington, D.C.: USAID), http://usaidlearninglab.org/sites/default/files/resource/files/USAID_Education%20Strategy_2011–2015.pdf (accessed on 14 April 2014).

Van Rijmenam, M. (2013) 'Big Data will Revolutionize Learning', *Smart Data Collective*, http://smartdatacollective.com/bigdatastartups/121261/big-data-will-revolutionize-learning (accessed on 15 April 2014).

Verger, A. and S.L. Robertson (2012) 'The GATS Game-changer: International Trade Regulation and the Constitution of a Global Education Marketplace' in Robertson, S.L., K. Mundy, A. Verger and F. Menashy (eds.) *Public Private Partnerships in Education: New Actors and Modes of Governance in a Globalizing World* (Cheltenham: Edward Elgar).

Vinokur, A. (2005) 'Avant-Propos', *Cahiers de la recherche sur l'éducation et les savoirs*, Hors-série, No. 1, pp. 7–14, http://cres.revues.org/1868 (accessed on 15 April 2014).

Warner, J. (2013) 'Resisting Big Data and Adaptative Software', *Inside Higher Education*, http://www.insidehighered.com/blogs/just-visiting/resisting-big-data-and-adaptive-software (accessed on 15 April 2014).

Winthrop, R., G. Bulloch, P. Bhatt and A. Wood (2013) *Investments in Global Education. A Strategic Imperative for Business*, Report of the Centre for Universal Education at Brookings (Washington, D.C.: The Brookings Institutions), http://www.brookings.edu/~/media/research/files/reports/2013/09/investment%20in%20global%20education/investment%20in%20global%20education%20final%20%20web.pdf (accessed on 14 April 2014).

World Bank (2011) *Learning for All: Investing in People's Knowledge and Skills to Promote Development*, World Bank Group Education Strategy 2020 (Washington, D.C.: World Bank), http://www-wds.worldbank.org/external/default/WDSContentServer/WDSP/IB/2011/09/15/000356161_20110915012555/Rendered/PDF/644870WP0Learn00Box0361538B0PUBLIC0.pdf (accessed on 15 April 2014).

——— (1974) *Education*, Sector Working Paper (Washington, D.C.: World Bank), http://www-wds.worldbank.org/external/default/WDSContentServer/WDSP/IB/1974/12/01/000009265_3961003052734/Rendered/PDF/multi_page.pdf (accessed on 15 April 2014).

World Conference on Education for All (WCEFA) (1990) *World Declaration on Education for All and Framework for Action to Meet Basic Learning Needs* (New York: UNESCO), http://www.ceses.it/docs/JOMTIE_E.pdf (accessed on 15 April 2014).

FIGURE 1.7 *Timeline: major milestones in international educational research and training.*
SOURCE: AUTHORS.

Annex

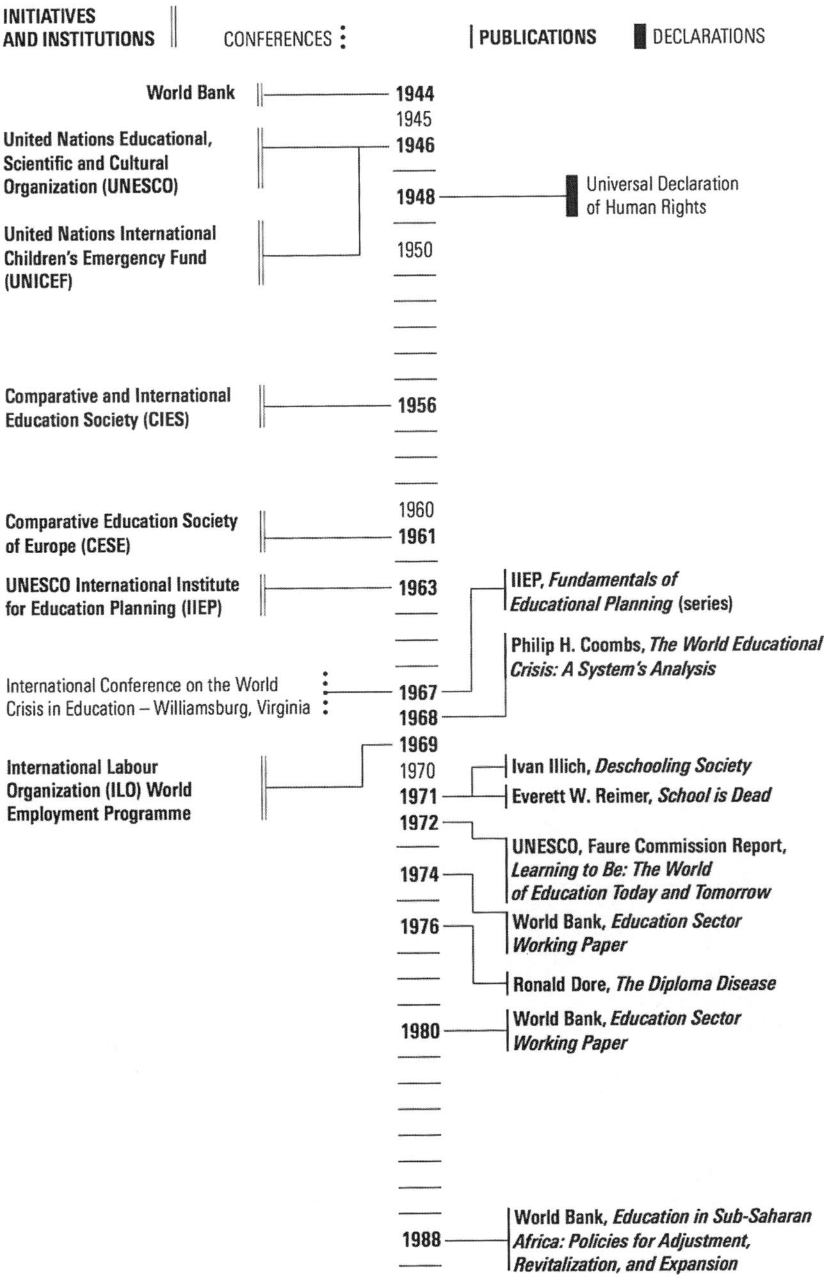

FIGURE 1.7 (*cont.*)

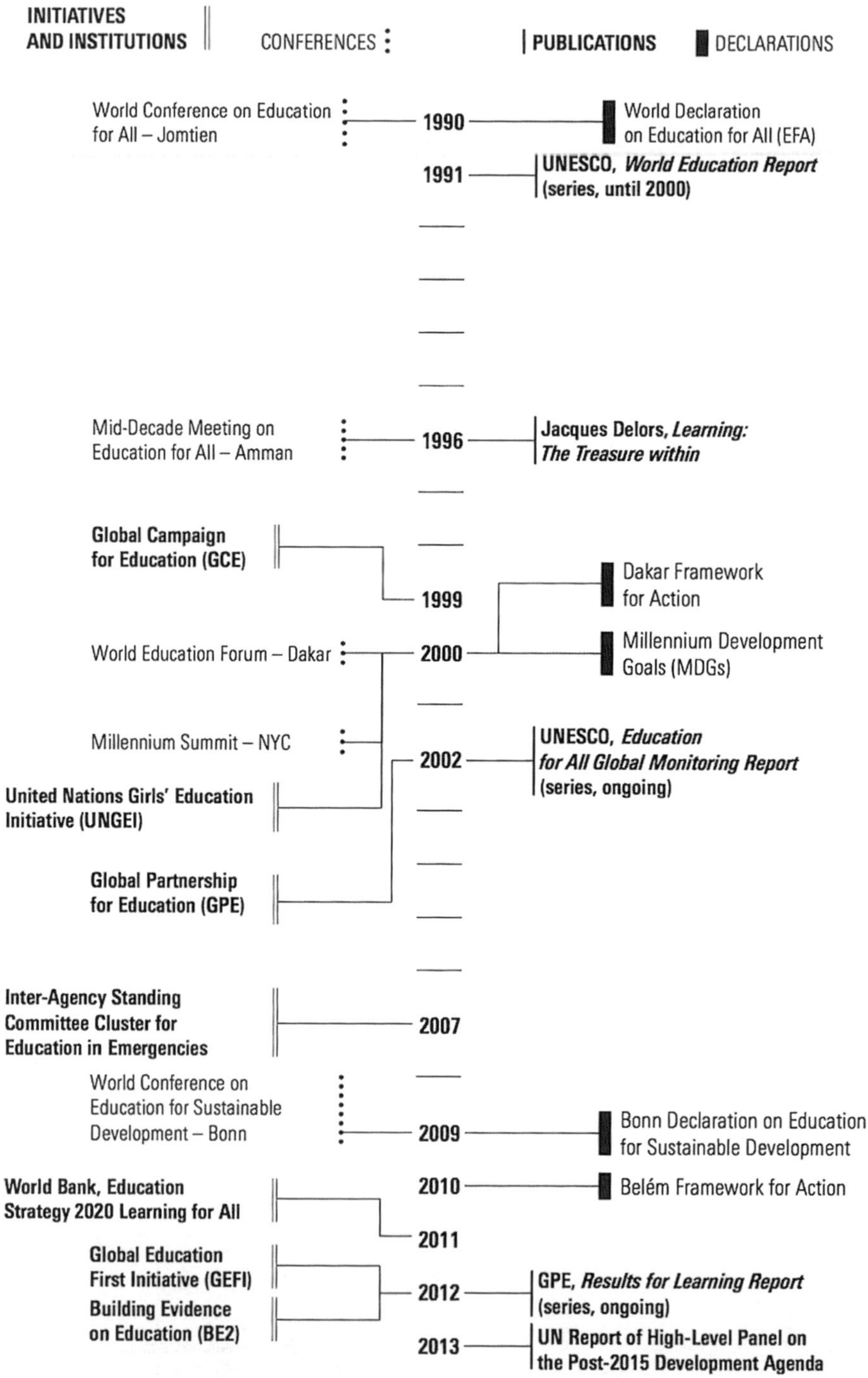

CHAPTER 2

International Education Policies, Issues, and Challenges

Nicholas Burnett

Abstract

This short chapter discusses the rights and capabilities of, and development approaches to, education in developing countries, the recent evolution of developing countries' education systems in the present century, the 'leaderless globalisation' of the international institutions currently responsible for education, and the initial effects of the data and evaluation revolution on education. It concludes with five recommendations: evidence should be used more in education strategies, policies and practices; innovation needs to be encouraged; international funding should target more the neediest countries; assessment, benchmarking, and evaluation should be further encouraged; and a new international governance mechanism is needed for education, possibly led from outside the education sector itself.

Education post-2015 was discussed at the Global Education Meeting in Oman in May 2014, and there seems likely to be one broad international goal for education, focused particularly on learning at all levels of education and throughout life, measured by some ten or so targets. This new goal, and its associated targets, will therefore go well beyond the overlapping six Education for All (EFA) and two education Millennium Development Goals (MDGs) currently in place since 2000, which are mostly to do with access.

The effectiveness of any new education goal, however, will depend on the extent to which it is grounded in (1) a consensus on why education matters for development; (2) the recent history of enrolment, learning, and financing, including the growing importance of private as well as public education for the poor; (3) the international institutional environment, including new players, and the ability to monitor and enforce the goal; and (4) the application in education of the broader data and evaluation revolution that has impacted on development thinking and development economics.

 | DOI 10.1163/9789004281158_003

1 Why Education Matters

For the EFA and MDGs set in 2000, the case for investing in basic education for all and basic schooling respectively rested largely on two planks. First, education, and especially elementary education, is a human right, enshrined in the 1948 Universal Declaration of Human Rights and many subsequent international and national documents, though taken together they do not clearly delineate exactly how many years of education are implied by its being a right that the state should ensure. Second, education results in increased productivity and leads to economic growth and so is essential for development. In particular, basic education was thought to be the priority, based on analyses that appeared to show that the rate of return to investments in primary education was higher than those in secondary and tertiary education. Even though these two planks each led to the same conclusion of the overarching importance of basic education, and thus could have been seen as complementary, in practice they were often presented as alternatives, respectively associated with the United Nations Educational, Scientific and Cultural Organization (UNESCO) and the World Bank. Frequent debates, in international meetings, about which plank was the fundamental reason for investing in education paradoxically undermined the powerful joint case that both could have made together. Echoes of these debates, which have not been helpful to the broader case that education must make against other priorities in international goal-setting, can be seen in Draxler's article in this volume (Chapter 3).

This state of affairs can be avoided with the post-2015 goals if it is recognised that the case for education has, since 1990, developed in three important directions, all of which are complementary if conceptually different:

a) The rights argument has been reinforced by the inclusion of education as a human right in the constitutions of major countries, such as India and Indonesia; by explicit statements by the World Bank, beginning under the Wolfensohn presidency, that education is a right, thereby reducing the artificial differences between the *rights* and *economics* arguments caused by their association with particular institutions; and by worldwide reaction to well-publicised attacks on education such as the shooting of the schoolgirl Malala Yousafzai in Pakistan in 2012 and the abduction of two hundred or more schoolgirls in northern Nigeria in 2014.
b) The *rights* and *economics* arguments have been complemented by a third and powerful argument from yet another perspective, that of *capabilities* as developed by Amartya Sen. Individuals can only reach their full

potential (capability) if they are equipped by education to do so. This argument has not achieved as great a visibility as the other two arguments but it has been very important in influencing key debates and discussions. For example, the Education for All Global Monitoring Report has since its inception taken a 'rights, capabilities and development' approach (UNESCO, 2002).

c) The economic growth argument has grown into a broader development argument, based not only on the economic benefits of education but also on those of social cohesion and especially health. On the economic side, it has become clear that much more than simply access to basic education is important to economic growth and poverty reduction; secondary education and quality matter too. The returns to education have continued to be estimated but now show that those for secondary education are generally higher than those for primary education (see, for example, Psacharopolous and Patrinos, 2004; Colclough et al., 2009). The quality of education (as measured by scores on the international PISA assessment) is more important in determining economic growth than is simply the number of years spent in education (see, for example, Hanushek and Woessman, 2010). In addition, education has been shown to reduce poverty directly (Bird and Higgins, 2011). Beyond the economic effects, education has been shown to contribute to social cohesion in general (Heyneman, 2003) and specifically to lower crime rates (Soares, 2004) and greater civic engagement (Mertaugh et al., 2009). Education results in better decisions about maternal and child health (see, for example, Feinstein et al., 2006) and delays the age of marriage (Majgaarden and Mingat, 2012), reducing fertility and improving health generally.

Thus, the broad case for investing in education now has three rather than two planks, and each plank is much stronger than it was before. Moreover, these planks are complementary and together make an overwhelming case for educating all and, in particular, for focusing on learning as suggested by the work of Hanushek and Woessman (2010). However, this case will only be effective in education's competition, for attention and indeed resources, with other sectors if it is made in this coherent fashion and not partially undermined, as in the past, by unhelpful debates about which plank is of prime importance. All three matter.

Some of these debates continue, as noted in Chapter 1 of this volume, though there is a growing consensus around all three planks of rights, capabilities, and development that make the case for education. An interesting exception to this growing consensus is the new debate stimulated by the growth of private education for the poor (see Section 2 of this chapter), the pragmatic analysis of which is complicated by those opposing it on principle on rights grounds and those supporting it on principle on economic grounds. Neither seems very helpful in explaining why private education for the poor has expanded and what policy options are relevant.

2 The Evolution of Education in Developing Countries Since 2000

The education MDGs and the EFA goals are not going to be met by 2015 (UNESCO, 2013—which is also the source of data in this and the next two paragraphs). Nonetheless enormous progress has been made as documented by the EFA Global Monitoring Reports. Major achievements between 1999 and 2011 include pre-primary gross enrolments increasing from 33 per cent in 1999 to 50 per cent in 2011; a halving of the number of primary school aged children out of school to 57 million; the proportion of countries achieving universal primary enrolment rising from 30 per cent in 1999 to 50 per cent in 2011 (for the 122 countries for which data exist); a vast expansion of secondary education with the gross enrolment rate increasing from 72 per cent to 82 per cent, including a doubling in sub-Saharan Africa to reach 49 per cent; major progress towards gender parity; government spending on education increasing from 4.6 per cent to 5.1 per cent of gross national product (GNP), with the increase being one full percentage point of GNP for low-income countries; and a steady increase in aid for education from 2002 to 2010.

Major problems nonetheless persist. The rate of decline in the numbers of children out of school has slowed, and such children are increasingly concentrated in conflict-affected countries where progress is difficult. The number of adult illiterates remains stubbornly constant at around 774 million, though the rate of illiteracy has declined slightly. Aid for education peaked in 2010 and has since declined, with the share of total education aid going to the neediest low-income countries being less than that going to middle-income countries.

Above all, however, there is now a general realisation, based on different sources of evidence, that many of those in school are not learning, or are not learning sufficiently. In one sense, this is not new knowledge, as discussed in Chapter 1 of this volume; in another it is, in that there is now an emerging consensus that something needs to be done about this 'learning crisis' and that efforts need to focus as much on learning as on access to education. There are today some 250 million primary and secondary school-aged children who are not able to read, write, or do basic mathematics—and 130 million of them are in school. Much other evidence, including from powerful citizen-led assessments in India, Pakistan, and East Africa, has highlighted this learning crisis. Learning is as much an equity issue as is enrolment, as those from more affluent backgrounds show higher levels of learning than do the poor and disadvantaged.

While skills for employability were included in the current EFA goals, if not in a well-defined way, they are not part of the current MDGs. This relative disregard of skills development is now changing and there has been a major renewal of interest in skills for employability, driven by the large youth 'bulge', by the global recession of 2008–11 with the consequent rise in unemployment, and by the increasing complaints of employers that school-leavers are not well equipped to join the workforce. Vocational education, and the need to link to employers, is very much back on the agenda having not featured strongly in 2000 when the present goals were set.

Yet it is surprising how little thinking has been devoted to meeting these new challenges. While most children now exit formal education with at least some secondary schooling, secondary education is less and less relevant, being generally still designed as a route towards higher education rather than one into the workplace. Indeed, education more generally remains a very conservative sector, largely doing things the way they have always been done, with insufficient innovation and adaptation to modern economies and societies. Innovation is not to be confused with technology, yet technology is the only area in which innovation is currently happening in education, with the growth of MOOCs and their applicability to higher education in developing countries.

In large part in response to the poor performance of the public sector in terms of both learning and relevance, there has been a major expansion of private education aimed at the poor. In urban India and in Lagos State in Nigeria, some 80 per cent of children now attend private schools (Day et al., 2014); about 80 per cent of pre-school age children in the slums of Accra, Johannesburg, Lagos, and Nairobi attend private preschools (Lowenstein et al., 2014). Chains of private schools for the poor are springing up, including, for example, Bridge International in Kenya and Omega in Ghana. The response of the education establishment to these developments has largely been to deplore them or to try to regulate them rather than to understand what has caused them in terms of poor parents' dissatisfaction with public education in many, though by no means all, countries.

These major developments in education in developing countries in this century are relatively absent from current discussions leading up to possible new international goals, with the important exception of the learning crisis which is now generally recognised. Even here, however, institutional developments make it hard to create a concerted focus on the problem, as the next section will discuss.

3 International Institutions and New Players

In addition to its inherent conservatism, the international education community's relative failure to adapt to these trends and to innovate can be traced to the weakening institutional environment at the international level. For a variety of reasons, UNESCO has not exercised leadership as it did from its foundation following World War II until the 1980s. These reasons include its increasing politicisation (Burnett, 2011) and also, most recently, the serious resource issues that have resulted from the non-payment of USD 130 million of dues by the United States in response to the organisation's admission of Palestine.

Yet no other institution has stepped in to fill the partial void and the international institutional framework for new global initiatives in education is thus one of 'leaderless globalisation' (Rodrik, 2011): there are many important trends and developments but there is no effective mechanism for prioritising and guiding them. The World Bank has launched a number of research and benchmarking initiatives, and has clearly signalled the importance of learning by titling its current strategy document *Learning for All*, but the Bank has not tried, nor does it have the mandate, to lead the global community on education. The Global Partnership for Education is too much a financing mechanism and too focused on basic education to perform this role. The regional development banks have largely moved away from basic education to focus more on higher and technical education. The United Nations International Children's Emergency Fund (UNICEF) has continued to concentrate particularly on equity and on the disadvantaged, though it is increasingly interested in innovation. The UN Secretary-General has also tried to fill the gap, with the launch of the Education First initiative, and the appointment of former UK prime minister Gordon Brown as a Special Envoy. A further interesting development is the expansion of the Organisation for Economic Co-operation and Development's (OECD) education activities towards developing countries, especially middle-income ones, which are not OECD members. None of these other institutional efforts has resulted in clear leadership at the international level. Rather there is a plethora of activity but insufficient coordination.

The situation is further compounded by increased globalisation. Countries increasingly understand that their economic futures depend in large part on the skills of their labour forces, and so in turn on their education systems. Ideally this should lead to both competition and cooperation around education.

Countries have yet to translate this into effective international cooperation; major emerging economies such as Brazil, China, India, and South Africa still exercise their influence as individual countries rather than through international institutions. The fact that most of these middle-income countries found the 2000 education MDGs and EFA goals largely irrelevant to them has also contributed to their reluctance to engage. A further important development is the entry of many new actors onto the international education scene, especially private foundations (such as the Hewlett and MasterCard foundations), private corporations (such as Pearson)—both directly and through their corporate social responsibility (CSR) functions—and non-traditional donors such as Qatar and China (see King, Chapter 8 in this volume). CSR is particularly interesting—in both South Africa and India it is now compulsory and, in both countries, education appears to be one of the major sectors receiving finance through this modality, as much as 40 per cent of the total in South Africa. Thus one of the major responses to the learning crisis, the establishment of a Learning Metrics Task Force, run jointly by the Brookings Institution and the UNESCO Institute for Statistics, has been driven and financed largely by private funding from foundations in OECD countries, resulting in high quality work that faces serious issues of wider legitimacy.

4 The Data and Evaluation Revolution

It is now a commonplace to talk about the impact of the data revolution on development. This largely consists of the availability of major datasets, especially internationally comparable ones, and the application of rigorous evaluation techniques.

These developments have affected education in four major ways. First, educational data have traditionally largely been administrative data, taken from school and institutional records. Increasingly, however, with the Living Standards Measurement Study (LSMS)[1] and Multiple Indicator Cluster Surveys (MICS),[2] population-based data have become available—it is instructive to

1 Established by the Development Research Group in order to improve the quality of household data collection in developing countries, http://econ.worldbank.org/WBSITE/EXTERNAL/EXTDEC/EXTRESEARCH/EXTLSMS/0,,contentMDK:21478196~menuPK:3359066~pagePK:64168445~piPK:64168309~theSitePK:3358997,00.html (accessed on 23 May 2014).

2 In order to fill gaps for monitoring the situation for women and children, UNICEF is assisting countries in the collection and analysis of data, http://www.unicef.org/statistics/index_24302.html (accessed on 23 May 2014).

compare the current EFA Global Monitoring Report with the early ones of a decade ago and to see this evolution of sources. Nonetheless, as discussions in the Learning Metrics Task Force have shown, there is still some reluctance to use population-based rather than administrative data, in part because of issues of control of such data. Departments and ministries of education tend to control administrative data more than they do population-based surveys.

Second, the OECD's Programme for International Student Assessment (PISA)[3] and other international assessments such as the Trends in International Mathematics and Science Study (TIMSS) and the Progress in International Reading Literacy Study (PIRLS)[4] have steadily increased their country coverage and are no longer confined just to OECD countries. PISA has been the most influential, comparing standardised measures of learning among 15-year olds across countries. These have reinforced the focus on learning and stimulated important action in some countries, the most recent example being Vietnam, which has improved very rapidly. Other countries have been provoked by their relatively poor rankings to try to take action; Thailand, for example, has recently established the Quality Learning Foundation to promote innovation and quality in its public schools following its ranking well below where it feels it should be as an upper-middle income country.

Third, and less positively, there remains a considerable reluctance to use evidence in education to determine 'what works'. OECD analysis of PISA results, for example, points towards important steps that can be taken to improve equity in learning; randomised controlled trials in education, all documented by the World Bank, show many things, including for example the importance of remediation; and there are examples of countries, such as Vietnam and South Korea, which have made tremendous progress with both enrolments and learning. Yet there remains a strong reluctance in the educational community to apply this evidence, as reflected in statements that education is not just about cognitive learning and that there is a danger of teaching to the test if excessive attention is placed on such assessments. These statements, while true, are disappointing; they appear to be the reactions of a conservative sector to data that show it has enormous scope to improve.

Fourth, there is the very interesting development of citizen-led assessments of learning, pioneered in India by the Annual Status of Education Report (ASER) and now applied also in Kenya, Mali, Mexico, Pakistan, Senegal, Tanzania, and Uganda. These assessments, so far carried out only at primary level, reinforce the opinion that there are major challenges in basic reading

3 http://www.oecd.org/pisa/ (accessed on 28 May 2014).

4 http://timssandpirls.bc.edu/ (accessed on 28 May 2014).

and mathematics; what is still unknown is to what extent resulting public and parental pressure will lead to reform.

5 Conclusion

This short chapter has outlined some of the major developments in international education. It has highlighted both progress made and the huge challenges that remain, especially around learning. It has noted important data developments but the sector's reluctance to embrace them, reflecting its inherent conservatism that is seen also in the relative failure to innovate, at least on a major scale. It has observed the institutional weakness present at the international level.

What should priorities be in this situation? What should the international community focus on?

Five key areas seem most important. First, there is already a vast amount of evidence but a reluctance to apply it—efforts should be stepped up to diffuse this evidence and to compare countries' practices and reactions to what is known. Second, innovation should be strongly encouraged in education systems, to make them more effective and more relevant—secondary education being a good place to start with its out-of-date curricula and increasing irrelevance to the labour force. Third, international funding, declining though it is, should target more those countries in greatest need. Fourth, assessment, benchmarking, and evaluation should be further encouraged in the full recognition that cognitive achievement is not the only purpose of education. Fifth, and most difficult probably, international actors should try to develop an effective new international governance system for international education—but this may require leadership from outside the education sector.

References

Bird, K. and K. Higgins (2011) *Stopping the Intergenerational transmission of poverty: Research highlights and policy recommendations*, Working Paper 214 (Manchester: Chronic Poverty Research Centre).

Burnett, N. (2011) 'UNESCO Education: Political or Technical? Reflections on Recent Experience', *International Journal of Educational Development*, 31, pp. 315–318.

Colclough, C., G. Kingdon and H.A. Patrinos (2009) *The Pattern of Returns to Education and Its Implications*, Policy Brief 4 (Cambridge, UK: Research Consortium on Educational Outcomes and Poverty).

Day A.L., C. Mcloughlin, M. Aslam, J. Engel, J. Wales, S. Rawal, R. Batley, G. Kingdon, S. Nicolai and P. Rose (2014) *The Role and Impact of Private Schools in Developing Countries*, Education Rigorous Literature Review (London: UK Department for International Development).

Feinstein, L., R. Sabates, T. Anderson, A. Sorhaindo, and C. Hammond (2006) 'What are the Effects of Education on Health?' in Desjardins, R. and T. Schuller (eds.) *Measuring the Effects of Education on Health and Civic Engagement—Proceedings of the Copenhagen Symposium* (Paris: OECD), pp. 171–313.

Hanushek, E. and L. Woessman (2010) *How Much Do Educational Outcomes Matter in OECD Countries?*, NBER Working Paper 16515, (Cambridge, MA: National Bureau of Economic Research).

Heyneman, S.P. (2003) 'Education, Social Cohesion and the Future Role of International Organizations', *Peabody Journal of Education*, 78(3), pp. 25–38.

Lowenstein, C., M. Ziswiler, K. Bidwell and L. Watine (2014) *Exploring Early Education Programs in Peri-Urban Settings in Africa: Summary Findings from Lagos, Nigeria* (Zurich: UBS Optimus Foundation).

Majgaarden, K. and A. Mingat (2012) *Education in Sub-Saharan Africa: A Comparative Analysis*, World Bank Study 70979 (Washington, D.C.: The World Bank).

Mertaugh, M.T., E.Y. Jimenez and H.A. Patrinos (2009) *The Global Challenge in Basic Education: Why Continued Investment in Basic Education is Important* (Washington, D.C.: The World Bank).

Psacharopolous, G. and H.A. Patrinos (2004) 'Returns to Investment in Education: A Further Update?, *Education Economics*, 12(2), pp. 111–134.

Rodrik, D. (2011) *The Globalization Paradox: Democracy and the Future of the World Economy* (New York and London: Norton).

Soares, R.R. (2004) 'Development, crime and punishment: accounting for the international differences in crime rates', *Journal of Development Economics*, 73, pp. 155–184.

UNESCO (2013) *Education for All Global Monitoring Report* (Paris: UNESCO).

——— (2002) *Education for All Global Monitoring Report* (Paris: UNESCO).

CHAPTER 3

International Investment in Education for Development: Public Good or Economic Tool?

Alexandra Draxler

Abstract

Is education a human right or a driver of economic development? How international organisations frame their strategies is determined to a great extent by their response to this question. This chapter argues that a sound education system is one that is rights-based and seeks to achieve social cohesion, equality of access, and equity of opportunity. Efforts to generate economic returns from education to individuals and societies, while important, should not dominate development policies. As the post-2015 Development Agenda emerges, tensions between those who perceive education as a human right and those who see it as a tool of economic development are increasingly coming to the fore, notably due to growing influence and interest among international private entities, both foundations and corporations, in steering the agenda towards the development of market opportunities. The author argues that preserving the role of the state as the ultimate democratic arbiter of rights, equality, and equity is the only way, albeit imperfect, of guaranteeing education as a public good.

1 Introduction

What are the purposes of education? An implicit answer to this question is the foundation for all public policy, private investment, and choices made by individuals concerning education for them or their children. The evolving policies for development cooperation in education respond to and reflect the underlying ideologies of the main protagonists. These protagonists include the United Nations (UN) system (principally the United Nations Educational, Scientific and Cultural Organization (UNESCO)), the World Bank, bilateral donors, and civil society organisations. This chapter will look at some of the lessons pertinent to the next stage in international cooperation that aims to achieve universal quality education after 2015. It has three underlying themes that highlight inherent policy choices and tensions:

 | DOI 10.1163/9789004281158_004

- The tension between two visions of education—on the one hand, education as human right and an end in itself, and on the other, education as a tool for economic development.
- Evolving definitions of equity, fairness, and equal opportunity, including the opportunity for all to have access to organised learning opportunities throughout life.
- Standardised assessment, evaluation, and measuring, and how they both reflect and structure policies and learning opportunities.

The right to education was originally broadly defined as the right to schooling,[1] and the right to schooling as a right that principally benefitted individuals. Demand for schooling has never ceased to grow. In spite of powerful economic and social obstacles and of criticisms of the imperfections of schools and school systems, parents and children continue to aspire to access ever-increasing levels of schooling and training. Targets for schooling continue to be the most scrutinised benchmarks for progress in education worldwide and meeting the aim of schooling for all has been arguably the dominant force to date in international education movements over the past twenty years. Education is, of course, much more than schooling, and although this chapter discusses mainly schooling, the tendencies it points out also apply to other kinds of training and lifelong learning opportunities.

This chapter identifies education as a public good. There is disagreement among experts on the validity of this claim. In the original and public-finance notion of public goods, they are non-rivalrous (use by one individual does not alter a good's availability to another individual) and non-excludable (they are freely available to all and cannot be restricted) (Samuelson, 1954). Knowledge, while commonly recognised as a public good, can be excludable. The classification of public services as public goods or non-public goods depends to a large extent on an ideological divide. On the one hand, there are those, including UN organisations, who support the notion that governments and international organisations are responsible for ensuring public services that are considered human rights, and are in consequence public goods. On the other, there are those who maintain that market forces can and should take care of many of these services, which are essentially private goods. Here we base our arguments on the United Nations Development Programme (UNDP) position

1 'Everyone has the right to education. Education shall be free, at least in the elementary and fundamental stages. Elementary education shall be compulsory.', United Nations, *Universal Declaration of Human Rights* (1948). http://www.un.org/en/documents/udhr/ (accessed on 24 April 2014).

(Kaul, Grunberg et al., 1999) and the continued inclusion, by the UN system, of education among public goods.

> Or take education, which benefits the person being educated. To calculate the benefits, we take the income a person earns over a lifetime with education, and subtract that which she would get without an education. But that figure does not tell the whole story. What about the numerous employers the person will have over a lifetime, and the savings realised because these employers do not have to train her in-house? What about the benefits that literacy brings to all the companies that rely on the written word to advertise? The benefits to those who issue public warnings, put out signs or seek to implement laws? If one were to put a figure on all these benefits, they would dwarf the amount that accrues strictly to the educated person. This difference between the public and the private benefits is called an externality. And because of its substantial externalities, education is a public good. (Kaul, Grunberg et al., 1999, p. xx)

2 Defining Education's Role in Development

In the years after World War II, and with growing force in the 1960s as the wave of African independence grew the number of sovereign nations by almost half in a decade, both economic growth and enthusiasm for the potential of global human rights—including the right to education—inspired the discourse and the policies of all those involved in international cooperation. Targets were set for universal schooling and adult literacy. A world in which education throughout life would be available for all and taken up by most was envisaged (Faure, Herrera et al., 1972). Literacy for all was a mobilising notion during the 1960s for a significant proportion of development programmes. Entire nations embarked on massive literacy programmes for everyone out of school, and some succeeded.[2] Education was seen, by most actors and observers, as an integral feature and driver of the betterment of the human condition. Not all agreed that formal learning was the answer. Indeed, thinkers such as Paulo Freire and Ivan Illich favoured dismantling education systems as they existed in order to rebuild from the beginning on the basis of local needs and local effort to favour the fulfilment of individual potential (Gajardo, 1993; Gerhardt, 1993).

---

2 See UNESCO *50 Years of Education* (online archives), http://www.unesco.org/education/educprog/50y/brochure/tle/124.htm (accessed on 19 February 2014).

Then, as public social sector spending came under scrutiny in both 'South' and 'North' during the 1970s, the scramble for economic arguments to support investment in education and health focused on outcomes the economic impact of which could be determined. Human capital had been defined and consecrated as a factor of economic prosperity (Vally and Spreen, 2012). Thus, academics, theorists, and eventually international policymakers developed concepts and translations into policies of 'manpower planning' (Samoff and Carrol, 2003), 'functional literacy',[3] and 'rates of return' (Tilak, 2007b) on investment for various levels of education.

In addition to the economic arguments, though, the notion that development was a process of ensuring basic needs are met for all (including education) was initiated by the International Labour Organisation (ILO) in 1976. Basic needs appeared to unite humanistic and practical aims through a vision of development that could be quantified and itemised, and for many years, including at the Jomtien Conference and afterwards, this approach exerted significant influence (Emmerij, 2010) on the policies of international and bilateral aid agencies. Another school of thought criticised basic needs as an approach based on a consumerist view of development and advocated for an approach based on capabilities (Sen, 2003). In any case, the fulfilment of basic needs could be estimated in terms of the growth needed to achieve targets, and so employment became both 'a means and an end' (Emmerij, 2010, 1). In more recent years, as manpower planning has lost its appeal, marketplace notions of education provision and delivery have been touted whereby learners and their parents, through 'school choice', become consumers who are individually responsible for the design and wisdom of their trajectories. Recommendations by the World Bank for the allocation of public investment in education still lean heavily on notions of rates of return and on the idea that much of the provision of education should rely on market forces and private sector providers. When structural adjustment programmes in the 1980s and 1990s forced drastic reductions in public sector spending and proposed increased roles for private sector entities, opponents to such programmes foresaw with fury their long-term negative effects on education.

These contrasting philosophical and policy trends, with correspondingly competing agendas, have had significant influence on education policy and practice internationally. On the one hand, there has been a renewed commitment to basic education as a right both on the part of the international com-

3 It has to be said that the notion of functional literacy emerged partly as a response to the failure of many classical literacy programmes in impoverished environments where the skills of literacy had no immediate relevance or application.

munity and on the part of governments. On the other, the search for greater accountability for education expenditure has often been played out in a search for functionality in terms of economic productivity. The notion of education being provided through marketplace mechanisms and of the learner as consumer to a large extent absolves the public sector for inequalities that originate outside the education system and persist or are aggravated through it. The justification of education streams, subjects, or levels in terms of rates of return implies lesser value for types of learning where rates of return are more elusive. Although rates of return are widely used by the World Bank, and references to rates of return have turned up in the report (High Level Panel on the post-2015 Development Agenda, 2013) tabled as a key document to inspire post-2015, they are subject to a great deal of controversy and criticism (Tinak, 2007a, 2007b). Use of rates of return has also has resulted in a wide and very successful push for a greater influence of the private sector in the provision of public goods, from the actual running of schools (Patrinos and Sosale, 2007), to the provision of vocational training (Adams, Middleton et al., 1992), to provision of learning materials and methods, and the devising of measurement and management tools. At the same time, while nominally defending a rights-based approach, the UN (and UNESCO) have increasingly shown quite uncritical acceptance of the role of the private sector and welcomed market-based approaches (UN Global Compact, 2013; UNESCO, 2013).

3 Tension or Equilibrium between Goals and Purposes

It is only recently that significant policy attention has been devoted internationally to the sad fact that the expansion of education opportunities does not result in more equal opportunity or outcomes. The equilibrium between the dual aims of education in individual and societal development, in terms of access to and content of education, has naturally varied widely over time according to the nature of governments and to societal events. Furthermore, the issue of tackling within-country inequalities has been approached somewhat gingerly in development circles until recently.

As already stated, the notion that human capital is an important feature in economic growth was very important for post-World War II reconstruction and then as a tenet of development in general (Spalletti, 2008). Therefore, 'manpower' forecasting as a way of organising the post-primary levels of education systems became an accepted and influential technique used by governments with an interventionist economic tradition. This included decisions about the creation and placement of vocational training, *numerus clausus* at different levels of the system, and incentives to attract learners to specific areas that were viewed as under-served. Education planning became a permanent part of the public sector landscape as a management tool to match and evaluate aims, resources, and competencies over time.

Once education became 'both a sign of wealth and a source of it' (Spalletti, 2008), the goals of education became inextricably entwined, for public policy purposes, with notions of national prosperity and growth. People can be seen as more an instrument of progress, however that is defined in public policy terms, than the other way around. The relevance of education, once it is defined as relevance for the marketplace, can distort the process away from the realisation of individual potential.

4 Some Milestone Reports

One of the first analytical report on education worldwide was produced for a joint US – UNESCO effort in 1967. The International Conference on the World Crisis in Education announced a crisis and attributed it to the tension between demand and available resources, to societal inertia, and to not enough understanding and information about education as a system. The book (Coombs, 1968) that emerged from the background papers and the conference did not ignore individual aspirations and needs. It was nevertheless a heavily economically oriented analysis, working on an analytical framework of objectives →inputs →process →outputs. The book formulated recommendations for more international cooperation as a way of improving education worldwide. It was also influential in giving weight and momentum to the development of analytical tools and collaboration in the collection and use of data for educational planning and management, and by extension the measurement of the economic value of education.

Fifteen years later, partially in response to student and worker demonstrations and violence in many parts of the world at the end of the 1960s, a seven-man commission, brought together by UNESCO to reflect on the future of education, issued a report entitled 'Learning to Be' (Faure, Herrera et al., 1972). This report carried a powerful message of faith in humanity and of the role of education in bringing out the best in humanity. It was both a plea and an affirmation of the right of each person to receive an education that develops critical thinking and allows full realisation of individual potential. 'The aim of development is the complete fulfilment of man, in all the richness of his personality, the complexity of his forms of expression and his various commitments—as individual, member of a family and of a community, citizen and producer, inventor of techniques and creative dreamer' (Faure, Herrera et al., 1972, 94).[4]

Around the same time, in 1971 (revised in 1974), the World Bank produced its first Education Sector Working Paper (World Bank, 1971). The paper talked about education largely in terms of production efficiencies: 'matching education with manpower needs', adapting content to the realities of primitive rural life, and positing that, given high youth unemployment, continued expansion of education systems would be unprofitable in the short term. At the time, nearly three-quarters of bank lending went to post-primary education. It is worth pointing out that educational television and programmed learning (for both of which countries took out large loans) were at the time completely unproven technologies for quality of education in wealthy countries, let alone poor ones. Their cost—benefit attraction for secondary schooling is still to be demonstrated to any scale.

Still, as a lender, the World Bank had not only to look for but to provide arguments for efficiencies in its social sector programmes in order to convince its board of the value of social sector support. It naturally looked at the inevitable resource constraints of poor countries that were already devoting 20 per cent of national budgets to education and could hardly aim at unlimited expansion of the education offer. The trade-off between quality and quantity was already very much present as an issue. The unavoidable financial constraints on education therefore provided the humus for the World Bank's thinking in which both rates of return and, ultimately, the expansion of sources of financing to embrace the private sector and privatisation sprouted and flourished.

At the end of the 1980s and the decade's period of structural adjustment, economic crisis, and stagnation in educational progress, UNESCO, United Nations International Children's Emergency Fund (UNICEF), UNDP, the United Nations Population Fund (UNFPA), and the World Bank joined forces to give a new impetus to the push for universal education. A secretariat was created under the leadership of Wadi Haddad, a senior World Bank official, to provide the conceptual and organisational underpinnings of a World Conference on Education for All (EFA), which took place in Jomtien, Thailand, in 1990. The background report of the conference (Secretariat of the World Conference on EFA, 1990), as well as the goals formulated and agreed by the conference itself (World Conference on Education for All, 1990) placed human development

4 It will not escape the attention of any reader that the equal rights of girls and women to participate fully in education did not become a serious preoccupation of international organisations until the 1980s with the gradual adoption of the Convention on the Elimination of all forms of Discrimination.

and basic learning needs firmly at the centre of development discourse, and for the first time proposed not only aims but also funding strategies to reach universal basic education. An international consortium kept up this impetus with follow-up studies. Ten years later, in Dakar, Senegal, a review of progress led to revised goals and to a permanent monitoring process that is expressed in an annual report.[5] These EFA reports have been influential, with annual updates of standard data and in-depth thematic reviews of particular challenges.

The notion of human development had joined the international development vocabulary, under the impetus of economist Mahbub ul Haq who pushed for an alternative to the purely economic models in vogue among funders. The UNDP Human Development report, launched in 1990, was influential in giving both ideological and factual ammunition to civil society organisations and policymakers regarding the inadequacy of structural adjustment, trickle-down economics, and laissez-faire in tackling inequality, lack of democracy, and weaknesses in the social fabric. Here is what it had to say about the conception and vision of the human development indicators in the first report: '[...] we are rediscovering the essential truth that people must be at the centre of all development. The purpose of development is to offer people more options [...] including long life, knowledge, political freedom, personal security, community participation and guaranteed human rights. People cannot be reduced to a single dimension as economic creatures' (UNDP, 1990, iii).

In the wake of the Jomtien Conference, and around twenty years after the publication of *Learning to Be*, UNESCO entrusted an independent commission of fifteen people, chaired by Jacques Delors, with the task of looking at the challenges of education for the twenty-first century. The commission's work consisted in hearings, and the examination of studies it requested. Its report (Delors, 1996) was a call for a humanistic, people-centred vision of education. It was framed in the light of, and was an alternative to, several decades of intense focus on the macro-economic benefits of schooling and training. Its foundation view of education, based on four pillars—*learning to know, learning to do, learning to be,* and *learning to live together*—resonated with a large constituency of educators, policymakers, and governments. Education was placed primarily in its social setting—in the light of the challenges of global interdependence, enhanced democratic participation, and sustainable development. Its plea was for the development of a learning society, in which citizens would be able and conscious actors in the construction of their environment and the world at large.

5 See documents from the World Education Forum, Dakar, http://www.unesco.org/education/efa/wef_2000/ (accessed on 8 May 2014).

The World Bank's 1995 education strategy (World Bank, 1995), while sticking to its rates-of-return calculations and maintaining throughout the text that education is principally aimed at economic growth (co-defined with poverty reduction) and knowledge creation, softened much of its language to take on board notions of human development. It discovered the virtues of general secondary education, including in poor countries and for poor people. Its introduction gives a nod to the Delors report's 'four pillars' of learning: education produces knowledge, skills, values, and attitudes. Still, most of the justification of education remains based on calculations of its economic value.

As already mentioned, the launch of the EFA monitoring system has federated and driven much of the thinking and discussion internationally since 2002. Its thematic reports (Education Global Monitoring Report Team, 2013) are firmly grounded in a rights-based approach, building on the Delors report's four pillars and inspired by Amartya Sen's theoretical development of the notion of individual capability (Unterhalter, 2003).

On the donor side, the Fast Track Initiative that has become the Global Partnership for Education has developed its own monitoring mechanisms, and launched in 2012 a series of annual reports (Global Partnership for Education, 2012) on progress towards national education sector plans on access and learning outcomes. The indicators regarding enrolments and quality certainly focus on the right to education and on learning outcomes, rather than economic indicators.

5 The Increasing Role of the Private Sector

However, beyond unity of discourse, as the World Bank has moved to using language more friendly to the notions of human development, the UN and its specialised agencies have enthusiastically embraced collaboration with the private sector.

It was at the 1990 World Conference on EFA that there was the first notable inclusion of the private sector among international and national partners working towards universal education.[6] Seeking to expand the range of actors involved in contributing to the EFA goals (World Conference on Education for All, 1990) was a logical response in the need to mobilise new resources,

6 'Achieving Education for All will also require more creative and sustained mobilisation of resources from other parts of society, including different levels of government, the private sector and non-governmental organisations.' World Education Forum 2000 website http://www.unesco.org/education/wef/en-conf/dakframeng.shtm (accessed on 30 March 2014).

particularly when classic development mechanisms were demonstrating intractable problems. It is now conventional wisdom that public—private partnerships for education (whether bilateral or multi-stakeholder), essentially aimed at increasing the contribution of business and civil society to the provision and monitoring of education at all levels, should be able both to generate new resources and to enrich skills and experience available for educational reform. The UN has embraced public—private partnerships and multi-stakeholder partnerships, as has the World Bank (Patrinos and Sosale, 2007; United Nations Global Compact website in the state of 2007).[7] UNESCO has courted private sector partners for more than a decade. It has working agreements in the field of education with Microsoft, Varkey GEMS Foundation, Procter & Gamble, the Packard Foundation, and others. UNESCO had, beginning in 1997 a multi-year programme with the World Economic Forum, has established working relationships and memoranda of understanding on education with a range of multinationals, has endorsed debt conversion development bonds for financing basic education, and has brought out a guide for corporations (UNESCO, 2013).

Unfortunately, the dialogue on the question of public—private partnerships is clouded by both meaning and ideology.[8] The very concept of partnership means different things to different people. Partnerships can be very different in nature depending on whether they involve business or the not-for-profit private sector. Furthermore, corporate foundations vary greatly in their organisational and funding independence from their corporate founders (Martens, 2007). Partnerships between the public sector and the for-profit private sector in which investment, risks, and benefits are shared equally are rare. Nonprofit contributions from the private sector to education are a tiny proportion of education costs. The overwhelming majority of so-called partnerships are simply sub-contracts by public entities to private firms, with the public sector shouldering most, if not all, of the risk. As for the amounts involved, there is no international tracking of private sector flows of funding for development in general. But except for cases in which all foreign sources of money—including remittances and foreign direct investment—are lumped together, evidence is scarce that the amounts destined for education are significant (van Fleet, 2012).

7 United Nations Global Compact webpage, http://www.unglobalcompact.org.

8 See NORRAG website http://www.norrag.org/en/publications/norrag-news/online-version/the-new-politics-of-partnership-peril-or-promise/detail/white-knight-or-trojan-horse-the-private-sector-and-education-for-all-1.html (accessed on 30 March 2014).

Why does this matter? It matters because as business becomes an accepted and active partner in the development of education policies and management, business interests creep into the formulation of aims and strategy. Furthermore, partnerships are often poorly regulated, with contracts being unclear about ultimate responsibility for problems and failure, and transparency is thus weakened (Utting and Zammit, 2006). Business interests are not, and cannot be, primarily to serve the public good. Long-term investment of businesses is rarely directed towards ensuring equity. Calls for making more of an effort are likely to be heeded, and as a modest contribution to overall education funding, by a small minority of large corporations with deep pockets. The global partnership on development data proposed by the UN's High Level Panel is a case in point, whereby the private sector is to be not a subcontractor but an equal partner in the push to 'develop a global strategy to fill critical gaps, expand data accessibility, and galvanise international efforts to ensure a baseline for post-2015 targets' (High Level Panel on the Post-2015 Development Agenda, 2013, chapter 4).

In recent years a standardised testing mania that began in a few wealthy countries has produced another divide regarding the purposes and potential of education. Proponents of standardised testing are convinced that it contributes to accountability and to improving the relevance of education as well as the performance of individual teachers and of entire schools. Evidence is scarce that this is true.[9] What is beyond argument is that the education industry now has a powerful financial interest in defending standardised testing, and in expanding it as a method worldwide. This results in, among other things, a narrowing and standardisation of curricula to focus essentially on the subjects covered by tests. Relevance and quality, then, can be defined and driven by what seems amenable to testing.

To be sure, education should be relevant to later life, and the education sector needs to be aware that business can help ensure such relevance. But that relevance should not be entirely decided independently of the learners and their families or standardised for the whole world to make testing simpler. Education is part of the process of preparing for adult life and adapting during adult life to a variety of needs, only one of which is related to the initial workplace. As businesses and corporations become more and more involved in the design of curricula, educational delivery, data collection, and assessment of outcomes, there is a strong risk of shifting priorities towards processes and contents that serve business interests. These interests lie both in having immediately employable school-leavers and in having processes that are profitable.

---

9 See Diane Ravitch's Blog at http://dianeravitch.net/ (accessed on 30 March 2014).

6 Education in the Next International Development Agenda

The EFA movement has certainly favoured the emergence of a relative unity of discourse among the main international actors, international governmental organisations, bilateral donors, and NGOs. Education as a human right is now the first statement and central argument of most international policy documents on the subject. The reality of permanent crisis in certain countries and between certain countries has now been integrated into the conversation, if not into sums dedicated to development assistance. The spectacular growth of income inequality has caught the attention of observers and features prominently in the yearly EFA Global Monitoring Reports and most of the documents leading up to the establishment of the post-2015 agenda. The World Bank now talks more about learning and less about knowledge (World Bank, 2011). Equity figures prominently in the texts outlining principles. Yet, the discrepancy between the announced aim of poverty reduction and the growth in unequal distribution of wealth is tackled mainly by academics and a few international NGOs. The lack of a general theory of development (McGrath, 2012) and the failure of most mainstream policy documents to consider the perverse effects of reform in the form of privatisation, limiting the role of and space for teacher involvement in reform and choices regarding priorities and the allocation of funds are also an unfortunate common theme.

The main trends affecting our topic in recent years—the equilibrium or lack of it between education as an economic tool and education as a public good—are related to

- widespread advocacy and acceptance of the role of the private sector in both the design and the provision of education;
- trends to generalise international tools of measurement and testing;
- the search for tools that can help education contribute to reducing poverty and unemployment, notably by insisting on the relevance of education to the economy.

The right to quality schooling does not, of course, mean that everyone will obtain equal results. But as with all public goods and services, governments' roles are to mitigate the circumstances that prevent individuals and groups from benefitting equally from schooling and other learning opportunities. While this chapter is not primarily focused on measurable benefits from schooling, it may be useful to examine briefly how the ideology of individual responsibility drives the education agenda and some of the perverse effects of standardised measurement.

One of the most important features of the last two decades or so is the growth, worldwide, of inequality of income. So, although education has, to a very significant extent, narrowed or even reversed the gender gap in access to schooling, it has not played its expected role in narrowing the gap in human development (United Nations Development Programme, 2013). This growth in inequality calls into question many of the main thrusts of education and development policy worldwide. Education is widely accepted as a human right and research overwhelmingly shows that economic disparities are the most reliable predictors of educational disparities. Yet, measures of learning outcomes are still generally focused on individual success or failure. We are still lacking indicators of progress towards narrowing disparities: in measuring the impact of policies that focus on marginalised groups and individuals.

Much of the contemporary education reform discussion, primarily driven by thinkers, funders, and other influential actors in English-speaking countries, assumes that improving schools can solve most of the problems around the learning outcomes of marginalised groups. Prominent funders of education and development like the World Bank, the Department for International Development (DFID, UK), USAID, focus on improving schools and the school environment. A further assumption is made that unemployment can be tackled by improving the skill sets of the unemployed, mainly by making the content of learning directly relevant to actual or hoped-for employment opportunities. Nearly all the recent papers and declarations leading up to the post-2015 agenda have made these two assumptions. Yet, the evidence is relatively thin to support either (Ravitch, 2013; Shierholz, 2013). Education does not create employment. What learners bring to school, in terms of advantage or disadvantage, is as important as what they find there.

Finally, testing individual learners on subject matter competence has emerged as the principal method for ascertaining the quality of learning and of schools. These processes have the ultimate consequence of failing to address a number of key features of education. Some that one can name are: the functioning of institutions, the social and ethnic composition of institutions that contributes to or detracts from learning, the skills and aptitudes that go beyond individual competence, or the way in which the status and functioning of the education profession impacts education quality. As long as these are treated only as background features, we may miss most of the essential things we need to know. As long as we are primarily testing individuals, there will continue to be winners and losers, and the essence of a complete, quality education for all will not be achieved.

Remedies for inadequate mastery of key skills centre around earlier entry into learning institutions, increased privatisation, or the use of private contractors so as to increase choice and/or efficiency, widespread standardised measurement and testing, and placing more responsibility on teachers for learning outcomes. Few of these policy proposals are costed (or calculated by rate-of-return methods for that matter) side-by-side with policy alternatives aimed at tackling fundamental socio-economic inequalities. The perverse effects of the focus on school efficiency (e.g. the narrowing of curricula and the disempowerment of teachers in the wake of widespread high-stakes testing) are not adequately assessed. In spite of widespread agreement that data on education systems and learning outcomes should be disaggregated to track inequality (United Nations, 2013; High Level Panel on the Post-2015 Development Agenda, 2013), we have every reason to fear that this will not happen with the necessary regularity or longevity to inform policies that can reduce the effects of disadvantage. Helping '[...] people build resilience to life's uncertainties' (High Level Panel on the Post-2015 Development Agenda, 2013, Executive Summary) is not the same thing as implementing policies that minimise egregious existing injustices and disparities among people, and even more importantly, groups.

In the meantime, much international data collection is about averages, and not enough about who is being left behind, why that is so, and what evidence there is regarding the effectiveness of measures to combat marginalisation (van Fleet, 2012). Most justifications of education aimed at donors or constituencies of donors are significantly rooted in the notion of education as an investment in human capacity for economic growth.

7 Conclusion

Clearly, in the push and pull of emphases of the importance of education, all actors shift emphases and attention over time. The UN system tends to favour idealism over messy reality in its policies, moving forward the rights agenda sometimes without enough attention to constraints even while increasingly embracing the notion of partnership with the corporate sector. The inevitable rationing of social services is not a popular theme in UN bodies. The funders, whether the World Bank, the International Monetary Fund (IMF) or bilateral agencies, have constituencies to which they are answerable. These constituencies do not always share the humanistic vision of the UN and have different or divided priorities, even more so when domestic public financing is under strain. Corporations in wealthy donor countries seek Corporations government assistance to reach new markets, and bilateral aid is often used to ease the way.

As the EFA goals and the Millennium Development Goals approach the 2015 target year, there has been intense activity to prepare the next stages (King and Palmer, 2013). The first proposals of the UN Secretary General's High Level Panel were released in 2013 (High Level Panel on the Post-2015 Development Agenda, 2013), and education was one of the twelve goals proposed.

How and by whom will quality be defined and measured? If the growing pressure for widespread international metrics results in significant expansion of standardised testing developed and administered by corporations, what resources will be diverted from the actual task of ensuring the most marginalised become included? How and by whom will inequality be defined, measured, and collected? Who will be the gatekeepers of the data revolution called for? Will the focus on a few limited outcomes of schooling not lead to a narrowing of the ambitions for education? Will the push for employability lead to a further narrowing of the ambitions for education and the learning experience of most? The answers to these questions will decide much about how the right to education will be offered and by whom it will be exercised.

The World Bank has already announced a major commitment to SABER (Systems Approach for Better Education Results), which intends to cover all the key domains of education (World Bank, 2011); Brookings and UNESCO's Institute for Statistics are moving quickly to flesh out for adoption international metrics for measuring school learning outcomes at all levels and in seven domains (LMTF (Learning Metrics Task Force), 2013); PISA for Development 'aims to increase developing countries' use of PISA assessments for monitoring progress towards nationally-set targets [...] in the post-2015 framework being developed within the UN's thematic consultations'.[10] Private entities have a lot to gain in the development and marketing of standardised measurement tools. Some have already been intimately involved in the development stages. Standardisation provides much better market opportunities for international corporations than nationally-tailored standards and measurements.

Of the five transformative shifts proposed by the High-Level Panel, the first is 'Leave no one behind'. The only sector that can and might make that happen is the public sector. If the goals of education are to ensure targeted preparation and support to the system so that each person can experience the possibility of discovering her or his own potential, then we need a much stronger commitment and the construction of more complex and differentiated tools for assessing how we are doing. If education is a public good, then it should be non-excludable. We are not there yet, in practice or in philosophy.

10 Programme for International Student Assessment (PISA), http://www.oecd.org/pisa/aboutpisa/pisafordevelopment.htm (accessed on 30 March 2014).

It seems reasonably clear that, in the near future at least, the combination of slow growth among donor countries, reduced support for public sector spending and influence, strategic planning for market opportunities by key technology and media corporations, and a desperate search for practical help from the education sector in alleviating poverty and youth unemployment, will favour economically led approaches to education planning. What will likely be missed out, if that is the case, will be policies that aggressively target disadvantage and that treat education, in the words of Jacques Delors, as a means to 'foster a deeper and more harmonious form of human development and thereby to reduce poverty, exclusion, ignorance, oppression and war'.

References

Adams, A.V., J. Middleton, A. Ziderman (1992) 'The World Bank's policy paper of vocational and technical education and training', *Prospects*, Vol. 22, pp. 127–40.

Coombs, P.H. (1968) *The World Education Crisis: A Systems Analysis.* (New York: Oxford University Press).

Delors J. (Chair) (1996) *Learning: The Treasure Within*, Report to UNESCO of the International Commission on Education for the Twenty-first Century (Highlights) (Paris: UNESCO) http://unesdoc.unesco.org/images/0010/001095/109590eo.pdf (accessed on 1 April 2014).

Emmerij, L. (2010) *The Basic Needs Development Strategy*, Background paper, World Economic and Social Survey 2010, https://www.un.org/en/development/desa/policy/wess/wess_bg_papers/bp_wess2010_emmerij.pdf (accessed on 1 April 2014).

Faure, E., et al. (1972) *Learning to Be: The World of Education Today and Tomorrow*, Report of the Edgar Faure Commission (Paris: UNESCO).

Gajardo, M. (1993) *Thinkers on Education: Ivan Illich*, originally published in *Prospects: the quarterly review of education* (Paris: UNESCO) http://www.ibe.unesco.org/fileadmin/user_upload/archive/publications/ThinkersPdf/illiche.PDF (accessed on 1 April 2014).

Gerhardt, H.-P. (1993) *Thinkers on Education: Paolo Freire*, originally published in *Prospects: the quarterly review of education* (Paris: UNESCO), http://www.ibe.unesco.org/fileadmin/user_upload/archive/publications/ThinkersPdf/freiree.PDF (accessed on 26 June 2013).

Global Partnership for Education (2012) *Results for Learning Report 2012: Fostering Evidence-Based Dialogue to Monitor Access and Quality in Education* (Washington, D.C.: Global Partnership), http://www.globalpartnership.org/content/all-children-learning-report-2012–2013 (accessed on 29 April 2012).

High Level Panel on the Post-2015 Development Agenda (2013) *A New Global Partnership: Eradicate Poverty and Transform Economies through Sustainable Development*, Report of the High-Level Panel of Eminent Persons on the Post-2015 Development Agenda, http://www.post2015hlp.org/featured/high-level-panel-releases-recommendations-for-worlds-next-development-agenda/ (accessed on 11 June 2013).

Kaul, I., I. Grunberg and M.A. Stern (eds.) (1999) *Global Public Goods: International Cooperation in the 21st Century* (New York: Oxford University Press), http://web.undp.org/globalpublicgoods/TheBook/globalpublicgoods.pdf (accessed on 1 April 2014).

King, K. and R. Palmer (2013) *Post-2015 Agendas: Northern Tsunami, Southern Ripple? The case of Education and Skills*, Working Paper 4 (Geneva: NORRAG), http://www.norrag.org/index.php?id=167&type=0&juSecure=1&locationData=167%3Atx_dam%3A297&juHash=947382fffb3ec4ebd9776691bc9c9cb9724cfdce (accessed on 27 October 2013).

Learning Metrics Task Force (LMTF) (2013) *Toward Universal Learning: A Global Framework for Measuring Learning*, Report No. 2 (Montreal and Washington, D.C.: UNESCO Institute for Statistics and Center for Universal Education at the Brookings Institution), http://www.brookings.edu/research/reports/2013/07/global-framework-measuring-learning (accessed on 2 August 2013).

Martens, J. (2007) *Multistakeholder Partnerships: Future Models of Multilateralism? Potential Pitfalls of Multistakeholder Partnerships* (Berlin: Friedrich-Ebert-Stiftung e.V.), http://library.fes.de/pdf-files/iez/04244.pdf (accessed on 29 July 2011).

McGrath, S. (2012) 'Education and Skills Post-2015: What Education; What Development?' *NORRAG NewsBite*, http://norrag.wordpress.com/2012/09/17/education-and-skills-post-2015-what-education-what-development/ (accessed on 1 April 2014).

Patrinos, H.A. and S. Sosale (eds.) (2007) *Mobilizing the Private Sector for Public Education A View from the Trenches* (Washington, D.C.: World Bank), http://siteresources.worldbank.org/EDUCATION/Resources/278200-1099079877269/547664-1099079934475/Mobilizing_PrivateSector_PublicEdu.pdf (accessed on 1 April 2014).

Ravitch, D. (2013) 'Stop Blaming Schools for Inequality', *authors personal blog*, http://dianeravitch.net/2013/04/29/stop-blaming-schools-for-inequality/ (accessed on 1 April 2014).

Samoff, J. and B. Carrol (2003) *From Manpower Planning to the Knowledge Era: World Bank Policies on Higher Education in Africa* Prepared for the UNESCO Forum on Higher Education, Research and Knowledge (Paris: UNESCO), http://portal.unesco.org/education/en/file_download.php/d23a168b1dbb956f3c63676d5842b6a3Samoff+doc.doc. (accessed on 8 August 2013).

Samuelson, P.A. (1954) 'The Pure Theory of Public Expenditure', *Review of Economics andStatistics,* 36(4), pp.387–389, http://links.jstor.orgsici?sici=0034–6535%28195411%2936%3A4%3C387%3ATPTOPE%3E2.0.CO%3B2-A (accessed on 1 April 2014).

Secretariat of the World Conference on EFA (1990) *Meeting Basic Learning Needs: A Vision for the 1990s World Conference on EFA, Jomtien, 1990*, Background document (New York: UNICEF), http://unesdoc.unesco.org/images/0009/000975/097552e.pdf (accessed on 08 August 2013).

Sen, A. (2003) *The importance of basic education*, Speech to the Commonwealth Education Conference, Edinburgh, http://www.theguardian.com/education/2003/oct/28/schools.uk4 (accessed on 1 April 2014).

Shierholz, H. (2013) 'We have a demand problem, not a skills problem', *Working Economics*, http://www.epi.org/blog/high-underemployment-young-college-grads/ (accessed on 1 April 2014).

Spalletti, S. (2008) *The History of Manpower Forecasting in Modelling Labour Market* (Macerata: University of Macerata), http://www.unimc.it/sviluppoeconomico/wpaper/wpaper00018/filePaper (accessed on 1 April 2013).

Tilak, J.B.G. (2007a) 'Best Practice in Education and Training: Hype or Hope?', *NORRAG News*, No. 39, http://www.norrag.org/es/publications/boletin-norrag/online-version/best-practice-in-education-and-training-hype-or-hope.html (accessed on 1 April 2014).

——— (2007b) 'Rate Of Return To Education: Best Practice?', *NORRAG News*, No. 39, http://www.norrag.org/en/publications/norrag-news/online-version/best-practice-in-education-and-training-hype-or-hope/detail/rate-of-return-to-education-best-practice.html (accessed on 1 April 2014).

UN Global Compact (2013) *UN—Business Partnerships: A Handbook* (New York: UN Global Compact), http://www.unglobalcompact.org/docs/issues_doc/un_business_partnerships/UNBusinessPartnershipHandbook.pdf (accessed on 5 December 2013).

United Nations (2013) *Global Thematic Consultation on Education and The Post-2015 Development Framework: Making Education for All a Reality*, Beyond 2015 Position paper, www.worldwewant2015.org/file/340073/download/369696 (accessed on 31 October 2013).

United Nations Development Programme (UNDP) (2013) *Human Development Report 2013* (New York: UNDP), http://hdr.undp.org/en/reports/global/hdr2013/download/ (accessed on 6 August 2013).

UNDP (1990) *Human Development Report 1990* (New York: Oxford University Press), http://hdr.undp.org/sites/default/files/reports/219/hdr_1990_en_complete_nostats.pdf (accessed on 1 April 2014).

United Nations Educational, Scientific and Cultural Organization (UNESCO) (2013) *The Smartest Investment: A Framework for Business Engagement in Education* (Paris: UNESCO), http://www.unglobalcompact.org/resources/391 (accessed on 5 November 2013).

UNESCO (2013) *Education for All Global Monitoring Report* (Paris: UNESCO), http://www.unesco.org/new/en/education/themes/leading-the-international-agenda/efareport/ (accessed on 1 April 2014).

Unterhalter, E. (2003) *Education, Capabilities and Social Justice*, Background paper prepared for the Education for All Global Monitoring Report 2003/4 (Paris: UNESCO), http://www.unesco.org/ulis/cgi-bin/ulis.pl?database=&lin=1&futf8=1&ll=1&gp=0&look=basic&sc1=1&sc2=1&ref=http://www.unesco.org/ulis/education/EFA/GMR_search.html&nl=1&req=2&by=2&au=Unterhalter,%20Elaine (accessed on 27 October 2013).

Utting, P. and A. Zammit (2006) *Beyond pragmatism: appraising UN-business partnerships What drives the Public Private Partnership phenomenon?* (Geneva: United Nations Research Institute for Social Development) http://www.unrisd.org/80256B3C005BCCF9/httpNetITFramePDF?ReadForm&parentunid=225508544695E8F3C12572300038ED22&parentdoctype=paper&netitpath=80256B3C005BCCF9/(httpAux Pages)/225508544695E8F3C12572300038ED22/$file/uttzam.pdf (accessed on 29 July 2011).

Vally, D. and C.A. Spreen (2012) 'Human Rights in the World Bank 2020 Education Strategy', in Klees, S.J., J. Samoff and N.P. Stromquist (eds.) *The World Bank and Education: Critiques and Alternatives* (Rotterdam: Sense Publishers), pp. 173–188, https://www.sensepublishers.com/media/1165-the-world-bank-and-education.pdf (accessed on 1 April 2014).

van Fleet, J.W. (2012) *Scaling Up Corporate Social Investments in Education: Five Strategies that Work* (Washington, D.C.: The Brookings Institution) http://www.brookings.edu/~/media/research/files/papers/2012/5/corporate%20investments%20vanfleet/05_corporate_investments_vanfleet.pdf (accessed on 20 May 2012).

World Bank (2011) *Learning for All: Investing in People's Knowledge and Skills to Promote Development. World Bank Group Education Strategy 2020* (Washington, D.C.: World Bank), http://siteresources.worldbank.org/EDUCATION/Resources/ESSU/Education_Strategy_4_12_2011.pdf (accessed on 3 April 2014).

——— (1995) *Priorities and Strategies for Education: A World Bank Review*, Development in Practice (Washington, D.C.: World Bank), http://siteresources.worldbank.org/EDUCATION/Resources/278200-1099079877269/547664-1099080118171/Priorities_and_Strategies_for_Ed_WB_Review.pdf (accessed on 06 July 2013).

——— (1971) *Education Sector working paper* (Washington, D.C.: World Bank), http://documents.worldbank.org/curated/en/1971/09/700922/education (accessed on 3 April 2014).

World Conference on Education for All (1990) *World Declaration on Education for All* (Jomtien, Thailand: UNESCO), http://www.unesco.org/education/efa/ed_for_all/background/jomtien_declaration.shtml (accessed on 29 July 2011).

PART 2

Shaping Training and Lifelong Learning

CHAPTER 4

Tertiary Technical Education and Youth Integration in Brazil, Colombia and Mexico

Claudia Jacinto and Ana García de Fanelli

Abstract

Vocational training versus a traditional university education. This chapter seeks to answer the question of whether 'tertiary technical education' has contributed to increasing economic and social opportunity for young people in Latin America, using three case studies from Brazil, Colombia and Mexico. It examines the extent to which tertiary technical education has contributed towards democratising access to education through institutional diversification, expanded enrolment and, at least theoretically, improved access to quality employment. The analysis shows that tertiary technical education has contributed to widening of opportunities by offering an alternative form of education to new generations of young people. Tertiary technical education is more accessible, shorter in duration, has a vocational orientation, and tends to be cheaper than a university education. However, the case studies also reveal that while a tertiary technical education diploma is an asset for young people seeking employment, it nonetheless does not have the same perceived value as a traditional university education. Available data appear to indicate that graduates of tertiary technical education earn less on average than university graduates and face several challenges in the labour market. Furthermore, the studies reveal that despite the presence of highly regarded tertiary technical education institutions in all three countries, these carry less prestige and status than universities.

1 Introduction

The acceleration of economic growth experience by Latin America during the 2000s (an average annual Gross Domestic Product (GDP) growth rate of about 5 per cent in 2003–08 (OECD, 2012) can be considered as offering a window of opportunity to ensure development sustainability. Changes in domestic productive systems and labour markets, on-going transformations of information and communication technologies and increasing integration into regional and

 DOI 10.1163/9789004281158_005

globalised markets have all combined to create new requirements, and new demands, for qualifications. At the same time, many key skills are found to crosscut different sectors and segments of the labour market (e.g. the ability to manage software, organise work, lead groups, etc.).

To accomplish the goal of sustainable development, it is key to invest in human capital and human development. In Latin America, the proportion of the total population aged 15 and over that had completed tertiary education grew 12 times over the past 50 years, from 0.6 per cent in 1950 to 7.1 per cent in 2000. Although this was a significant increase, it still lags considerably behind developed countries, where 14.5 per cent of the population aged 15 and older had completed some form of post-secondary education (Barro and Lee, 2010). Within a context of low unemployment across Latin American countries from 2005–10, tertiary education increased the probability of attaining both some form of employment and a better quality of employment (García de Fanelli, 2013a). Moreover, the private rate of return of higher education is quite high in some Latin America countries, averaging 15 per cent per annum for post-secondary education (García de Fanelli, 2013a).

Unfortunately, data that discriminates between tertiary non-university and university programmes is very scarce. A few studies from the mid-2000s claimed that tertiary technical education in Latin America was insufficient, inadequate and incompatible with the demands of globalisation (Espíndola and García, 2005). According to these studies, negative features of tertiary technical education (also 'TTE') included weak ties with the productive sector, high drop-out rates, a deficient coordination with the university sector, as well as public policies that were more concerned, until very recently, about supporting universities than developing the sector more generally. This critical diagnosis stands in contrast to the fact that the continual, though insufficient, expansion of secondary education throughout the region has boosted the demand for higher education. Increasingly, young people aspire to tertiary education because secondary diplomas no longer pave the way to good jobs. To respond to this social demand, the 2000s witnessed a renewed dynamism in public policies aimed at developing tertiary technical education.

In the context of these concerns, from 2009–12 the International Institute of Educational Planning (IIEP) operated a research project focused on equity and the entrance of tertiary technical education graduates into the labour market.[1] To acquire the fullest possible understanding of the issue, the IIEP employed a comparative approach, examining three case studies: Brazil, Colombia and

1 The results of the research are published in Jacinto, C. (ed.) (2013) *Incluir a los jóvenes. Retos para la educación terciaria técnica en América Latina* (Paris: IIPE-UNESCO).

Mexico. These three countries have very different linkages between education and employment, and help illustrate some of the paths followed in the region.[2]

The tertiary technical education programmes studied consist of short degree programmes (lasting approximately two or three years) at the post-secondary level geared toward developing technical qualifications that combine both theory and practice. At first, they were generally associated with non-university institutions. Today, however, tertiary technical education is taught at both non-university institutions and universities alike, in both the public and, particularly, the private sector. Moreover, institutional and curriculum integration is progressively blurring the line between university and non-university education (García de Fanelli, 2013b). At the same time, tertiary technical education courses have increased in length as they incorporate the additional knowledge and skills of information and communication technologies, English language competence and other crosscutting skills.

The study analyses the ways in which, from the perspectives of human capital and human development, tertiary technical education works to create opportunities for new graduates. It explores the various advances and contradictions in democratising access to higher education (including universities and tertiary technical education institutions) via institutional diversification, increased enrolment and the possibility of transfer with a tertiary technical education degree to earn a university degree. In doing so, we examined tertiary technical education's contribution to graduates' job placement (e.g. quality of employments, salaries, etc.) to the extent permitted by available quantitative data, but also considered the subjective perspectives of the students themselves regarding their own personal development.

Methodologically, the study proceeded in two steps. First, we analysed the available statistical and archival information to describe the trends in the development of tertiary technical education, its respective policies, and its corresponding employment placement for graduates. Additional details regarding the sources and type of quantitative data are provided, as relevant, through the various sections of this chapter. In the second step, a number of qualitative studies were carried out at several conventionally prestigious institutions (three in Colombia, six in Mexico and two in Brazil). These institutional studies included both initial interviews with heads of administration, teaching faculty, students and business leaders, and follow-ups intended to illustrate the

2 The diversity of models adopted in Latin America and their different historical roots make it hard to generalise about the region. As of yet, there has been no substantive progress on cross-national recognition of technical diplomas within the region. As such, we have preferred to limit ourselves to the three countries mentioned above.

educational processes and perceptions of the various actors. In total, more than 100 interviews were conducted in each country. Obviously, this information is not statistically representative and is limited by the dearth of panel data tracer studies tracking graduates' labour market progress over time. This means that, by and large, it is difficult to determine the independent effect(s) of qualifications on employment possibilities. The conclusions of the chapter, therefore, should be read both as a contribution to a crucial, yet often overlooked, subject and a hypothesis for future studies, as well as a source of comparison for similar tertiary technical education-related phenomena in other regions. Based on the above-mentioned research, this chapter examines the extent to which this educational experience offers young people better employment opportunities and improved well-being.

Informed by this overarching question, we focus on some specific objectives: to determine the extent of, and rationale for, expansion of this offer; to explore differences in admissions processes and overall between tertiary technical education and university institutions; to investigate the ease (or lack thereof) of tertiary technical education students' transition to universities or postgraduate studies, with respect to both technical regulations and actual practice; and finally, to examine tertiary technical education graduates' transitions into the labour market.

The chapter is divided into four sections, each based on a specific working hypothesis and aimed at discussing and organising the relevant data (though by no means meant as a definitive verification thereof). The first section discusses the current configuration of tertiary technical education in terms its relation to higher education, technical education and vocational education as a whole. The second section shows that increasing proportions of young people have been able to access higher education through this avenue, and examines the causes underlying the surge in tertiary technical education enrolment from 2000–10. The subsequent section presents the legal framework that enables tertiary technical education graduates to go on to university, and the institutional and individuated obstacles to putting it into practice. The fourth and final section analyses maps the labour market destinations of young graduates and the employment quality and career opportunities offered therein.

2 Institutional Diversification of Tertiary Technical Education: The Democratisation of Higher Education?

In what follows, we first focus on the institutional differentiation of the higher education sector, highlighting the emergence of the tertiary technical education sector and the types of students it usually attracts. We then present some provisional answers to the questions about the prestige or social status of tertiary technical education institutions in each national and local context and with respect to the selection process for admission to higher education in general.

2.1 *The Emergence of Tertiary Technical Education in the Context of Higher Education Expansion*

Higher education enrolment in Latin America is concentrated in undergraduate university programmes, with a preponderance of students pursuing a professional (rather than bachelor's) degree. Only in Argentina, Chile, Colombia, Peru and Venezuela do we see that over 25 per cent of post-secondary enrolment is found in the tertiary, non-university higher education sector (Brunner and Ferrada Hurtado, 2011).

Low-income students are more attracted to these tertiary, non-university programmes than to undergraduate university courses. Firstly, admittance to the best public and private Latin American universities is based on entrance exams and, in some cases, only a limited number of places are available (as, for example, in Chile, Brazil, Bolivia and Peru) (Brunner and Ferrada Hurtado, 2011). In general, secondary school students from disadvantaged socio-economic backgrounds seeking a higher education lack access to the leading public or private secondary schools.[3] They are often the first in their family to attend university, and thus often receive less support in pursuing their educational goals than do middle- and upper-middle class students. Secondly, non-university higher education institutions are far more regionally dispersed, thus saving students the high cost of moving to the large cities where most universities are located. Finally, these programmes are short term, thus reducing the opportunity cost of foregone earnings for students and their families, and have a vocational or technical orientation (García de Fanelli and Jacinto, 2010).

The working hypothesis that grounds our examination of this process of institutional diversification and integration in tertiary technical education holds that that it actually broadened the graduates' job opportunities, though this was somewhat tempered by variations in educational quality. The overall process of higher education institutional diversification processes converges with international trends, and raises the question as to whether this reflects greater democratisation or merely greater segmentation of the supply in higher education (Varghese, 2009).

---

3 The proportion of young people from the poorest strata who manage to complete their secondary education is also very low. See García de Fanelli and Jacinto (2010).

In principle, tertiary technical education is not only connected to higher education, but also to the history of technical and vocational education in each country. Since the 1950s, vocational training in the region has chiefly taken the form of tripartite arrangements (i.e. run jointly by the state, labour unions and businesses vocational education institutes) or institutes dependent on the states' respective education ministries. The Latin American system of tertiary technical education is distinguished by the considerable participation of the business sector in the creation and maintenance of the system, particularly in countries such as Brazil (Caillods and Jacinto, 2006).

In Brazil and Colombia, the *institutos tecnológicos* and *institutos de formación de técnicos superiores* (literally, 'technological institutes' and 'higher institutes of technical training') were generally 3-year programmes for professionally oriented post-secondary education in technical fields, historically based on technical and vocational training courses. As qualifications became more complex and education grew in scope, social and productive demand raised them first to the level of secondary technical education and/or vocational training, and later to tertiary technical education (García de Fanelli and Jacinto, 2010). The three countries studied feature diverse modalities of tertiary technical education institutional models.

In Brazil, four modes of technological education can be discerned, each with its own background and characteristics: (1) a state-run network of technical colleges and technological institutes that provide further education from the secondary to postgraduate level; (2) the so-called 'S' system, which includes the *Serviço Nacional de Aprendizagem Industrial* (SENAI) (National Service of Industrial Apprenticeship), the *Serviço Nacional de Aprendizagem Rural* (SENAR) (National Service of Rural Apprenticeship) and the *Serviço Nacional de Aprendizagem Comercial* (SENAC) (National Service of Trade Apprenticeship) and is managed in partnership with business;[4] (3) the federal network of technological education;[5] and (4) private technical schools and institutions that concentrate on training programmes for the service sector.

4 Traditionally strongly informed by the demands of the industrial sector, they provide a single institutional home for various levels of education, ranging from secondary technical education to higher education. The institutions in the 'S' system also provide technical consultation to the productive sector and develop technological innovations to meet its needs (Moura Castro and Bernasconi, 2005).

5 They began with 19 schools for craftsmen and apprentices in 1909, later becoming industrial and technical schools. Most of these schools were then turned into *Centro federal de educação tecnológica* (CEFETs—Federal Centres of Technological Education).

In Colombia, tertiary technical education forms part of the National System of Training for work: it is offered at public and private institutes and in the *Servicio Nacional de Aprendizaje* (SENA) (the National Apprenticeship Service), a public institution with considerable input from the business sector. Although the tertiary technical institutions arose as a parallel institutional model to that of universities, university degree programmes have been created at the higher technical and technological institutes, and graduates from tertiary technical education may now go on to pursue degrees at university.

In countries such as Mexico, in contrast, the history of tertiary technical education owes less to a tradition of technical education than it does to the development of the university system. Technological institutes were created in the 1950s to offer higher technological degrees. By the 1990s and 2000s, these institutes evolved into new technological 'universities', or public polytechnics, specifically mandated to offer tertiary technical education. The *Técnico Superior Universitario* (tertiary technical university) degree is mainly offered at technological universities but also at some state and private universities. The trajectory of tertiary technical education's development in Mexico was strongly informed by a policy commitment to national economic modernisation through education of the labour force, underscored by an overall goal of facilitating the transnational integration of trade and production, particularly with the United States (Flores and Mendoza, 2013).

These institutions were originally considered to be stepping stones enabling the middle classes to enter university (Tedesco, 2012). In recent decades, and particularly over the last ten years, the institutional diversification of higher education and development of tertiary technical education should undoubtedly be understood as contributing to democratisation of access to higher education where lower middle classes have been also included. The fact that tertiary non-university students come from lower socio-economic backgrounds than university students, and that tertiary non-university institutions were often created in places that had no other opportunities for higher education, speaks to this trend (García de Fanelli and Jacinto, 2010; Turbay, 2013).

2.2 *Admission Processes and Prestige in the Diversification of Higher Education*

According to interviews conducted with business people and civil servants of different levels, all three countries were found to have a core of public institutions considered superior in quality and prestige. In Brazil, this includes institutions within the 'S' system. The case studies conducted on prestigious institutions in Colombia, Mexico and Brazil indicate that the choice of short tertiary technical education programmes is not a matter of opting for the second-best, as, particularly in Colombia and Mexico, students select tertiary technical education even when they had, or continue to have, aspirations of pursuing a university degree.

Studies of Brazil and Colombia, however, include testimonials that cast doubt on the quality of private tertiary technical education education centres (García de Fanelli, 2013b), which are especially oriented toward the service sector. It may be that private tertiary technical education grew without sufficient regulation and quality control.

In the case of Brazil, this situation may change. Since 2004, Brazil has developed the *Sistema Nacional de Avaliação da Educação Superior* (SINAES) (National System for Higher Education Evaluation) to assess the quality of higher education through the use of, among other tools, a test to measure learning outcomes at the undergraduate level. The SINAES has also developed criteria for the accreditation of programmes and institutions, and has been used to regulate the growing private (for-profit) sector of Brazilian higher education (Pedrosa et al., 2013).

In Colombia, the poor quality of many private *Institutos de Educación Superior* (Higher Education Institutes) is reflected in their students' low scores on academic achievement tests designed to assess the impact of the ACCES (*Acceso Con Calidad a la Educación Superior*) student loan system, aimed at increasing access to higher education. The higher technical institutions are among those most rated as having average, low and very low academic standing; technological education fares little better (Turbay, 2013). Another study (Gómez, 2011) indicates that private higher technical education programmes concentrate on a few low-investment areas: accounting, financial administration, information systems, sales and so forth. Few technical and technological programmes are in modern fields involving in new technologies, as this would require considerable investment in equipment, laboratories and infrastructure.

In Mexico, where education is essentially public, youth and business people alike (in so far as they value training) note a segmentation in potential educational routes, differentiating between tertiary technical education and other universities (Flores Crespo and Mendoza, 2013). Admissions procedures that include exams, a fixed number of places and other selection devices act as an additional constraint on the democratisation of access. Similarly, tuition fees in the private sector in Brazil, and both sectors in Colombia, also constitute obstacles to more inclusive admissions practices.[6]

---

6 For more information regarding the higher education costs in tertiary education in Brazil, Colombia, Mexico and Peru, see Murakami and Blom (2008).

Although public policy strategies have been developed to improve inclusion and retention, such as the provision of scholarships (Brazil and Mexico) and student loans (Colombia) and/or improving the integration of secondary education and higher education through tutorials and remedial courses, the results still seem insufficient. According to research examining the financing of tertiary education in Brazil, Colombia, Mexico and Peru, Colombia is the only Latin American state where student assistance results in a significant improvement in the affordability of tertiary education (Murakami and Blom, 2008). Overall then, while that tertiary technical education might bring wider opportunities for education, it may also widen the gap between different tertiary education segments. Thus, the democratisation of access to tertiary education has been relative. Differences in quality and prestige continue to exist between tertiary technical education programmes and longer university degrees, and young people find it difficult to access and finish their studies.

3 Expanding Tertiary Technical Education: Between Social Demand and Public Policy

In all three countries, the expansion of higher education has been accompanied by the growth of secondary education, as indicated by table 4.1.

TABLE 4.1 *Net rate of enrolment (NRE) at secondary and tertiary levels, 2000 and 2010, in Brazil, Colombia, and Mexico*

	2000		2010	
	Secondary NRE	**Tertiary NRE**	**Secondary NRE**	**Tertiary NRE**
Brazil*	41.5	10.9	59	17
Colombia	66.2	17.1	79.1	24
Mexico	67.9	18.3	75.2	23.7

* Data from Brazil are from 2001 and 2011.

Source: Socio Economic Database for Latin America and the Caribbean (SEDLAC); Centro de Estudios Distributivos (CEDLAS), Laborales y Sociales Universidad Nacional de La Plata, Argentina.

The tertiary level demonstrates a clear increase in tertiary technical education enrolment. In Brazil, student enrolment in tertiary technology courses increased seven-fold between 2001 and 2010. The number of technological degrees granted also rose from 9 per cent of undergraduate enrolment in 2008 to 17.8 per cent by 2011. In Colombia, tertiary technical education enrolment soared in the last decade; while enrolment in university grew by 40 per cent from 2002 to 2010, enrolment in tertiary technical education increased 241 per cent over the same period. This is primarily considered to be the effect of government policies aimed at stimulating technical and technological education at the tertiary level, especially through the direct action of SENA and the participation of private institutions (Montañez, 2012). Even in countries like Mexico, where tertiary technical education accounts for only 3.2 per cent of total enrolment in higher education, the number of students in tertiary technical education nearly quadrupled between 1998 and 2008 (García de Fanelli, 2013b).

Our hypothesis suggests that in addition to the development of new technologies and other transformations in the demand for skilled labour, the increase in tertiary technical education has been mainly a response to social demands for more openings in higher education. This demand, in turn, can be attributed to a significant divergence in the ability to access higher education, highly dependent upon the family's socio-economic status. In Brazil, for instance, enrolment in higher education is 15 times greater amongst the wealthiest 20 per cent of the population (the fifth quintile) than amongst the poorest 20 per cent (the first quintile). In Colombia, this gap is five times wider and in Mexico the net enrolment of the wealthiest quintile is three times that of the poorest. That said, none of the countries show evidence of gender discrimination, as women's net enrolment equals or slightly exceeds that of men in all the cases (García de Fanelli, 2013b).

Thus, one reason for the rise in tertiary technical education enrolment may be the incorporation of students from low- and low-middle income groups into secondary education and the corresponding increase in the number of students who complete this level. Pressure placed upon access to higher education by lower-income portions of the population is particularly evident in Colombia: the secondary education graduation rate for students from lower socio-economic sectors reached 70 per cent in 2010 (Jacinto, 2013). In this context, enrolment in tertiary technical education comprises 30 per cent of total higher education enrolment.

Private education played a key role in this regard in Brazil and Colombia. In Brazil, eight of every ten institutions are private, as are seven out of ten in Colombia. Brazil's private sector is composed of universities, schools and technological centres.[7] In Colombia, private higher education consists of a network of professional technical institutes, technological institutes, university institutes and universities.[8] Education in Mexico, in contrast, is predominantly public.

Faced increasing demand for higher education, public policies have responded by creating a few public institutions on the one hand, and by enabling the private sector to provide such education on the other. Moreover, the creation of new public education institutions offering tertiary technical education programmes are often linked to decentralised, regional initiatives that address demands for local development. The new regional centres in Colombia and the increasing federal school system in Brazil are particularly good examples of this process (Jacinto, 2013).

Although this expansion initially took place without clear state regulation, to address the heterogeneity in quality and relevance of this expansion, over the last decade governments have been developing quality assurance systems. Recently, all three countries have developed accreditation and evaluation criteria to be applied to all institutions, be they public or private, thus strengthening the role of the state in the field of tertiary technical education.

Overall, across contexts and in its various institutional forms, tertiary technical education offers an alternative for secondary school graduates who are also seeking rapid employment opportunities or an intermediate degree prior to university studies. According to statements of the young people interviewed, they have no other options in their places of residence.

4 Does Tertiary Technical Education Increase Access to University?

To examine the issue of opportunity creation in higher education, we begin with the working hypothesis that, despite the existence of formal regulations in each of the case studies, there are insufficient practical means of bridging the gap between tertiary technical education and university education. For young people to be able to go on to university or post-graduate studies, personal matters (for example, balancing work and study) must be addressed and assurances given as to the quality, pertinence and relevance of the tertiary

7 During the last decade, a significant for-profit private higher education sector has also gained greater importance (Rama, 2012).

8 For more information about the programmes offered at these types of institutions, see García de Fanelli (2013b).

technical education on offer. The section proceeds by developing arguments to support this hypothesis.

In all three cases, progress has been made in connecting tertiary technical education to university level education. In line with international trends in the promotion of lifelong learning, credit transfer systems are being designed to enable coursework to cross over from one institution to another. The development of vertical institutional models, wherein technological institutions include everything from technical and vocational secondary education to doctorate programs, follows a similar logic. This model is exemplified by Brazil, where the tertiary technical education certificate was turned into an undergraduate degree, thereby allowing students to go on to postgraduate studies. Colombia is following a similar path by enabling tertiary technical and technological institutes to award university degrees. This represents an attempt to address the difficulties tertiary technical education graduates encountered in having their diplomas recognised by universities (Turbay, 2013). In Mexico, the situation is slightly different. The Mexican system does have rules enabling transfer between the different subsystems of technological higher education, but, somewhat ironically, these regulations have served to complicate institutional and curricular reorganisation. In Colombia and Mexico, tertiary technical education graduates may, at least in theory, go on to study for a university degree, but in practice there are institutional, cultural and economic obstacles that often prevent them from doing so. Both countries attempt to integrate these institutions by other means, such as the partial transfer of select modules within university education. Again, in theory, this option would be facilitated by a skills-based system of evaluation from which equivalencies across the different levels might be determined.

The institutions analysed in the case studies have also tried to either integrate the different modalities of teaching within the same organisation, or make arrangements with other institutions to further the same goal (García de Fanelli, 2013b). That said, integrating and coordinating institutions with different traditions and levels of social prestige is not easy. This is compounded by competition between universities and non-universities for funding, as an asymmetry of influence is quite typical amongst the different types of higher education. These practical obstacles are exacerbated by the curricular tensions between the predominantly theoretical training of universities and the theoretical-practical training of technical colleges and technological institutes (Gallart, 2002; Bernasconi, 2006). In summary, the process of articulation and integration between non-university and university education remains incipient. While we lack statistics on the educational continuity between one level and another for tertiary technical education graduates, anecdotal evidence suggests the actual number is low across all three studies.

From the perspective of promoting lifelong learning, improving the articulation between educational systems and opportunities must be a priority in struggle to realise the right to education and training. Although technically permitted by the rules and regulations of each of the three countries, both personal and institutional conditions must be improved if young people are to make these kinds of moves. Furthermore, in Latin America, the formal recognition of the skills of employees working in higher technical positions is weak.

5 Does the Tertiary Technical Education Diploma Lead to Greater Opportunities in the Labour Market?

What is the productive sector demand for graduates of tertiary technical education? Is there any demand, moreover, for them specifically? In answer to these questions, we hypothesise that while tertiary technical education helps graduates to find employment, their subsequent upward mobility hits a 'ceiling'. It should be noted that the data we gathered on this subject differs from country to country, and even in countries with greater and more representative data, the question at hand is not fully addressed.[9]

With respect to Colombia, quantitative studies from the *Observatorio Laboral*, as well as a study of graduates from three institutions (Turbay, 2013), show that tertiary technical education degrees play a significant role in finding employment. For graduates from technical schools and institutes of technology, the percentage of graduates finding employment in the formal sector (66.4 per cent and 73.6 per cent respectively) is slightly lower than that of university graduates (76.7 per cent) (Observatorio Laboral para la Educación, 2011).[10] In general terms, the demand for tertiary technical education graduates is driven by the service sector, for degrees in areas such as accounting, secretarial skills, tourism, computer science, etc. For tertiary technical education graduates in industrial occupations, demand is more disaggregated, and linked to specific companies and sectors.

9 As we use aggregate data, it is not possible to discern what may be very dissimilar patterns in different subsectors of technical qualification. Some evidence about this matter was collected in the qualitative studies, however, as will be discussed shortly.

10 This source only provides data regarding the formal sector of the economy.

In terms of the income earned by graduates of the different modalities of higher education, from 2005–07, though tertiary technical education graduates, on average, earned less than university graduates, their income growth rate slightly exceeded that of university graduates (García de Fanelli, 2013b). As would be expected, analysis of the salaries of recent graduates by type of education and gender shows that the higher the level of education, the greater the average starting salary. It also demonstrates that, across the board, the average salary of women is lower than that of men. As a whole, recent female graduates that work as wage earners earn 12.6 per cent less than men. For men, a university degree equated to a starting salary 52 per cent higher than that of a graduate of a technical college and 34 per cent higher than that of a graduate of a technological institute. For women with a university degree, the gap between their starting salary and the starting salary of female graduates from technological institutes is similar to the gap between men, but even greater with respect to female technical college graduates. The average starting salary of a female university graduate is 56 per cent higher than that of a female technical college graduate. Whatever the sector men's salaries are 10 to 15 per cent higher that those of women (García de Fanelli, 2013b).

In short, this data shows that the marketplace of occupations and income for graduates from technical college and institutes of technology is not on par with that of university graduates. The percentage of workers employed in the formal sector is high, however, and their salaries have tended to increase more sharply than those of other graduates of higher education. The qualitative data following up the tertiary technical education graduates in the study indicates that after graduation, their incomes improve by 20 to 35 per cent and they are promoted from operators to supervisors, technicians or area managers. That said, they are extremely likely to encounter an income ceiling during their career, as well as other conditions that limit their social and work life. A technical certificate does not enable upward employment mobility in subsequent occupations (Turbay, 2013).

In Mexico, the data on tertiary technical education graduates' average monthly income in 2005 indicates that they earn roughly only half of what a university graduate earns.[11] There is, however, some variance depending on the professional field, for tertiary technical education and university graduates alike (García de Fanelli, 2013b).

Why are tertiary technical education graduates paid less than their university-educated counterparts? On the one hand, the rates of return on education

11 Regrettably, there is currently no data available that would enable comparison of this variable with that of graduates of secondary education.

are usually higher for those with scarcer qualifications. On the other hand, the qualitative case studies reveal that even when filling a technical position, employers tend to prefer people with academic qualifications to those with technical qualifications. This is primarily due to the fact that in Latin American countries, as a result of a highly credentialistic process, the university degrees are more valued in firms (Bourdieu and Passeron, 1973; Rodriguez Gomez, 1999).

One of the findings in the Mexican qualitative study is consistent with the 'ceiling' on upward mobility observed in the other two countries (Flores and Mendoza, 2013). Graduates from technical universities, however, show greater horizontal mobility than engineers and holders of bachelor's degrees. Interview data suggests that this may be because the employment conditions encountered by the technological university graduates do not meet their expectations.

It is worth considering whether the demand for tertiary technical education graduates is a result of greater *credentialism* stemming from the devaluation of secondary level diplomas. An alternative explanation is that tertiary technical education graduates respond better to the overall demand for greater computer and management skills in at least the formal sectors of the economy. Their greater horizontal mobility could thus perhaps be interpreted as some kind of *screening*. All of these reasons are most likely involved. In regard to Brazil, Barato (2013) argues that, from the perspective of labour force structure, there is no evidence that tertiary technical education is, or should be considered, a distinct, self-contained category. In some cases, tertiary technical education courses are created for emerging occupations in the new information and communication technologies sector. In others, higher-level professional education stems from the increase training requirements—in terms of both time and skill—of professions that demand mid-level technical certification (such as nursing), and/or regulation by professional associations. In the service sector, however, for example, it is quite common to find technologists in positions a technician could perform. Studies suggest that this overlap may be due to some combination of the process of credential devaluation, a possible glut of higher technologists, and the existence of some overlap in the training of mid-level technicians and higher-level technologists (Jacinto, 2013). Regarding this last point, it should be noted that recent efforts have been made to reorder and reorganise technical and higher technological education. In Brazil, the curriculum is set out in two catalogues: one for mid-level technical education and the other for the higher level. In Mexico and Colombia, a similar process was conducted through the (re)organisation of the national systems of labour skills.

Despite of these efforts, in practice there is considerable tension and overlap between technical and technological education. The study of Brazil, for instance, found that there are several degree programmes, such as medical radiology, in which 60 per cent of the content is similar in both modalities.

An additional perspective on labour market entry is provided by surveys and interviews with employers, who, by and large, are satisfied with these graduates. For example, in a study of the Brazilian job market for engineers and technologists (cited by García de Fanelli, 2013b), employers emphasised the shorter duration of the technologists' education as an advantage over engineers, as it enables their training to adjust more quickly to changes in technology and better adapt to the changing needs of the labour market, as well as costing significantly less. Across the businesses interviewed, 7.5 technologists were employed per company, as opposed to 12.7 engineers. That said, 34 per cent of the people interviewed believed future demand for technologists would increase sharply, whereas only 22 per cent thought that for engineers. When asked to assess the quality of the technologists in meeting the needs of the market, survey respondents gave an average of seven points out of ten; technologists were most recognised in the fields of mechanics, computer science and civil construction (CNI et al., 2008). Similarly, the employers interviewed in the Brazilian study noted that even if they remain in operational positions, technologists can generate higher quality products and services (Barato, 2013).

In Mexico, data from the *Coordinación General de Universidades Tecnológicas* from 2011 finds, according to the 53 businesses surveyed, a high degree of employer satisfaction with graduates' knowledge, technical skills and attitude (Flores Crespo and Mendoza, 2013). On the other hand, amongst the less favourable characteristics reported, some employers mentioned a lack of humanistic education in some tertiary technical education graduates. Others noted that tertiary technical education graduates lacked the ability to do independent research and be pro-active regarding matters that need settling.

Similarly, in Colombia, 87.5 per cent of the employers surveyed stated their satisfaction with the work done by tertiary technical education graduates. Compared to university graduates, the technicians and technologists were valued by employers for their ability to carry out practical tasks and routine operational work. When employers compared these graduates to those who came from SENA, they observed that the university graduates acquire more general, social and humanistic skills. Nevertheless, most also pointed out that due to out-dated university curricula, gaps in practical training, underdeveloped reading, writing, and communications skills, and inexperience in team management, these graduates require significant on-the-job training to be able to do their job correctly. In terms of tertiary technical education graduates' own subjective assessment, those interviewed in the case studies expressed overall satisfaction with their studies, placing particular emphasis on the value of concrete links with the labour market through internships. Aside from a few criticisms of the quality of some of the internships, this work-study tool proved to be relevant for the companies and students alike. The study by Barato (2013), for instance, points out that a great many students in these courses are offered paid internships because business owners consider the courses to be of good quality and they may want to hire these students in the future. In fact, many young people go on working at their placement companies even after completing the official internships. At the same time, most of the young people pointed out that their degree programme itself was very important in getting their current job.

In Mexico, the data from both the survey done by the *Coordinación General de Universidades Tecnológicas de Mexico* and our own case study indicated that young people assess their academic education, practical training, and quality of institutional instruction quite positively. According to the survey of graduates in the qualitative study, 31.3 per cent reported that their salary met their expectations, 25 per cent felt their salary was fair and satisfactory, and 23 per cent stated that their salary was fine, but they expected a raise in the future (Flores and Mendoza, 2013).

In Colombia, 70 per cent of the graduates interviewed valued the contribution of their technical and technological training in providing opportunities for upward career mobility; 75 per cent were satisfied with the improved social recognition they received in comparison to that of professionals; 91.7 per cent believed their professional training proved beneficial to both their personal life and their social and cultural skills; and 58 per cent felt their training improved their employment stability. In terms of earning power, 33 per cent reported that their income increased significantly, 29 per cent partially, 18 per cent, that it remained the same, and 4.2 per cent, that it decreased (Turbay, 2013).

Indeed, these alternatives in higher education are highly valued by the young people who are able to finish their studies. Turbay (2013) notes that due to their flexibility, the institutions analysed in her research are highly inclusive, as enable students to work while they study. Graduates improve their living conditions, income, self-esteem and social and cultural capital. They appreciate the opportunity to receive further education, as they perceive it to have increased their competitiveness in the job market.

The relevance of this form of professional education for young people stands in stark contrast with the now-discredited views found in some earlier studies comparing tertiary technical education-style training to university degrees. This contrast is worth exploring. On one hand, this positive evaluation of alternative higher education may derive from segmentation within the tertiary technical education level of education and the fact that the case studies chose prestigious institutions with good results. On the other hand, it also reflects recent changes in tertiary technical education in responding to the demands of society, politics and the job market, all of which should be considered in greater detail.

Overall, our research finds that most tertiary technical education graduates find employment in the formal sector of the economy, but are paid considerably less than university graduates. From a certain perspective, this gap is understandable; the investment in human capital (by states, families and occasionally individuals) for these degrees is correspondingly lower than that of university degrees. That said, in terms of improving work conditions and/or obtaining better employment upon graduation, the higher technical degree seems to be a good investment. Later in tertiary technical education graduates' careers, however, there are indications of a ceiling on the chances for upward mobility.[12] Regrettably, there is no data available with which to observe the evolution of this 'ceiling' effect on tertiary technical education graduates in the labour force.

6 Conclusion

This chapter synthesised data from case studies carried out in Brazil, Colombia and Mexico to analyse recent developments in tertiary technical education, including the reasons for diffusion and the extent and ways in which it contributes to broadening young people's opportunities for education and work. It may be concluded that tertiary technical education contributed to democratising opportunities for advanced study, as it offers an alternative in educational continuity for new generations of young people who, often uniquely in their family history, have completed their secondary education. In each section we have explored different dimensions of this contradictory democratisation.

Our first objective was to determine the extent of, and rationale for, the expansion of tertiary technical education. We conclude that tertiary technical education constitutes a higher education option that is easier to access, takes less time, is more vocational and/or technical in orientation and costs less than a university degree. The recent increase in tertiary technical education enrolment (at different levels, depending on the country) seems to be due to social

12 It should noted, however, that this provisional conclusion rests on the analysis of data that should be regarded with a degree of caution. (The conclusion relies on: data from the Observatorio in Colombia, some partial follow-ups in Brazil and Mexico, and qualitative studies conducted at high-quality institutions in Brazil, Colombia and Mexico).

and political demand. Pressure from social groups newly and regularly completing their secondary education, matched by subsequent policy responses, is largely responsible for the recent surge in tertiary technical education activity.

Our second objective was to explore differences in social prestige/status and selection/admission processes amongst tertiary technical education and university institutions. Most tertiary technical education institutions have lower prestige and status than universities, though there are a core of extremely well regarded public tertiary technical education institutions in terms of quality and prestige. Although public policy experts have developed strategies attempting to improve the inclusiveness, permanence and quality of these programmes, thus far, the results remain insufficient.

Our third objective was to investigate the continuity of access of tertiary technical education students to universities or postgraduate studies, from both a regulatory point of view and that of practical, empirical experience. We conclude that even if regulations aimed at easing this transition have been developed, the process of articulation and integration between non-university and university education remains incipient. Successful transitions between tertiary technical education and the university system appear to be scarce, a topic which bears further, systematic investigation.

Our fourth objective was to collect evidence about tertiary technical education graduates' transitions into the labour market. tertiary technical education graduates positively value their training. The diploma has value for those entering the service sector, some regulated occupations and, in some cases, the industrial sector. The data also indicates, however, that tertiary technical education graduates earn less than university graduates, and, due to limited demand, are more constrained in their placement in the labour market. In terms of human resource demand, graduates' job placement was largely linked to the generalised spread of information and communication technologies, which sparked the demand for more education, while simultaneously devaluing secondary education diplomas. Overall national growth in job creation during the period of study may also explain improvements in demand for tertiary technical education graduates but, at this time, the longitudinal data required to confirm this hypothesis is not available. Social, political and economic demands all converge in the development of new, broader tertiary technical education programmes in ways that are both complementary and contradictory.

Finally, we note the need to develop databases and research projects capable of lending depth to the understanding of the processes now underway. We suggest three steps in that regard. First, more data is needed on the entrance of tertiary technical education graduates into the job market, paired with representative data that can be used to draw comparisons with university graduates and holders of secondary diplomas. This would help clarify the value of tertiary technical education education and better measure social recognition of the youths' general and specific technical skills within the hierarchy of occupational qualifications. To do so, a closer examination of the supply side of employment is required. As such, systematic studies of the most useful qualifications in technological organisations, by specific economic sector, and their linkages with the tertiary educational supply should be conducted. Second, research is needed into the parameters of institutional quality more broadly; we must develop quality parameters that encompass, for instance, not only the demands of the labour market but also the human development needs and expectations of the young people, as well as sustainable social development and technology transfer and innovation. Finally, public-private alliances, which may support tertiary technical education in its mandate to provide more young people with access to quality work and education, also bear further investigation.

References

Barato, J. (2013) 'Educación técnica y tecnológica os-secundaria. Tendencias, enfoques y desafíos en Brasil' in Jacinto, C. (ed.) *Incluir a los jóvenes. Retos para la educación terciaria técnica en América Latina* (Paris: IIPE-UNESCO).

Barro, R. and J. Lee (2010) *A New Data Set of Educational Attainment in the World, 1950–2010*, Working Paper No. 15902 (Cambridge, MA: National Bureau of Economic Research (NBER)).

Bernasconi, A. (2006) *Donde no somos tigres: problemas de la formación técnica en Chile en el contexto latinoamericano*, En Foco vol. 72 (Santiago de Chile: Expansiva).

Bourdieu, P. and C. Passeron (1973) *Los estudiantes y la cultura* (Madrid: Taurus).

Brunner, J.J. and R. Ferrada Hurtado (eds.) (2011) *Educación Superior en Iberoamérica: Informe 2011* (Santiago de Chile: Centro Interuniversitario de Desarrollo (CINDA)-UNIVERSIA).

Caillods, F. and C. Jacinto (2006) *Mejorar la equidad en la educación básica: lecciones de programas recientes en América Latina* (Paris: IIEP).

CINDA (2006) *Repitencia y deserción universitaria en América Latina* (Santiago de Chile: CINDA-IESALC-Universidad de Talca).

CNI, Serviço Social da Indústria (SESI), SENAI, Instituto Euvaldo Lodi (IEL), Conselho Federal de Egenharia e Agronomia (CONFEA) (2008) *Mercado de Trabalho para o Engenheiro e Tecnólogo no Brasil*, http://www.univasf.edu.br/~edmar.nascimento/iee/RelatoriodaPesquisaRevisado2008.pdf (accessed on 15 March 2011).

De Moura Castro, C. and A. Bernasconi (2005) *Los institutos técnicos superiores norteamericanos y América Latina: ¿Clonación, inspiración o rechazo?* (Washington, D.C.: IADB).

ECLAC (Economic Commission for Latin America and the Caribbean) (2009) *Statistical Studies*, No. 37, http://www.eclac.cl/cgi-bin/getProd.asp?xml=/prensa/noticias/comunicados/0/37110/P37110.xml&xsl=/prensa/tpl-i/p6f.xsl&base=/tpl/top-bottom.xslt (accessed on 15 January 2013).

Espíndola, V. and N. García (eds) (2005) *Modernización de la educación técnica post-secundaria: opciones y desafíos para América Latina y el Caribe* (Washington, D.C.: Inter-American Development Bank).

Flores Crespo, P. and D. Mendoza (2013) 'Educación Superior Tecnológica. El caso mexicano' in Jacinto, C. (ed.) *Incluir a los jóvenes. Retos para la educación terciaria técnica en América Latina* (Paris: IIPE-UNESCO).

Gallart, M. (2002) *Veinte años de educación y trabajo: la investigación de la formación y la formación de una investigadora* (Montevideo: Cinterfor).

García de Fanelli, A. (2013a) 'Training the 21st Century Knowledge Workers: Higher Education and Workforce Development in Latin America' in Balán, J. (ed.) *Latin American's New Knowledge Economy: Higher Education, Government and International Collaboration* (New York: Institute of International Education (IIE) and American Institute for Foreign Study (AIFS) Foundation).

——— (2013b) 'Modelos institucionales, tendencias y desafíos de la educación superior técnica y tecnológica no universitaria en Brasil, Colombia y México' in Jacinto, C. (coord.) *Incluir a los jóvenes. Retos para la educación terciaria técnica en América Latina* (Paris: IIPE-UNESCO).

García de Fanelli and C. Jacinto (2010) 'Equidad y educación superior en América Latina. El papel de las carreras terciarias y universitarias', *Revista Iberoamericana de Educación Superior*, 1(1), pp. 58–75.

Gómez, V.M. (2011) *Sesgo universitario, subvaloración de la educación 'no universitaria' y desigualdad social en educación superior*, Paper presented in the Congreso Nacional de Sociología, Universidad ICESI—Universidad del Valle (UNIVALLE)—Universidad del Pacífico UNPA, Cali, Colombia, 2–4 November.

Jacinto, C. (2013) 'La educación post-secundaria técnica: contexto, interrogantes y aportes de la investigación' in Jacinto, C. (ed.) *Incluir a los jóvenes. Retos para la educación terciaria técnica en América Latina* (Paris: IIPE-UNESCO).

Murakami, Y. and A. Blom (2008) *Accessibility and Affordability of Tertiary Education in Brazil, Colombia, Mexico and Peru within a Global Context*, Policy Research Working Paper 4517 (Washington, D.C.: The World Bank).

Observatorio Laboral (2011) *Salario de entrada de los recién graduados de la educación superior*, http://www.graduadoscolombia.edu.co/html/1732/article-195406.html (accessed on 10 April 2011).

Organisation for Economic Co-operation and Development (OECD) (2012) *Latin American Economic Outlook 2012: Transforming the State for Development*, http://www.oecd.org/dev/americas/48965859.pdf (accessed on 28 February 2014).

Pedrosa, R.H. et al. (2013) 'Assessing Higher Education Learning Outcomes in Brazil', *Higher Education Management and Policy*, 24(2), pp. 55–71.

Rodriguez Gómez, R. (1999) 'La universidad latinoamericana en la encrucijada del siglo XXI', *Revista iberoamericana de Educación*, 21 (septiembre–diciembre), pp. 55–77.

SEDLAC (CEDLAS y BANCO MUNDIAL) (2013) *Base de datos socioeconómica para América Latina y el Caribe*, http://sedlac.econo.unlp.edu.ar/esp/index.php (accessed 14 April 2011).

Sistema de Información de Tendencias Educativas en América Latina (SITEAL) (2005) *La educación superior. Acceso, permanencia y perfil social de los graduados comparados con los egresados de la educación media*, Documento para el Foro de Debate no. 5 (Buenos Aires: SITEAL).

Tedesco, J.C. (2012) *Educación y justicia social* (Buenos Aires: FCE).

Turbay, C. (2013) 'Educación Técnica y Tecnológica Superior en Colombia y sus efectos para la inserción laboral e inclusión social de las juventudes. Estudio de caso en tres instituciones de Bogotá—Distrito Capital' in Jacinto, C. (ed.) *Incluir a los jóvenes. Retos para la educación terciaria técnica en América Latina* (Paris: IIPE-UNESCO).

UNESCO Institute for Statistics (UIS) (2012) *International Standard Classification of Education (ISCED) 2011* (Montreal: UNESCO).

Varghese, N.V. (2009) *Higher Education Reforms: Institutional Restructuring in Asia* (Paris: IIEP-UNESCO).

CHAPTER 5

Why Commodity Booms Have Not (Yet?) Boosted Human Capital: Bolivia's Struggle to Create a Skilled Workforce

Fritz Brugger and Kathlen Lizárraga Zamora

Abstract

Do windfalls from the extractive sector help developing countries invest in human capital? To date, empirical studies remain inconclusive. Using Bolivia as a case study, this chapter examines the specific political-economic dynamics that led the country to increase spending on education yet at the same time failed to build a skilled workforce. Overall, the study finds that while the mining sector continued to seek unskilled, cheap labour, the capital-intensive hydrocarbon sector, for its part, developed on-the-job training programmes. Meanwhile, education policies failed to anticipate evolving demand from the labour market. As a result, vocational training suffered, a situation further compounded by efforts of powerful groups in the education sector to protect their own, somewhat narrow interests, at the expense of educational achievements. It concludes that the rise of private education and popular skills-based training programmes cannot substitute for development of a functional vocational training system, capable of supporting the country's ambition to develop a world-class lithium processing industry with linkages in strategic sectors.

1 Introduction

Bolivia flooded the Spanish crown with silver, and later supplied the minerals that fuelled the Industrial Revolution. Today, Bolivia has the world's largest lithium reserves, which may be critical to the green, low-carbon economy. Bolivia's President Evo Morales wants this looming extractive boom to differ from those of the past. Rather than exporting the primary commodity, Morales seeks to develop strong downstream linkages by manufacturing lithium batteries domestically; he has even expressed a desire to assemble battery-powered cars in Bolivia (Bajak and Valdez, 2009). The government intends to invest USD 902 million, of which USD 485 million would be earmarked for the

 | DOI 10.1163/9789004281158_006

industrialisation of lithium (Stroebele, 2012). In 2013, Morales inaugurated a USD 19 million lithium carbonate pilot plant in the Uyuni salt flat. In February 2014, a USD 3.7 million pilot plant for the production of lithium batteries followed, built by the Chinese company Lin Yi Dake Trade Co. Ltd. Once running at full capacity, the plant is expected to produce 1,000 mobile phone batteries daily, as well as 40 batteries for electric vehicles (Agencia EFE, 2014; BNA, 2014). Recently, a declaration of intent with a Dutch consortium and a joint venture contract with a South Korean consortium have also been signed, South Korea being the world's largest manufacturer of rechargeable lithium batteries (GoN, 2013; Dyson, 2012).

Will Bolivia live up to these ambitious objectives? Does the country have the skilled workforce required to jumpstart such an industrialisation process? Endogenous growth theory posits that investment in human capital and innovation and technology is instrumental to promoting economic development. History shows, however, that resource-dependent developing countries often do not allocate extractive revenues to the development of human capital. Gylfason (2001), for instance, finds that natural resource extraction negatively affects human capital, as measured by education expenditure as a share of national income, secondary school enrolment and total years of girls' schooling. He concludes that the neglect of education is one mechanism by which natural resource abundance slows economic development. Stijns (2006), on the other hand, finds subsoil wealth to be significantly correlated with human capital accumulation. The discrepancy between the findings of the two is primarily due to the indicators used to measure natural capital: Stijns employs subsoil wealth per capita and resource rent per capita, while Gylfason considers the share of natural capital in total national wealth (i.e. as a portion of total physical, human and natural capital, wherein natural capital is the sum of subsoil wealth, timber, non-timber forest benefits/products, cropland, pastureland and the opportunity cost inherent to protected areas).

Bolivia spends around 8.5 per cent of its GDP on education in 2011—more than most other Latin American state. A closer look at the Bolivian labour market, however, reveals that despite this significant investment in education, Bolivia has a smaller middle class and higher youth unemployment rate than the Latin American average. The informal sector absorbs 75 per cent of the non-agricultural workforce, compared to an average of 50 per cent across the region (LO/FTF, 2013). In addition, over 67 per cent of the working population between 24 and 65 have no vocational training (INE, 2011). As this data demonstrates, the Bolivian case clearly illustrates that allocating extractive revenues to education does not necessarily translate into a skilled workforce. Export statistics mirror this finding, as Bolivia's economy has one of the world's lowest shares of manufactured (7 per cent) and high-tech (4 per cent) exports (World Bank, 2009).

The interaction between political imperatives, the vagaries of the extractive economy, and the co-option of the education sector by powerful stakeholders resulted in a dysfunctional system unable to produce the skills required by the Bolivian economy. On the contrary, this situation has served to sharpen inequality:

- 56 per cent of 19–24 year-olds are excluded from tertiary education.
- 38 per cent attend public universities at no cost. Given that the vast majority of this group belongs to the upper income quintile, the public education system largely finances the professional education of the wealthy.
- A mere 3 per cent of 19–24 year-olds attend technical or vocational training; they belong to the second, third and fourth income quintiles (INE, 2011; UNDP, 2011). Hence, the 77 per cent of Bolivians living in moderate or extreme poverty scarcely benefit from tertiary education, where per student spending is typically much higher than that of primary and secondary education.

How can the current stalemate and lack of consistent strategic interplay between education, industrial and scientific policies in Bolivia be explained? Our analytical framework examines three key factors, the first of which is the *political pattern* reflecting the political orthodoxy of the time. The second factor, referred to here as the *education governance pattern*, represents the dominant political discourse's influence on education policy and its corresponding influence on the state's vision and actions in building an educated society and skilled workforce. Finally, *principal-agent dynamics* highlight the challenges of motivating operational actors (the 'agent') to act in the best interests of the 'principal', in this case, the Ministry of Education. The existence of asymmetric information distribution, conflicts of interest or moral hazards may cause the agent to prioritise his own interests.

2 The Emergence of Contemporary Education Power Brokers

Bolivia's economic status as a single-commodity exporter dates back to early colonial times, when the Spanish crown extracted silver to expand and maintain its empire. At the time, the ready availability of cheap, unskilled labour was by far the most critical production factor. The Spaniards instrumentalised pre-colonial models of community organisation. *La mita*, a social institution that required each household to contribute labour to communal projects (e.g. building and repairing roads or bridges), was transformed into a colonial system of forced labour quotas that benefitted private mining interests and the Spanish crown (Acemoglu and Robinson, 2005 and 2012). By 1825, independence and the rise of the Republic saw the emergence of a new economic and political elite: the *criollos* (locally born people of 'pure' Spanish ancestry) and the *mestizos* (people of mixed Spanish and indigenous descent). They took ownership of the mines and confiscated the land of indigenous people (Gray-Molina, 2009).

Bolivia's economic dependence on commodity export became even more pronounced when the incipient Industrial Revolution in Europe triggered a sharp increase in demand for minerals and metals. During the First World War, moreover, Bolivia emerged as one of the foremost producers of tin, a vitally important war materiel. A host of unskilled labour, working in precarious conditions and under tight control, facilitated capital accumulation, but acted as a disincentive to the development of an employment-oriented youth education system. In 1900, 81.5 per cent of the population was illiterate and only 2 per cent attended primary school. The illiteracy rate decreased to 77.5 per cent in 1920 following the founding of the first teacher training college in Sucre by the Belgian missionary in 1909 (Contreras, 1999).

When the onset of capital-intensive oil extraction in the early twentieth century suddenly required qualified skilled workers, Bolivian companies sent employees on scholarships to Argentina and Mexico rather than training them domestically due to a lack of adequate education facilities (Miranda, 1999). Hence, the demand and need for an adequate education system in Bolivia grew.

As such, the institutional dynamics present at the inception of the formal education system have had far-reaching consequences. Teachers began to organise in the early 1920s and were granted labour union status in 1936. Ideological disagreements between rural and urban teachers resulted in the creation of separate urban and rural teachers' unions, both of which still exist as distinct and influential entities. At the same time, the government of Bolivia made two important educational governance decisions. The first was to set up independent commissions tasked with developing an organisational and administrative model for national education. The commissions were to act as education trustees, while the state was to provide the resources necessary to fund the system without exerting political influence. The second key decision was to grant autonomy to public universities (Lizárraga, 2002).

From a principal-agent perspective, this reform set out the basic educational governance structures that inform the system's evolution until today. The state, as the principal, placed itself in a weak position by granting independence to the commissions and refraining from the exertion of strong political influence. This allowed the agents, particularly the teachers' unions and autonomous universities, to grow stronger. The former were able to influence the independent commissions' work from the outset. The latter managed to bolster their autonomy by securing independent funding guaranteed by law. Universities receive 5 per cent of overall tax revenue, 8 per cent of tax revenue collected on hydrocarbon production, in addition to royalty participation devolved to the department level (UDAPE, 2013).

3 The Nationalist Project

3.1 *Putting Unions in the Driver's Seat*

The next phase of the cycle began in 1952 with the political project of the national revolution, led by the unions and the *Movimiento Nacionalista Revolucionario* (MNR), a political party that united the demands of interest groups and a society weary of the elite's privileges. On the economic front, the state nationalised the most important mining companies and took control of the production and sale of minerals. While, as owner, the state did nothing to upgrade and improve the means of production, it did grant concessions to the unions in return for their role in leading the revolution: Mining unions were granted job guarantees until retirement, the availability of small shops and social services at the mines, and an 8-hour work day. In the hydrocarbon sector, children retained the right to their parents' jobs (Lizárraga and Neidhold, 2011). In this context of excessive job protection and poorly developed means of production, union membership was more important than qualifications or skills in gaining and keeping employment. As a result, neither the workers nor the government perceived a need for technical training.

The revolution also rewarded the teachers' unions for their active support with a dramatic change in education governance. The organisation and administration of the education system (with the exception of the already autonomous universities) was, for all intents and purposes, handed over to the *Sindicato de Maestros*, or teachers' unions. The power of the unions was legitimised in the Education Code of 1955, which granted them major decision-making authority in the Ministry of Education, including, notably, the right to appoint all undersecretaries. Only the nomination of the minister was left to the incumbent government (Contreras, 2004).

This take-over of the Ministry of Education by the teachers' unions weakened the position of the principal—the state—and reinforced the influence of a key agent in the educational system, with far-reaching consequences.

First, in primary and secondary school, the teachers' unions gave priority to the humanistic teachings inherited from the colonial system, thereby neglecting technical and vocational training. Second, they promoted their members' interests through the codification of a number of privileges in the regulations governing job promotion (*Escalafón Docente*). The unions were successful in securing, for instance, a monopoly on teaching for graduates of the teacher training colleges, a guaranteed job for all graduates upon completion of their studies, and a system of promotion based on seniority rather than merit or education (Ministerio de Educación,, 1964). As indicated by the concession described above, the *Sindicato de Maestros* became a powerful agent of the education system. It sought less to ensure the quality of education than to protect the groups' privileges and gain economic independence in resource allocation and expenditure. The teachers' unions requested more and more money while the state, as principal, struggled to exercise control within the education system, leaving little room to craft clear policies, let alone develop vocational and technical education (see Lizárraga, 2002).

3.2 *Building a National Workforce to Curb Imports*

The prospects for vocational and technical training changed when dependency theory began to dominate the political thinking of leaders in the developing world, and Latin America in particular. They began to place greater emphasis on industrialisation and foster domestic production to curb imports. The import substitution development model demanded strong state intervention in domestic markets ('state capitalism'), as well as policies to protect national production. As successful industrialisation required skilled labour, in the early 1970s this new ideology both prompted and required innovation in the education governance system. The government created the *Servicio Nacional de Formación de Mano de Obra* (or FOMO, the national labour training service) as a decentralised institution, modelled on those of other Latin American countries, to promote vocational training (Jacinto, 2013). In order to finance the operations of the FOMO training institutions, the government introduced a 1 per cent payrolld tax on private, public and mixed companies. Notably, mining companies were exempted from this tax. Overall, industrialisation policy was aimed almost exclusively at import substitution rather than developing the capacity to process and add value to minerals prior to export (Jordán, 1999).

Institutionally, the FOMO branches were not placed under the supervision of the Ministry of Education, as one might expect, but under the Ministry of Labour. On the one hand, this has insulated the FOMO branches from the power dynamics of the established education sector and the influence of the teachers' unions. On the other hand, it has also resulted in the creation of two parallel education systems with no opportunity to navigate between them. Despite this isolation, or perhaps enabled by it, the FOMOs increased the skills and knowledge of metalworkers, lathe operators, automobile mechanics, carpenters and other tradespeople and enjoyed broad social acceptance throughout the 1970s and early 1980s (Lizárraga and Neidhold, 2011). Many of the trained professionals entered the petroleum and gas sector, especially the construction of gas pipelines. Integration with the mining sector never developed, however, as the industry maintained simple methods of production, for which on-the-job training was sufficient, and refused to participate in the FOMO system.

The creation of the FOMOs, therefore, left the traditional configuration of the education sector untouched and, instead, added a second principal-agent pattern with the Ministry of Labour as principal and the FOMOs as agents. In this case, it appears that the principal has been more successful in aligning the interests of the agent with its mission. This may be at least partially due to the fact that the special-purpose tax paid by the future employers of the trainees created a more stringent feedback loop, thus strengthening the principal's position. The promotion of vocational training was also facilitated by the affinity between nationalist industrialisation policies and those aimed at upgrading human capital as a factor of production.

For their part, the universities expanded tremendously during the 1970s and 1980s. This surge was partially driven by changes in class structure, wherein a university degree was a near-guarantee of social mobility, and was enabled by the robust funding from extractive activities and tax revenue. The downside of this rapid growth, however, was a decline in the universities' internal efficiency, and correspondingly in their external value, institutional reputation, and degree valuation (Lizárraga, 2002).

4 The Privatisation of Vocational Education?

4.1 *Addressing Structural Deficits in Education Governance*

State capitalism had accumulated a significant debt burden by the mid-1980s. At the same time, the country's export-based economic model was thrown into crisis when the prices for tin, silver and natural gas—which together accounted for more than 50 per cent of total Bolivian exports—fell dramatically. Most of the state-owned mines were forced to close. As a result, Bolivia implemented its first structural adjustment programme in order to stabilise the economy. This marked the beginning of the next political cycle, dominated by aggressive reform policies intended to liberalise prices, exchange rates and interest rates;

abolish export and import controls; and reduce public sector deficit by cutting spending and increasing tax revenue.

The austerity measures also abolished job protection for workers and relentlessly exposed the limits of the mining industry's learn-by-doing approach to training. Out of work miners were unable to get new jobs in different sectors due to their lack of formal qualifications and transferrable skills. Workers were relocated to lower lands and given a small amount of seed money, which they often used to relocate to the major cities (Milenio, 1998). The former labourers had little choice but to join the informal economy and try to make a living through petty trade and commerce. Others were given land in the headlands of the Amazon, where they practiced farming and later grew coca leaves.

The structural adjustment package also affected the education system, as tax expenditure on basic education temporarily fell to 2.5 per cent of GDP. This tax reform also cut off the FOMOs' sole source of funding. As a result, it was privatised and moved to the Confederation of Private Businesses (under the name INFOCAL). The infrastructure and workshops were transferred as loans. To run INFOCAL, private businesses were asked for voluntary contributions towards equipment and monthly student fees were introduced. Over time, the contributions from the *Confederación de Empresarios* became minimal and INFOCAL was transformed into a fully private institution.

Third, as response to the transfer of FOMO to the private sector, until the mid-1990s universities offered a number of professional training programmes. From 1985 to 1996, enrolment in vocational training programmes accounted for 13.5 per cent of total university enrolment. Later, the widespread desire for upward social mobility, combined with a glut of university graduates applying for jobs traditionally reserved to technical school graduates, resulted in the devaluation of technical certificates, and the transformation of many vocational programmes into full university degree programmes. Today, enrolment in university technical education courses is only about 5 per cent (CEUB, 2013). At the same time, the ITC and services age created new professions and demanded new skills, inspiring a surge of private universities and vocational institutes. Due to a lack of regulation, these institutions spread in a haphazard fashion, often failing to provide the quality of education required by industry standards (Lizárraga and Neidhold, 2011).

The education system thus saw the disappearance of the principal-agent structure in vocational training. Public universities, on the other hand, were strengthened, as their legislated participation in tax revenue protected them from austerity measures. These concessions were maintained by the universities' autonomous status and the state's inability to carry out substantive reforms within the education system. The same was true of the teachers' unions, which also managed to protect their interests from potential intervention or reform.

As Bolivia entered the 1990s, its primary education system was vast but weak, and educational quality was poor. It encompassed some 12,000 schools, 1.5 million students and 90,000 teachers. Only three-quarters of teachers, however, had completed some form of teacher training. Of the remaining teachers, particularly those in rural areas, few had finished secondary school. Although the budget allocated to education had recovered to 4 per cent of GDP, and represented the largest single category of public spending, over 95 per cent went to salaries. The absence of a reliable, timely reporting system for the number of teachers or schools eligible for, and receiving, funding illustrates the weakness of the Ministry's control over the sector. Innumerable pay cheques were cashed by 'ghost teachers' under false names, a reflection of the often-rampant political graft that characterised the educational sector (Contreras, 2004).

4.2 *Undermining Foreign Direct Investments Impact by Failing to Invest in Skills Education*

The 1990s saw a second package of structural adjustment reforms focusing on privatisation, increasing foreign direct investment (FDI) and the decentralisation of state power to municipalities and their elected mayors.

As part of the move towards the privatisation of state-owned enterprises (referred to in Bolivia as 'capitalisation') the national oil company YPFB (*Yacimientos Petrolíferos Fiscales Bolivianos*) was put up for sale. Investment-friendly policy frameworks gave foreign companies the opportunity to access Bolivia's oil, gas and mineral reserves. Correspondingly, between 1996 and 2001, over 40 per cent of all FDI went into the extractive sector (Andersen et al., 2004); the companies recruited university graduates and trained them according to their needs. The discovery of large natural gas reserves at the end of the 1990s and the resurgence of the mining industry, driven by soaring mineral prices, have restored extractive activities to their former status as pillars of the economy. Many of the previously shuttered, state-owned mines were re-opened by cooperatives, but did receive FDI and continued to rely on primitive extraction methods and unskilled labour.

FDI is generally promoted as a means of encouraging economic growth through the introduction of, among others, an influx of capital, new technologies and better management practices. The realisation of these benefits, however, is dependent upon the existence of certain channels through which these positive effects can be generated, such as backward-forward linkages between local companies and education and training. The educational reform of 1994, therefore, was, and continues to be, a critical factor in the success (of failure) of economic reform.

In terms of education governance, the reform of 1994 represented the most decisive attempt to date to reorganise the system. It was supported by the international donor community, which once again began to place greater emphasis on education (see the 1990 Jomtien Declaration of Education for All, for instance) and agreed to resume funding Bolivia's education sector, subject to credible reform plans, for the first time since suspending their support in the late 1970s (Contreras, 2004). Overall, the reforms were aimed at increasing the primary school enrolment rate, improving the quality of education, and introducing technical and vocational training. At the organisational level, the reform programme sought to strengthen the position of the Ministry of Education. Municipalities were given the responsibility and resources to run the infrastructure of primary schools.

The reform succeeded in increasing the enrolment rate, as funds from HIPC and HIPC II, the debt relief initiative targeted at Heavily-Indebted Poor Countries, supported the launch of programmes such as school breakfasts. Similarly, in 2006, the Juacinto Pinto school voucher system was created to strengthen the incentives to attend school. Provided he or she attended at least 90 per cent of school days, each child received BOB 200 (approx. USD 29) at the end of the calendar year. Government-issued bonds financed the programme. Municipalities spent a large percentage of their resources upgrading primary school infrastructure and supported an increase in public spending on teachers' salaries. As a result, the net primary school enrolment rate rose to 93 per cent by 2006, though according to World Bank data, it dropped to 83 per cent between 2006 and 2011. This focus on access, however, once again overshadowed the question of the quality of education, where once again little progress was made.

At the time of educational reform, the ambitions for improvements in technical education were also high and policy coherence was achieved between the promotion of FDI and increasing human capital. Originally, the government planned to introduce technological apprenticeships in grades 9 and 10, which would result in a Basic Technical Certificate and thus enhance graduates' employment prospects. Two different types of secondary school programmes were also considered: a humanistic and a technical programme, each designed to help students enter the labour market with certified skills (República de Bolivia, 1994). In the end, however, for a number of reasons, this technical training scheme was never developed, let alone implemented. First, the Ministry of Education did not have the expertise and resources to tailor its work to the needs of both the productive and services sectors, as had been the case with FOMO and the Ministry of Labour. Second, all three vice-ministries (for formal, alternative and higher education respectively) were authorised to teach vocational training at each level and according to their own philosophy. This resulted in different entrance conditions, unequal lengths of study and varying approaches to the curriculum in each system, preventing the development of a strong, unified technical education system. Third, there was no teachers' vocational education college and thus, no trained teachers. Most vocational education instructors are normal teachers who have done some vocational coursework, but lack practical work experience. The hiring of other types of teachers, such as university professionals or practitioners, was prohibited by job hierarchy, which only allows hiring graduates from teacher training colleges (proCap, 2011).

Given the fate of the proposed technical and vocational training reform, it comes as no surprise that the evaluation of FDI promotion in Bolivia does not find any complementary effects between FDI and education (Andersen, 2004). This failure to realise spill-over effects is compounded by the fact that only 8 per cent of all FDI between 1996 and 2001 went into manufacturing, while over 50 per cent went to sectors with few linkages with the local economy (i.e. 40 per cent to the extractive sector and 14 per cent to telecommunications). This is in stark contrast to the drive for industrialisation in the 1970s.

In light of the continued lack of vocational training, the 'skills-based training' concept proffered by organisations of international cooperation gained importance. Many municipalities started investing in technical skills-based training education centres, where courses and topics are determined based on local needs. This approach responds to both regional industry demand for skilled workers and public demand for further education (Lizárraga and Neidhold, 2011). Although this alternative form of education has demonstrated some worthwhile results, particularly in terms of public perception, it is not a systemic approach capable of producing effective vocational training at national level. It also depends on the support of whoever happens to be mayor at the time. Moreover, due to the lack of independent funding, the costs between centres differ significantly. A 2004 analysis indicates that the cost can range from between USD 114 and 534 per year per training for the same course (CIESS-Econométrica, 2004).

The 1994 education reform also attempted to change the existing principal-agent relationship by strengthening the position of the Ministry of Education and removing some of the agents' power base. As we will see, the agents' engrained position allowed them to successfully defend their interests and maintain the previous pattern. At first glance, the Ministry of Education appeared to strengthen its position as the governing body of education in

Bolivia. Processes were modernised and a system was put in place for collecting and managing statistical data. The hiring of teachers was now done in coordination with municipalities, in keeping with their new functions following decentralisation. The reform process stalled, however, with the attempt to shift resources from higher to primary education. There was a fear that as this appeared to alter their codified financing mechanism, this would weaken the universities' autonomy. Despite the fact that as universities were already overfunded, the redistribution of funds would have not diminished their capacity, the universities completely resisted any movement in this direction and the original text of the reform had to be modified.

The universities also managed to fend off impending regulation and oversight by a new Vice-Ministry for Higher Education, which was to regulate public and private universities, determine curricula and establish degree programmes. Shielded by their historical autonomy, the public universities successfully opposed the new body and retained their independence. The Vice-Ministry of Higher Education was thus left in charge of regulating the work of the private universities alone.

The teachers' unions, for their part, have been extremely successful in protecting their control over public education. For example, proposals for parental control of attendance and input on teacher quality by means of a School Board, as granted in the Reform Act, were vehemently resisted by the unions and not put into practice. The teachers' unions, and the urban organisations in particular, claimed the reform process lacked teacher participation and was imposed by neo-liberal actors (Contreras and Talavera, 2005).

5 Remaking the Nationalist Project

5.1 *Meeting the Innovation Demands of the National Lithium Industry*

The current political cycle is determined by the incumbent president's ideology of indigenisation, nationalisation and anti-imperialism. In accordance with these ideological commitments and delivering on his election campaign promise, Evo Morales nationalised the hydrocarbon industry on his hundredth day in office. The technology- and capital-intensive, externally-backed mining companies San Cristobal and San Bartolomé, in contrast, have remained in private hands. This change in ownership, however, has not made a difference to Bolivia's resource-dependency, nor has it changed the incentives for vocational training. Capital-intensive businesses maintain their own job training programmes, and small- and medium-sized cooperative mines continue to work with traditional methods, i.e. unskilled labour.

With the dawning of the lithium age, this should change. Morales' goal of not only maintaining control of at least 60 per cent of the sector's earnings, but also of creating an industrial economy (Bajak and Valdez, 2009) has changed the demand for skilled professionals. The lithium mining process is complex and requires advanced technology, as does the production of batteries and, eventually, electrical vehicles. To manage this growing industry, the President created the National Bureau of Evaporative Resources in 2008 (Decreto Supremo no. 29496), which is responsible for facilitating the lithium project, including ensuring the proper education and training of engineers, chemists and technicians.

As Bolivia is currently unable to draw on domestic expertise, it must rely on foreign partners in the pursuit of 'know-how', or technical competence, and technology transfer. The keen interest in Bolivia's lithium certainly helps, as about ten countries are actively competing to partner with Bolivia, including the US, Japan, France and Brazil. The partnerships drafted thus far make for a mixed picture regarding the extent of training and technology sharing. The deal closed with China's LinYi Dake Company for the pilot battery production project, for instance, mimics the approach of the hydrocarbon industry, as training is practically oriented and aimed at qualifying operators to run the plant. The agreement therefore provides for the training of two Bolivian engineers through a one-month internship in China. Further, during the first four months of operations, two Chinese experts will train the 21 Bolivian technicians in understanding and operating the relevant technology (Agencia EFE, 2014).

The cooperation with South Korea has two components, wherein the extent of knowledge transfer remains unclear. A 2010 Memorandum of Understanding covers joint exploration and production. The state-owned mining company KORES is intended to provide lithium expertise while, at the same time, Bolivia will be included in Korea's Knowledge Sharing Programme, designed to help Korea's trade and investment partners strengthen their capability for poverty reduction and economic development (Frank et al., 2010). That said, though Bolivia claims its National Bureau of Evaporative Resources (GNRE) has developed a technological lithium extraction process suitable for the particular conditions of the *Salar de Uyuni*, the only scientific paper on the subject was written by Korean researchers (some working for KORES) without participation of Bolivian scientists (Dyson, 2012; Woong et al., 2012). Moreover, the Korean consortium is said to have patented the methodology in such a way that excludes Bolivia from participating in any associated profits (Metals Pages, 2012). The second part of the partnership, an agreement signed in 2012, is a joint venture with a South Korean public-private consortium for the pilot production of lithium cathodes, a key component of lithium-ion batteries. The Korean consortium will provide applied training to Bolivian personnel in the processes and technology required to produce cathode materials (Latinomineria, 2012).

Finally, Bolivian cooperation with a public-private Dutch consortium has a scientific focus, with most of the training provided by the public partner. The declaration of intent includes plans for establishing a company to produce lithium-ion batteries (led by the Dutch company BTI Technical Support & Innovations) and a state-of-the-art research centre (set up by Da Vinci Laboratory Solutions). The Delft University of Technology will be responsible for training of most of the staff. In addition, Delft University will create research positions for 40 Bolivian Masters students, and Bolivian PhD students will have an opportunity to deepen their knowledge of lithium batteries in Delft over a four-year period. To this end, Delft University has partnered with universities in La Paz, Potosi, Oruru and Cochabamba, where Delft staff will also give lectures (GoN, 2013). The Dutch consortium is also intended to provide technical support for the development of a lithium industrialisation master plan (GNRE, 2013).

5.2 *Seeking to Recover Traditional Knowledge*

Contemporary discussions of education governance juxtapose the existing educational system, often unfavourably, with the country's lithium ambitions. The current educational system, which is still based on the European tradition of humanistic and integral teaching, has been harshly criticised by the government for its 'colonial' and 'classist' curriculum. The 2010 law on education (*Ley de Educación Avelino Siñani*—Elizardo Perez) calls for the 'recovery of traditional knowledge' and the development of curricula in coordination with the community. These precepts have yet to be implemented, however, and are fraught with challenges. Improvements in primary and secondary school enrolment, in conjunction with reduced dropout rates, are putting pressure on higher education. 77.3 per cent of all pupils finish primary school, and the percentage of students completing secondary education rose from 46.7 per cent in 2001 to 54.7 per cent in 2008 (UNDP, 2011). Since the tertiary sector cannot keep up with demand, university admission is becoming increasingly demanding. This, in turn, unmasks the persistence of the poor quality of primary and secondary education. Many young people find themselves ill-prepared and unable go on to university, especially public institutions.

The supply of vocational training remains minimal while the proliferation of information and communication technologies has created increased demand for qualified professionals. The gap in technical and vocational training continues to be partially addressed by skills-based training programmes, designed to help people develop the skills they need to find a job or start a business, rather than offering a generic certificate. The two largest programmes are offered by the Bolivian foundation Autapo (FAUTAPO) and the Catholic Church's Episcopal Commission on Education, both of which collaborate with international cooperation agencies. Instead of creating new training avenues, they strengthen existing public and private centres at the municipal level to improve the quality of courses offered. Their support consists of upgrading the centres' infrastructure and equipment, providing supplies and training and (in part) paying teachers and other staff. They also support municipalities as a strategic partner and co-funder independent of the usual interest groups.

The skills-based training model has helped to reach 50 per cent of rural municipalities and caters to a population otherwise traditionally excluded from education. In the larger cities, technical education is also provided for other students, such as Vocational Training for Young Baccalaureates (FAUTAPO, 2010). Unfortunately, the expectations of the target group do not correspond with a technical profession. As a result, the students demand and pursue courses while they wait for admittance to university, rendering the resources put into these programmes useless for the productive sector.

The limited navigability and recognition of skills-based training diplomas has now been addressed by the Bolivian System of Skills Certification (BSSC), created to certify people's skills regardless of where they were acquired, as a way of acknowledging and valuing traditional and empirical knowledge. As of yet, however, a system capable of integrating all the programmes and setting a universal technical training curriculum does not exist. This prevents the existing endeavours from making full use of the potential synergy amongst them.

In this phase, innovations in tertiary education continue to be outside the traditional principal-agent pattern. On a positive note, skills-based training is not co-opted by traditional agents' interests. At the same time, however, as they operate outside the existing formal education structure and the skills-based training system does not produce the forward-looking skills required by the economy, skills-based training agents lack influence over education governance. The original principal—the government—still suffers from a lack of competence and vision, unable to develop (or implement) sound policies for either the second and third sectors of the economy or corresponding policies for education and science and technology. Correspondingly, a piecemeal vocational educational system has developed, as exemplified by the devolution of responsibility to municipalities in the case of skills-based training. The provision of skills-based training by municipalities on a voluntary basis renders the vocational training system both limited and vulnerable, at the mercy of the local mayor's foresight.

Meanwhile, the teachers' unions and autonomous public universities still enjoy considerable power and influence over the education system. As previously discussed, the financial situation of public universities is a case in point, as the legislatively-mandated flow of funding is significantly higher than the universities' capacity to spend. In 2012, they only managed to spend 60 per cent of the official budget. This not an exception; in 2012, the unused resources from previous budgets reached BOB 2.6 billion, or 7.2 per cent of GDP (Ministry of Economy, 2013). In light of this wealth, unlike many of their counterparts in other states, universities can afford not to engage in research and development and refuse to agree to improve their technical education programmes in coordination with the productive sector. Their autonomy also allows them to refuse to transfer a fraction of their unused resources to other levels of education.

The state, and Ministry of Education in particular, continue to be co-opted by the universities and teachers' interests, rendering the government unable to enforce quality standards or to set its own policies for technical education. As a result, industry's demand for skilled, qualified labour often goes unanswered.

6 Conclusion

Our analysis reveals that the principal-agent dynamics established in the first half of the 20th century have prevented Bolivia from developing a comprehensive and effective education governance system. Despite allocating significant resources to education, the country did not succeed in developing its human capital. The universities' autonomy, together with their ring-fenced funding sources, allowed them to fend off potential challenges from vocational training. The extractive sector, moreover, failed to provide an incentive for the promotion of vocational and technical training. Similarly, the mining sector did not spur demand for a skilled workforce, and its absence from the FOMO initiative speaks for itself. Needless to say, investment in the human capital required to support backward or forward linkages and further economic diversification requires a political will that, thus far, has been sorely lacking.

Human capital indicators are biased towards a focus on primary and secondary education enrolment rates. To better capture human capital accumulation in resource-rich economies, indicators should prioritise educational attainments, particularly vocational training and the overall level of training in the workforce. Additionally, without significant improvements in the quality of primary education, increased primary enrolment rates are poised to result in higher, not lower, inequality, as has been witnessed in many developing countries (Gruber et al., 2014). Overcoming co-optation mechanisms, deeply entrenched teachers' privileges and university insensitivity to future labour market demand remains a formidable challenge.

Principal-agent dynamics emerged as one of the most important structural determinants preventing the development of a suitable vocational training system. The relative success of vocational education during the 1970s, however, suggests that developing a system isolated from existing power dynamics might be a more promising, pragmatic approach than fighting the entrenched interests, such as the unions, that represent an important electoral base the Morales regime.

Bolivia's approach to acquiring the skills and expertise required for the development of a lithium-based industry reflects this pragmatic mind-set. Capitalising on worldwide competition for access to Bolivia's lithium reserves, Morales sought to secure strategic FDI and conclude scientific cooperation agreements incorporating strong research and training components with knowledgeable foreign partners. The diversification of partners aims at reducing the possibility and risks of dependency. Within this framework, the first steps towards addressing the technological and human capital challenges related to the development of a world-class lithium industry have already been taken. Paradoxically, however, even within this context, limited attention is paid to vocational training, reflecting the extent to which the lack of progress in Bolivia's vocational training policy remains an obstacle.

The exclusive promotion of lithium also raises concerns. Unresolved technical and environmental extraction challenges could make it cheaper to expand on-going operations in Chile, Argentina and Australia, lowering demand for Bolivia's lithium (Brown, 2011; Tegel, 2013). Similarly, the discovery of a substitute material or method for powering electric vehicles may yet counter Bolivia's dramatic bet on lithium. The ensuing bust in lithium prices would recall dramatically past experiences of commodity booms in Bolivia and, correspondingly, bring the wisdom of the thus far substantial investment in battery plants into question. Even if the lithium boom materialises, it may be too limited a basis for the industrialisation of Bolivia. Battery production is capital-intensive, highly automatised and may not offer many jobs (Mares, 2010). It risks creating another enclave industry with few linkages to the rest of the economy and a limited impact on poverty.

Under such circumstances, sustaining economic diversification would, and does, require a broader, complementary vocational and tertiary education policy to nurture a skilled workforce. Forward linkages should go beyond those that are currently envisioned and enable the domestic industry to create clusters around the lithium and e-vehicle manufacturing industry. Matching the projected demand for particular skills with training must be a priority. This requires anticipating future labour market requirements and proactively assessing the quality and relevance of existing training programmes, in a collective effort involving government ministries, public and private training providers, and employers' and workers' representatives. Such a broadened skills-initiative would be complementary to the on-going scientific collaboration and training plans in the lithium sector. It is time to start enabling the Bolivian working and middle classes to buy electric cars, if and when the country succeeds in its ambitions to become a world-class producer.

References

Acemoglu, D. and J. Robinson (2012) *Why Nations Fail: The Origins of Power, Prosperity, and Poverty* (New York: Crown Business).

——— (2005) 'Los Origenes Coloniales del Desarrollo Comparativo: Una Investigación Empirica', *Revista de Economia Institucional*, 7(13), Segundo Semestre, pp. 17–67, http://www.economiainstitucional.com/pdf/no13/dacemoglu13.pdf (accessed on 24 April 2014).

Agencia EFE (2014) 'Bolivia Inaugurates Pilot Plant for Making Lithium Batteries', *Global Post*, 18 February, http://www.globalpost.com/dispatch/news/agencia-efe/140217/bolivia-inaugurates-pilot-plant-making-lithium-batteries (accessed on 17 March 2014).

Anaya, A. (2009) 'Magisterio y Reforma Educativa en Bolivia', *Sindicatos Docentes y Reformas Educativas en America Latina* (Rio de Janeiro: Konrad Adenauer Stiftung), http://www.kas.de/wf/doc/6774-1442-4-30.pdf (accessed on 24 April 2014).

Andersen, L. and D. te Welde (2004) *Trade, FDI, Growth and Poverty in Bolivia*, Development Research Working Paper Series No. 03/2004 (La Paz: Institute for Advanced Development Studies).

Bajak, F. and C. Valdez (2009) 'Bolivia Pins Hopes on Lithium, Electric Vehicles', *Associated Press*, 28 February, http://www.bolivia-us.org/downloads/news/AP%20-%20Bolivia%20pins%20hopes%20on%20lithium%20-%20electric%20vehicles.pdf (accessed 17 March 2014).

BNA (Business News Americas) (2014) *Construction Complete on Lithium Battery Pilot Plant in Bolivia*, http://www6.lexisnexis.com/publisher/EndUser?Action=UserDisplayFullDocument&orgId=102513&topicId=165230010&docId=l:2051269450&Em=7&start=28 (accessed on 17 March 2014).

Brown, D. (2011) *China and Bolivia Enter Lithium Resource Agreement*, http://lithiuminvestingnews.com/4140/china-and-bolivia-enter-lithium-resource-agreement/ (accessed on 17 March 2014).

CEUB (Comité Ejecutivo de la Universidad Boliviana) (2013) *Estadísticas universitaria*, http://www.ceub.edu.bo/index.php?option=com_content&view=article&id=103&Itemid=102 (accessed on 25 November 2013).

CIESS-Econométrica (2004) *Sistematización y Diagnóstico Actualizado de la Operación y Extensión del Sistema de Formación Técnica y Tecnológica*, Informe (La Paz: Programa de Fortalecimiento de la Formación Técnica y Tecnológica).

Contreras, M. (2004) *Education Reform in Bolivia: From Skepticism to Change*, Teaching materials for use in INDES training (Washington, D.C.: World Bank).

——— (1999) 'Reformas y Desafíos de la Educación' in Campero Prudencio, F. (ed.) *La Formación de la Bolivia Contemporánea* (La Paz: Harvard Club de Bolivia).

Contreras, M. and M. Talavera (2005) *Examen Parcial de la Reforma Educativa Boliviana 1992–2002* (La Paz: Fundación PIEB).

——— (2003) *The Bolivian Education Reform 1992–2002: Case Studies in Large-Scale Education Reform*, Country Studies, Education Reform and Management Publication Series, Vol. II No. 2 (Washington, D.C.: World Bank).

Dyson, J. (2012) 'Bolivian Lithium Production Moves Forward on South Korea', *Industrial Minerals*, 26 July, http://www.indmin.com/Article/3066997/Bolivian-lithium-production%E2%80%93moves-forward-on-South-Korea-jv.html?ArticleID=3066997 (accessed on 27 March 2014).

Frank, R. et al. (2010) *Korea 2010: Politics, Economy and Society* (Leiden: Brill Academic Publishers).

Fundación FAUTAPO (2010) *Sistematización de aprendizajes y buenas prácticas del Programa de Formación Técnica Laboral para Jóvenes Bachilleres* (La Paz: Fundación FAUTAPO).

Fundación Milenio (1998) *Las Reformas Estructurales en Bolivia*, Serie: Temas de la Modernización (La Paz: Fundación Milenio).

GNRE (Gerencia Nacional de Recursos Evaporiticos) (2013) *Memoria 2013*, http://www.evaporiticos.gob.bo/wp-content/uploads/2014/01/memoria2013.pdf (accessed on 17 March 2014).

GoN (Government of the Netherlands) (2013) *The Netherlands Helps Bolivia Make Most of Its Lithium Reserves*, http://www.government.nl/news/2013/08/26/the-netherlands-helps-bolivia-make-most-of-its-lithium-reserves.html (accessed on 17 March 2014).

Gray Molina, G. (2009) 'Relaciones Estado Sociedad en Bolivia: La fuerza de la debilidad' in Cabthree, J. et al. (eds) *Tensiones Irresueltas* (La Paz: Plural Editores, La Paz).

Gruber, L. and S. Kosack (2014) 'The Tertiary Tilt: Education and Inequality in the Developing World', *World Development*, 54, pp. 253–272.

Gylfason, T. (2001) 'Natural Resources, Education and Economic Development', *European Economic Review*, 45, pp. 847–859.

INE (Instituto Nacional de Estadística) (2013) *Household Survey 2011*, http://www.ine.gob.bo (accessed 12 January 2014).

Jacinto, C. (2013) *Tertiary Technical Education in Latin America: An Instrument for Youth Economic and Social Integration?* (mimeo).

Jordan Pozo, R. (1999) 'Siglo XX: la Era de Estaño' in Campero Prudencio, F. (ed.) *La Formación de la Bolivia Contemporánea* (La Paz: Harvard Club de Bolivia).

Laserna, R. et al. (2011) *La Trampa del Rentismo y Cómo Salir de Ella*, Tercera Edición (La Paz: Fundación Milenio).

Latinomineria (2012) Bolivia—Firms Sign Contract to Produce Lithium Cathode Materials, *Latinomineria*, 9 July, http://www.latinomineria.com/en/2012/07/bolivia-firman-contrato-para-producir-materiales-de-catodo-de-litio/ (accessed on 27 March 2014).

Lizárraga Zamora, K. (2006) 'Descentralización de la Educación en Bolivia' in Filgueira, F. and M. Fritsche (eds.) *Descentralización de la Educación Pública en América Latina* (Rio de Janeiro: Konrad Adenauer Stiftung).

——— (2002) *Educación y Universidad Pública* (La Paz: Plural editores).

Lizárraga Zamora, K. and C. Neidhold (2011) *Educación Técnica y Producción en Bolivia* (La Paz: Fundación PIEB).

LO/FTF Council (2013) *Bolivia—Labour Market Profile 2013*, http://www.ulandssekretariatet.dk/sites/default/files/uploads/public/PDF/LMP/bolivia_2013_final.pdf (accessed on 25 February 2014).

Mares, D. (2010) *Lithium in Bolivia: Can Resource Nationalism Deliver for Bolivians and the World?* (Huston: Baker Institute for Public Policy, Rice University).

Metals Pages (2012) *Bolivia's Development of Salar De Uyuni Lithium Project Takes Step Forward Following South Korea Deal—Analyst*, 6 April, http://seekingalpha.com/instablog/241014-juan-carlos-zuleta/482851-bolivia-s-development-of-salar-de-uyuni-lithium-project-takes-step-forward-following-south-korea-deal-analyst (accessed on 27 March 2014).

Ministerio de Educación y Bellas Artes (1964) *Código de la Educación Boliviana* (La Paz: Servicio de Ayuda Técnica Escolar).

Ministry of Economy (2013) *Memoria de la Economía 2012*, http://www.economiayfinanzas.gob.bo/index.php (accessed on 16 August 2013).

Miranda Pacheco, C. (1999) *'Del Descubrimiento Petrolífero a a Explosión del Gas'* in Campero Prudencio, F. (ed.) *La Formación de la Bolivia Contemporánea* (La Paz: Harvard Club de Bolivia).

proCap (Programa de Capacitación Laboral) (2011) *Análisis de las Condiciones Socioeconomicas en Areas de Incidencia del proCAP* (La Paz: Informe de Consultorí).

República de Bolivia (1994) *Ley 1565 de Reforma Educativa del 7 de julio de 1994* (La Paz: República de Bolivia).

Stijns, J.P. (2006) 'Natural Resource Abundance and Human Capital Accumulation', *World Development*, 34(6), pp. 1060–1083, http://dx.doi.org/10.1016/j.worlddev.2005.11.005 (accessed on 26 May 2014).

Ströbele-Gregor, J. (2012) *Litio en Bolivia*, Working paper no. 14, http://www.desigualdades.net/bilder/Working_Paper/14_WP_Str__bele_Gregor_online_sp.pdf (accessed on 17 March 2014).

Tegel, S. (2013) 'The Bolivian Dream: Lithium Batteries Included, *Global Post*, 28 March, http://www.globalpost.com/dispatch/news/regions/americas/bolivia/130321/bolivian-lithium-exports-smartphone-electric-car-battery (accessed on 17 March 2014).

UDAPE (Unidad de Análisis de Políticas Sociales y Económicas) (2013) *Esquema de Distribución de Ingresos por Hidrocarburos* (La Paz: Presentación PP).

UNDP (United Nations Development Programme) (2011) *El Camino Hacia el Desarrollo en Bolivia*, Boletines sobre el estado de situación social, Bolivia (La Paz: UNDP Bolivia).

Woong, J. et al. (2012) 'Recovery of Lithium from Uyuni Salar Brine', *Hydrometallurgy*, 117–118, pp. 64–70, http://dx.doi.org/10.1016/j.hydromet.2012.02.008 (accessed on 26 May 2014).

World Bank (2009) *World Development Report 2009: Reshaping Economic Geography* (Washington, D.C.: World Bank), http://www-wds.worldbank.org/external/default/WDSContentServer/IW3P/IB/2008/12/03/000333038_20081203234958/Rendered/PDF/437380REVISED01BLIC1097808213760720.pdf (accessed on 24 April 2014).

CHAPTER 6

Lifelong Learning in a Learning Society: Are Community Learning Centres the Vehicle?

Manzoor Ahmed

Abstract

This chapter provides a historical perspective on the evolving concepts of lifelong learning and the learning society and makes the case for the community learning centre as a potential institutional vehicle for the promotion of adult and lifelong learning. It highlights the pertinence of lifelong learning/learning society in the post-2015 Development Agenda discourse. Arguments in favour of the community learning centre as a vehicle for lifelong learning/learning society are illustrated using the example of Bangladesh and drawing on parallels and contrasts with China and India. Finally, lessons derived from a recent review of the Asia-Pacific region are evaluated with respect to the development of strategic actions intended to offer adult and lifelong learning within and through community learning centres.

> [O]nly an over-all, lifelong education can produce the kind of complete man the need for whom is increasing with the continually more stringent constraints tearing the individual asunder. We should no longer assiduously acquire knowledge once and for all, but learn how to build up a continually evolving body of knowledge all through life—'learn to be'.[1]

1 Lifelong Learning and the Learning Society—A Historical Perspective

'Lifelong education' and 'the learning society' were the key takeaways of the 1972 report of the Faure Commission. The former was seen as the keystone

1 Excerpt from letter of Edgar Faure, Chairman of the International Commission on the Development of Education, to René Maheu, Director-General of United Nations Educational, Scientific and Cultural Organization (UNESCO), in regard to the presentation of the report of the Commission, *Learning to Be: The World of Education Today and Tomorrow*, 18 May 1972, vi.

 | DOI 10.1163/9789004281158_007

of education policy, the latter a strategy to involve society as a whole as a participant and actor in education (Faure et al., 1972). How have the two related ideas, innate in learning as a social function, evolved with the institutionalisation of education? Have they gained new relevance in the globalised world of knowledge economies and information societies? Do they call for creating or re-inventing an institutional mechanism distinct from, yet complementary to, traditional formal educational institutions? This chapter explores these questions. As stated by the Faure report, 'If learning involves all of one's life, in the sense of both time-span and diversity, and all of society, including its social and economic as well as its educational resources, then we must go even further than the necessary overhaul of 'educational systems' until we reach the stage of a learning society' (Faure et al., 1972, xxxiii).

In the 1970s, at about the time of the Faure Commission report, the three-fold typology of education—formal, non-formal and informal—gained currency. Recognising that 'education is obviously a continuing process, spanning the years from earliest infancy through adulthood and necessarily involving a great variety of methods and sources', Coombs and Ahmed distinguished between the three modes of education as 'analytically useful, and generally in accord with current realities'. They went on to argue that 'the need now is to visualise the various educational activities as potential components of a coherent and flexible overall learning system that must be steadily strengthened, diversified and linked more closely to the needs and processes of national development'. They underscored the emerging consensus that nations should strive to build 'lifelong learning systems', offering every individual diverse learning opportunities throughout her or his lifetime (Coombs and Ahmed, 1974, 9).

This theme was picked up again, two decades later, by the United Nations Educational, Scientific and Cultural Organization (UNESCO) International Commission on Education for the Twenty-first Century in its report *Learning—The Treasure Within*:

> The concept of learning throughout life is the key that gives access to the twenty-first century. It goes beyond the traditional distinction between initial and continuing education. It links up with another concept often put forward, that of the learning society, in which everything affords an opportunity of learning and fulfilling one's potential [...]. In short, 'learning throughout life' must take advantage of all the opportunities offered by society. (Delors et al., 1996, 38)

The Belem Framework for Action, announced at the 6th International Conference on Adult Education (CONFINTEA VI), affirmed that 'lifelong learning 'from cradle to grave' is a philosophy, a conceptual framework and an organising principle of all forms of education, based on inclusive, emancipatory, humanistic and democratic values' (UIL, 2009, 1). Lifelong learning is as old as humanity itself. As observed by Ye, 'lifelong learning was there before education was invented' (Ye cited in UIL, 2010, 6). It was only as social functions became increasingly specialised and institutionalised that the idea of lifelong learning was eclipsed by the ascendancy of formal education in childhood and early adulthood (Ye cited in UIL, 2010). Today, the idea highlighted in the 1970s by the Faure Commission, among others, has gained new relevance in the context of a learning society where the acquisition and use of knowledge and information have taken on still greater importance, giving rise to the evocative terms 'knowledge economy' and 'information society.'

2 Two Sides of a Coin

The notion of the learning society underscores learning as an activity, rather than something tied to a specific place or an institutional setting. It emphasises the social context, purpose and character of learning and its existence both inside and outside educational institutions. More importantly, the concept of the learning society highlights the exigency of learning occurring not only within, but also out of, and around, formal institutional settings (Cisco Systems, 2010). In his book, *The Learning Society*, Robert Hutchins framed the learning society as a response to the ever-changing nature of the modern state and society and the correspondingly inability of institutional education to keep pace. Torsten Husén, in revisiting the concept, highlighted the need for a 'fluidity' of learning, in line with the free movement of knowledge required by the organisations and systems of global society (Hutchins, 1970; Husén, 1986).

2.1 *The Premises of the Learning Society*

Cisco Systems, a multinational information technology corporation, amongst others, saw the links between information and communication technology, the potential change in the nature and modalities of learning, and explored the notion of the learning society. It argues that the principles that characterise the learning society 'are informed by the demands of the 21st century, by emergent innovations at the very leading edge, and by what we now know about how learning happens' (Cisco Systems, 2010, iv). The company proposes the following set of principles to help meet society's new demands for learning and realise the learning potential of both societies and individuals.

The learning society:

- Engenders a culture of learning throughout life.
- Aims to develop motivated, engaged learners who are prepared to conquer the unforeseen challenges of tomorrow as well as those of today.
- Takes learning to the learner, seeing learning as an activity, not a place.
- Believes that learning is for all, and that no one should be excluded.
- Recognises that people learn differently, and strives to meet those needs.
- Cultivates and embraces new learning providers, from the public, private, and non-governmental (NGO) sectors.
- Develops new relationships and new networks between learners, providers (new and old), funders, and innovators.
- Provides the universal infrastructure they need to succeed—still physical but increasingly virtual.
- Supports systems of continuous innovation and feedback to develop knowledge of what works in which circumstances (Cisco Systems, 2010, v–vi).

Does the summation of the characteristics of the learning society by a multinational IT company make it a North American or European idea, alien to the reality of sub-Saharan Africa or South Asia? As noted below, the learning needs and solutions of today's diverse, globalised world are, to a degree, common, a fact emphasised by a forward-looking technology pioneer and relevant to the developing world.

2.2 *Lifelong Learning—A Corollary of the Learning Society*

Lifelong learning offers a holistic perspective on the role of education in a person's life cycle. It affirms that learning, as a continuous process in life, plays an essential role in enabling individuals to adapt to, and deal with, new challenges and changes in their lives and surrounding environment. Lifelong learning, embracing all forms of educational and learning experiences, helps individuals to engage in purposeful interactions with their environment through the development of their knowledge, skills and critical thinking abilities. Implicit to the idea of lifelong learning is the concept of 'life wide' learning. While the former emphasises the continuity of learning throughout the human life cycle, the latter recognises that people find it necessary to engage in multiple learning activities simultaneously, through different modalities and in varying settings. Lifelong learning is intended to enable individuals to become active social agents—people who are able to act, reflect and respond appropriately to the cultural, social and development challenges they face both as individuals and as members of society (Medel-Añonuevo et al. cited in Ahmed, 2009, 7). Life wide learning thus relates to the multiple and parallel roles of a person in society, as an added dimension of lifelong learning.

To sum up, in human life cycle in today's world, the traditional emphasis on building the foundation of basic knowledge and competencies and acquiring the intellectual and technical tools of learning in the first quarter of life has to be complemented by lifelong learning in a learning society where all participate in and contribute to learning throughout life.

3 Antecedents of Lifelong Learning Discourse and the Post-2015 Agenda

Despite a half-century of discussion and discourse aimed at innovation and progress, traditional paradigms and ways of thinking persist in education. The Education for All (EFA) movement, launched in 1990 at the World Conference on Education for All in Jomtien, Thailand and followed up by the EFA Dakar Framework for Action in 2000 with the adoption of six global education goals—which are in themselves a remarkable initiative of the international community—is a testimony of the endurance of conventional, narrow perceptions of education and learning. This limited view was again reflected in the education component of the 2000 Millennium Development Goals (MDGs) for global development, to be achieved by 2015. The same issues arise with new urgency as global development dialogue turns to the post-2015 development and education agenda.

The Jomtien Education for All conference in 1990, in fact, attempted to articulate a broad vision of education and learning. It visualised adult education as a key component of lifelong learning and argued that beyond universal and compulsory basic education, youth and adults are entitled to a wide range of opportunities as his or her own agent of learning and personal development. In specifying concrete goals and strategies and formulating programmes, however, this rhetoric was largely unfulfilled in practice (see Ahmed, 2009).

Ten years hence, in 2000, upon reviewing progress thus far, the Dakar Framework for Action attempted to redress a perceived imbalance in the Jomtien 'framework for action' in the relative neglect of elements of basic education other than primary education, such as early childhood education and development, literacy in a broader sense, and adult and continuing education. The Dakar Framework for EFA, however, did not specify quantitative goals or targets for early childhood development. As a result, progress in this area has been slow.

While some attention has been paid to preschool education, primarily in terms of school preparedness, there has been a relative neglect of the care and development needs of young children in the critical early years of life. The Dakar Framework set two goals related to adult learning and education—one in the area of adult literacy (Goal 4) and the other in life skills and lifelong learning (Goal 3). It also indicated targets for literacy and outlined the kind of actions that might be pursued by countries to achieve this goal, but, interestingly, failed to do likewise for 'life skills and lifelong learning.'

The commentary on Goal 3, related to lifelong learning, held that 'All young people must be given the opportunity to gain the knowledge and develop the values, attitudes and skills that will enable them to develop their capacities to work, to participate fully in their society, to take control of their own lives and to continue learning' (UNESCO, 2000, 12). In the commentary on literacy (Goal 4), the Dakar Framework document appropriately noted that there were some 880 million people who could not read or write, two thirds of them women, and 'yet, the education of adults remains isolated, often at the periphery of national education systems and budgets' (UNESCO, 2000, 13).

A close reading of the two EFA Goals and their elaboration suggests an attempt to differentiate between the ends to be achieved by the two goals—in terms of relevant content, objectives and potential learners—leading to an untenable dichotomy. The life-skills and lifelong learning goal was not quantified, and strategies for its achievement were not articulated. It referred simply to learning content and objectives; essentially, in a process of continual learning, the learners should be able to acquire values, attitudes and skills that would serve them throughout life. Unlike primary education and adult literacy, concrete programme strategies, actions or targets for lifelong learning were not mentioned. The adult literacy goal, in contrast, emphasised the mechanics of literacy skills and the importance of equipping learners with literacy as a tool with which learners might continue their education. This somewhat narrow and restrictive view of literacy skills, and its separation from life-skills and lifelong learning, represents a lost opportunity to place literacy and adult education firmly within a common framework that would be meaningful and relevant to each learner (Ahmed, 2009).

The Education for All initiative proclaimed in Jomtien in 1990 and the subsequent Dakar Framework of 2000 influenced policy-making and programme strategies in developing countries. Some Asian nations that have long-established non-formal and continuing education programmes have been able to overcome, to a degree, the apparent disjunction implied in Dakar between the mechanical acquisition of literacy and learning content and objectives. The conceptual and definition incoherence of adult and lifelong learning in many countries around the globe reflects, in part, the influence of what may be called the 'Dakar dichotomy' between adult literacy on the one hand, and the skills and learning needs of youth and adults on the other (Ahmed, 2009). The tension inherent to understanding this limited conceptualisation of literacy as a component of lifelong learning is more evident in countries where adult illiteracy remains a serious problem than in those where major progress has been made in expanding basic education opportunities. These latter states have had significantly more experience in developing the wide array of literacy, non-formal and continuing education activities that are the building blocks of lifelong learning (Ahmed, 2009, 16–17). It is a classic paradox of national development that those countries most in need of adult learning and education to fulfil their developmental aspirations are those least capable of providing such opportunities. This pattern is a persistent and formidable challenge for the post-2015 development agenda.

4 The Relevance of Lifelong Learning / Learning Society to the Post-MDG Debate

The experience and progress (or lack thereof) achieved thus far, informed by the restrictive view of education in MDG 2015 and its limited scope in EFA, underscore the need for a (re)conceptualisation of development as human capability enhancement, emphasising individual agency, empowerment, and the ability to make and exercise choices. Such a conceptualisation is essential to the promotion of human rights, human dignity and just societies. The discourse on the post-2015 development agenda, both domestically and globally, is an opportunity for civil society and other education and development stakeholders to articulate a human capability approach to development, installing it as the measure and criterion for selecting goals and indicators of development, and the basis for adapting and adjusting global goals to national contexts (see Ahmed, 2013). The question thus arises as to how, precisely, an overarching vision for development—the 'world we want'—can place human capability enhancement at the centre. Can the human capability, understood as the empowerment and agency of people, for achieving human rights and dignity for all be the touchstone and rationale for post-MDG sectoral/thematic goals in poverty reduction, sustainability, public and individual health promotion, lifelong learning and skills training, good livelihoods and generally meaningful, productive and rewarding lives?

Such an overarching vision, the proponents of the human capability approach (as advocated by Amartya Sen and others) argue, does not undermine the sectoral/thematic goals listed above. Rather, it offers a means of justifying their pursuit and prioritisation in diverse regional and national contexts. An overarching vision of human capability and agency, human rights and human dignity places education and learning, the key mechanism for enhancing human capability, at the centre of development agenda, rather than the sectorally differentiated margins. Capabilities are not to be equated with a narrow definition of outcomes, qualities or competencies related to educational programmes, though these deserve due attention in designing and implementing learning activities. In Sen's view, capability is both a goal and an indicator of development (Walker and Unterhalter, 2010). The enhancement of human capability as a *dimension* of development thus differs from the orthodox economic notion of human capital as the *driver* of development, wherein the human being is a mere tool of economic production.[2]

Sen has generated debate by asking why India has lagged behind China in economic development and poverty reduction. According to Sen and his co-author Dreze:

> China made enormous progress (especially in comparison with India) very early towards universal access to elementary education, health care and social security—much before embarking on market-oriented economic reforms in 1979. [...] China's growth oriented policies during that period benefited a great deal from the solid foundations of human development that had been laid earlier, but also retained that commitment in many ways. (Dreze and Sen, 2013, 67)

Sen argued the case for the human capability approach by invoking the Asian historical experience:

> [M]any Indian policy analysts may have missed that human capability is not only important in itself, but that human capability expansion is also a kind of classic Asian way of having sustained economic growth. It started in Japan, just after the Meiji restoration, where the Japanese said: 'We Japanese are no different from the Europeans or the Americans; the only reason we're behind is that they are educated and we are not'. They then had this dramatic expansion in universal education and then, later,

2 See also Chapter 7 in this volume regarding the significance of the capability approach in the context of skills development in South Africa.

> widespread enhancement of healthcare. They found that a healthy, educated population served the purpose of economic growth very well. That lesson was later picked up in South Korea. Korea had quite a low educational base at the end of the Second World War. But following Japan, they went in the same direction. The same happened in Singapore, Hong Kong, Taiwan and, to some extent, even Thailand. And gradually, in a smaller way, in Indonesia. Of course, they reaped as they had sown. So human capability expansion is very important for Asian economic growth. (Interview with Sen, Derbyshire, 2013)

The pivotal role of lifelong learning within the vision of human capability expansion makes building the learning society a goal of paramount importance. Industrial and post-industrial societies—members of the Organisation for Economic Co-operation and Development (OECD), for instance—have already acquired the paraphernalia of lifelong learning and the learning society. Their progress in this regard is evident in the widespread opportunities provided for the continuation of youth and adult education outside formal institutions (Hasan, 2012). In these states, the pursuit of lifelong learning may not, therefore, have the same level of priority as it does in developing countries, though the effort to broaden and deepen the concept and attendant practices should continue in wealthier states as well.

The concern thus arises as to whether adult and lifelong learning is being neglected in the post-2015 global development discourse and accorded only secondary priority in the formulation of the post-2015 EFA agenda. The work of the Centre for Universal Education, based in the Brookings Institution, an influential American think-tank, for instance, relating to the definition of learning objectives and measurement of progress in achieving them, heightens the concern. The Centre for Universal Education learning metrics project largely restricts itself to the examination of formal compulsory education from preschool to the lower secondary level. Yet, surely, it cannot be presumed that education and learning are completed by age 15. And what of early childhood development, covering the years between birth and institutional preschool, at age 5 or so? There is now overwhelming scientific evidence relating to early brain development and the importance of social-intellectual stimulation in the first thousand days of life, casting new light on the critical role of parents and early childhood care-givers. It is thus essential that they be supported through parenting and adult education—especially in disadvantaged segments of society (CUE, 2013a and 2013b).

It is worth recalling that EFA was launched in 1990 with the ambition of meeting basic learning needs, including adult literacy and education in a framework of lifelong learning. The fact that EFA and the MDGs have failed to do justice to this broad vision of education cannot be a justification for merely staying the wrong course in the post-2015 era (Ahmed, 2013, 45–47). Clearly, the challenge for developing countries will be to transform their educational systems and institutions into elements of the learning society, unconfined by time, space, delivery mechanisms and credentials imposed by the institutions and structures of conventional formal education. The modern explosion of human knowledge, revolution in information and communications technology, and rapid pace of change in the globalised world have converged to render the learning society and lifelong learning not only essential, but also eminently achievable.

5 Overview of Lifelong Learning in Bangladesh and Asia

A review of the state of adult and lifelong learning in the Asia Pacific region undertaken in preparation for the 6th Global Conference on Adult Education in Belem, Brazil in December 2009 provides an overview of concepts, strategies and programmes currently employed in the region. Conference reports and studies produced by the UNESCO Regional Office in Bangkok, an early and ardent promoter of the community learning centre (also known as CLC) as the vehicle for adult and lifelong learning, add to the understanding of the overall picture.

Such information is particularly important as many governments of developing countries in Asia Pacific do not have the specific policies, programmes or resources to place non-formal and adult education programmes within a lifelong learning framework. One way of making sense of the diversity in lifelong learning (also known as LLL) and adult education policies, programmes and strategies is to categorise countries according to the common features among them. Based on empirical assessment of the various states' progress in adult and lifelong learning, the afore-mentioned regional review developed a five-part taxonomy of the regional, consisting of: a) low basic education states; b) Asian giants (China and India); c) advanced basic education countries; d) developed Asia; and e) 'foreshadowing the future', illustrated by the Republic of Korea (Ahmed, 2009). This is clearly not a rigorous, mutually-exclusive classification, but does represent a convenient heuristic for generating a broad understanding of the diverse situations and contexts of adult education and lifelong learning in the region. Within this typology, Bangladesh and other South Asian countries, with the exception of Sri Lanka, fall under the category of low basic education, a key feature of which is weak and relatively ineffective adult and lifelong learning provisions. Most East Asian and South-East Asian countries, including Indonesia, Malaysia, Thailand and Vietnam, come under the advanced basic education group. Due to their size, China and India are categorised separately, but India could also be considered a low basic education country and China an advanced basic education country.

5.1 *Bangladesh: Lifelong Learning and the Potential of Community Learning Centres*

In 2006, the Government of Bangladesh adopted a forward-looking non-formal education (also known as NFE) Policy Framework. The principal features of the policy are listed below.

- The framework's mission is to provide lifelong learning opportunities to improve the quality of life of children, youth and adults, including those with special needs, who have missed out on formal education. An early priority is the reduction of illiteracy by at least 50 per cent by 2015.
- It emphasises alternate learning opportunities through non-formal channels for the basic education of children unable to participate in formal primary schools, second-chance learning opportunities for adolescents and adults, and a 'menu' of need-based continuing education.
- The framework aims to build a 'culture of quality' in all non-formal education programmes. Third party involvement in the assessment of effectiveness is seen as a means of quality improvement.
- It promotes non-formal channels for vocational, entrepreneurial and employment-related skills and seeks to establish equivalency between formal and non-formal qualifications.
- It proposes moving to a decentralised non-formal education operation system, with coordination and linkages among governmental organisations, non-governmental organisations (NGO), community-based organisations, the private sector and civil society.
- The framework encourages community ownership as a means of ensuring the sustainability of non-formal education programmes (Ahmed, 2009).

At present, the central Bureau of Non-Formal Education (BNFE) manages a number of post-literacy and continuing education projects. Building the organisational structure and mechanisms required to implement the policy framework with the involvement of major stakeholders, such as non-government development organisations, community organisations and research and academic institutions, is recognised as the primary challenge for the future.

A recent study of mapping the extent of existing non-formal education, however, indicates that the coverage of on-going projects is generally very low and inequitably distributed amongst the potential target population. With respect to programme delivery, the teaching-learning process, the development of curriculum and materials, and the ability of learners and providers to exercise choice were very limited. The technical capacity in non-formal education, especially in the public sector, is inadequate to the extent that 'it would be an uphill task to launch the programmes ideally required unless a massive professional skill development programme is planned' (Bangladesh Country Report cited in Ahmed, 2009). A comprehensive non-formal education sub-sector plan considered necessary was to be developed in line with the non-formal education Policy. As of 2013, this comprehensive plan has yet to be written. The absence of an overall strategy to give effect to this progressive policy statement is reflected in the fragmented efforts, ineffective outreach, and lack of coordination between the government and active NGO sector. As a result, the problems of quality, efficiency and sustainability, all of which would benefit from increased cooperation, go unaddressed.

The state of community learning centres is a case in point. The Bureau of Non-Formal Education claims to be operating some 7,000 community learning centres under the auspices of its donor-supported post-literacy and continuing education project (in the context of a population of 160 million and 60,000 villages, this number is not necessarily particularly high). These centres offer a curriculum combining a consolidation of literacy and income-earning skills identified as locally relevant. The teachers are appointed by the Bureau of Non-Formal Education and centres are managed in conjunction with a local committee. In addition to the deficiencies in quality assurance, efficiency and accountability, the centres are also constrained by total dependence on donor funds, which may run out in 2015. A sustainability strategy incorporating resources from community, NGOs, local government and regular government budgets has not been developed.

A number of NGOs have been engaged in running community learning centres, under various labels, for over a decade. About 5,000 such centres are estimated to be in existence, with the preponderance run by a half dozen NGOs, including the Bangladesh Rural Advancement Committee (BRAC), Dhaka Ahsania Mission, Friends in Village Development Bangladesh (FIVDB) and Rangpur-Dinajpur Rural Services (RDRS). Such centres also rely on donor funding, but the NGOs have worked with communities to establish firm local embeddedness and mobilise support, with an eye to sustainability. The fact that many of these centres have been in operation for ten or more years testify to both their prospects for sustainability as well as their relevance and responsiveness to community needs. Multi-purpose Community Learning Centres, or *Gonokendros*, were established in the mid-1990s as community reading rooms as part of the continuing education programmes of BRAC and other NGOs. Centres established by BRAC are registered as trusts and have become mostly self-financing, as users pay a small membership fee and funds raised by the community are matched by a capital grant from BRAC. These centres are open to adults, children and students and, in addition to their literacy promotion activities, provide IT and vocational training (in electronics, livestock rearing, horticulture, fish culture, poultry, etc.) in collaboration with the Department of Youth Development and other government agencies (BRAC, 2012).

Clearly, Bangladesh does not yet provide a good example or a workable model of the community learning centre as a vehicle for effective lifelong learning. But does this necessarily imply that such an option is unworkable and should not be considered? One could imagine, for instance, an agreement between the Bureau of Non-Formal Education and the successful literacy NGOs to jointly operate the 7,000 donor-supported centres and use the funds and technical capacities to develop a community-based sustainability model, supported by the government, NGOs and the private sector, as well as the various communities and local government. As it currently stands, without a strategic plan for government support to community learning centres, NGOs are struggling to keep the centres open. Potential donors justifiably raise questions about the future of the centres in the absence of a demonstrable national commitment. At the same time, Bangladesh could use several times the current number of community learning centres to bring the more than 60,000 villages within the reach of a functioning centre.

With a network of NGO-run community learning centres already in operation, and following the major expansion of primary and secondary education in recent decades, the basic building blocks for lifelong learning already exist. The forum of education NGOs established by the Campaign for Popular Education (CAMPE) provides a strong and lively platform for debate and dialogue amongst education stakeholders, including the government. The efficiency and efficacy of service delivery may be, and must be, enhanced by leveraging advances in information technology. Similarly, the renewal and enrichment of learning content must be responsive to learners' needs and demands. With this in mind, the mode and modalities of feasible partnership(s) between the government and civil society must be critically examined.

The multi-sectoral Bangladeshi civil society body, known as the People's Forum for MDG (PFM), established in 2005, has taken it upon itself to engage with the discourse of the new Global Agenda and make the case for human capability enhancement. In doing so, it has proposed a total of 12 development goals, two of which relate to education and human capacity development, as shown in Table 6.1.

TABLE 6.1 *Proposed education goals, targets and indicators for the post-2015 Development Agenda, as put forward by the Bangladesh People's Forum for MDG*

Goal	*Targets*	*Indicators*
4. All children up to the age of prohibition of child labour (age 14) will complete compulsory education of acceptable quality	4.1. All children from birth to transition into primary school participate in organised ECD programmes, including preschool;	4a. Proportion of children with birth registration, broken down by urban-rural locale and gender;
		4b. Proportion of parents/care givers of young children from birth to 8 years participating in organised parenting skills and knowledge programmes, with income quintile and urban-rural breakdown;
	4.2. Ensuring acceptable educational quality with adequate provisions for primary and post-primary education, including teaching personnel;	4c. Proportion of children 3–5 years participating in ECD programmes, with income quintile and urban-rural breakdown;
	4.3. Completion of primary and post-primary education by all eligible children;	4d. Proportion of children 5–6 years participating in preschool programmes, with income quintile and urban-rural breakdown;
	4.4. Major expansion of secondary education.	4e. Proportion of primary and secondary schools meeting essential quality standards for physical facilities, learning equipment and environment, and teaching personnel standards;
		4f. Proportions of students entering and completing primary school at designated age, with gender and urban-rural breakdown;
		4g. Gross and net enrolment in primary and secondary education;

TABLE 6.1 (*cont.*)

Goal	*Targets*	*Indicators*
		4h. Assessed achievement of students against competency standards in languages (first language and English), mathematics, and science at primary and secondary levels, with gender and urban-rural breakdown.
5. All youth and adults have opportunity to participate in lifelong learning related to livelihood, work, citizenship and personal fulfilment	5.1. Universal availability of learning centres, spaces, programmes, and learning technology networks;	5a. Proportion of youth and adults making regular use of learning centres, spaces, programmes, and learning technology networks, with gender, income quintile and urban-urban/slum-rural breakdown;
	5.2. 80 per cent of youth and adults participate in lifelong learning;	5b. Proportion of youth and adults participating in literacy and post-literacy, work, and livelihood skills training and personal fulfilment in community learning centres and other education programmes. with gender, age and urban-urban/slum-rural breakdown;
	5.3. Assessed basic literacy competency achieved by all youth and adults, with self-sustaining functional competency achieved by 80 per cent of youth and adults.	5c. Assessed competency achievement of youth and adults in literacy at basic and functional or self-sustaining levels.

Source: PFM (2013) 'A New Global Partnership: For Sustainable Human Development through Eradicating Poverty and Transforming Economies', Draft post-2015 Development Agenda based on a synthesis of position papers prepared for Bangladesh People's Forum for MDG (PFM), 8 July, cited in Ahmed, 2013, 47–48.

The PFM proposal highlights the fact that along with strengthening basic and post-basic education in both the formal and non-formal sectors, the structures and content of lifelong learning must be created and enhanced in Bangladesh.

China's progress in massively expanding lifelong learning opportunities and creating 'learning cities and communities' since the 1990s may serve as a reference point for the issues, challenges, and potential currently facing Bangladesh. Although the circumstances and contexts differ, lessons derived from the Chinese experience, while not necessarily transferrable directly, may point up issues and concerns that are crucial to lifelong learning's success.

5.2 *China: From Literacy Towards Lifelong Learning*

China, which viewed universal literacy as key to its revolutionary struggle for social and political change even before its liberation in 1949, has since advanced further, broadening the literacy effort into a lifelong system of adult and continuing education. It must be acknowledged, of course, that China does not often use the label 'community learning centre' to refer to the diverse and widespread national continuing learning opportunities and its experience is not directly comparable to the fledgling adult and non-formal education activities in Bangladesh. The point, however, is that an institutional, community-level base, whatever the name, is necessary for the furtherance of lifelong learning.

Similarly, support mechanisms for determining educational content and methodology as well as mobilising human and financial resources must also be in place. Such efforts must be guided by a theory of nation-building that places education at the centre. This is where the Chinese experience becomes pertinent, not as a model to be transplanted, but as a diagnostic tool for identifying potential problems and solutions in developing a learning system.

Literacy as the vehicle for nation-building and economic development has been a dominant theme in Chinese revolution and reform throughout the twentieth century. The communist movement led a nationwide struggle to overcome mass illiteracy. As observed by Peterson: 'Indeed, the literacy programs mounted in China after 1949 constitute what is perhaps the single greatest educational effort in human history' (Peterson, 1997, 3). When confronted with the twin challenges of ensuring prosperity for its people and becoming a global leader, China recognised the necessity of broadening the scope and mandate of adult learning to make it an instrument of lifelong learning. By one estimate, the potential scope of lifelong learning in China is at least three times that of formal schooling: there are a billion candidates for lifelong learning, composed of 790 million workers who need to renew their knowledge and skills; 120 million rural-urban migrants who need to adapt to new work and living environments; and 144 million elderly who want to be active citizens and pursue a meaningful and enriched life of leisure (Hao cited in UIL, 2010, 3).

A major expansion of opportunities in China has occurred to enable rural people with no formal education beyond primary school to acquire relevant knowledge and skills. Continuing education is offered at adult secondary vocational schools and adult higher education institutes, which grant diplomas. There are also provisions for non-diploma continuing education, such as secondary vocational schools for farmers, which have provided training to over 1.1 billion people since the mid-1980s. Workplace training, moreover, is offered to around 90 million participants every year. Continuing education opportunities are also provided to administrative cadres and other professionals in government, industries and non-governmental organisations, and are often aimed at women, youth and workers (UIL, 2010).

Additionally, China has constructed a distance education and service platform utilising satellite, television networks and the Internet. The number of registered distance learning students in regular higher education institutions recently reached 1.1 million (UIL, 2010). A national learning communities pilot project has been initiated in 114 locations, offering various forms of continuing education coordinated effectively to ensure a consistently high quality of service.

Provincial governments also have set up over 400 provincial learning communities (UIL, 2010). The city of Shanghai alone, for example, has more than 6,000 learning stations as well as other basic and tertiary level distance, face-to-face and combined educational facilities outside the formal education and training system. Shanghai is thus a striking example of the emerging architecture of lifelong learning. These are the building blocks for the 'learning city' that Shanghai has pledged to become and will, in time, form the basis of a learning society (Li cited in UIL, 2010, 5).

Key 'enabling measures' for the development and promotion of lifelong learning either currently underway or identified as necessary are:

- An overall legislative framework for lifelong learning, which will clarify the rights and responsibilities of the government, civil society organisations and individuals;
- A national lifelong learning support and service system that covers both urban and rural areas through the use of information and communication technology, including satellite, broadcast networks and the Internet;
- Improved learning outcomes assessment and accreditation, and credit transfer systems;
- Research into ways of developing personal accumulation of lifelong learning credit and integrating this, step by step, into the continuing education system;

- A national qualifications system in which knowledge, skills and competencies are equally weighted, and diploma and professional qualifications are mutually transferable;
- A learning budget assurance and cost-sharing system which clarifies the responsibilities of the government, employers and individuals, thereby ensuring that more support is given to disadvantaged and vulnerable groups; and
- Research into mechanisms to incentivise increased spending on workplace learning by industries, organisations and civil departments (Hao cited in UIL, 2010, 5).

The contrast between China and Bangladesh could not be greater. China's diverse and vast adult and continuing education efforts are seen as elements of a comprehensive national lifelong learning system backed by strong political, legal and resource support. Particularly remarkable in this system are what are referred to as 'enabling measures' underway or identified, including the overall legislative framework, an information and communication technology-based national support and services system; learning outcomes assessment and accreditation, and credit transfer systems; various steps to enhance resources for lifelong learning, and the creation of learning communities and learning cities. These elements, are essential to building a network of community learning centres as an effective institutional tool for lifelong learning.

6 What Can Be Done?

A complex mosaic of needs, constraints, actions and possibilities exist in Bangladesh and its South Asia neighbours. Within this rich mosaic lie the elements of a strategy for action capable of guiding the future development of lifelong learning, with the community learning centre serving as a major vehicle.

Since the UNESCO regional office in Bangkok first promoted community learning centres in the 1990s, they have spread to more than two dozen countries in the region. As illustrated by the range of activities and initiatives present in China, the nomenclature used to refer to community learning centres varies by national context, as does the scope and emphasis of the services. Correspondingly, it has been relatively difficult to count and compare the numbers in various countries. A 2009 report indicates the existence of 28,500 community learning centres in 16 developing countries in the Asia Pacific region, but notes that data from Bangladesh, China, India, and Sri Lanka were not available and several states, despite general knowledge of their more expansive offerings, reported relatively small numbers (Oyasu and Riewpituk, 2013). There is no doubt that the actual number of institutions resembling community learning centres is several times larger than the estimate given above. There is also no doubt that reaching and serving the over 60,000 villages in Bangladesh, or 600,000 in India, for example, will require many times more than whatever number of community learning centres exists at present. Bangladesh has some 80,000 primary schools; what would be a valid argument for not having a comparable number of community learning centres?

Of course, it is not just a numbers game. The centres must clearly define goals and learning objectives, identify the people to be served, and have the wherewithal to provide relevant services of acceptable quality.

As indicated above, the debate and discussion regarding the concepts and practices of lifelong learning and community learning centres as a potential institutional base has continued. Leading up to the CONFINTEA VI in 2009, this discourse was summarised in the Asia Pacific synthesis of progress in Asia. Subsequently, the outcome of CONFINTEA VI was expressed in the Belem Framework for Action, and the follow-up Second Global Report on Adult Learning and Education (GRALE 2) on progress since 2009 was recently released. Various conference reports and studies conducted under the auspices of UNESCO Bangkok Regional Office and UNESCO Institute of Lifelong Learning (UIL) have also been added to this body of work.[3] Together, they provide a strong basis for proposing principles and strategies regarding what might be done in Bangladesh and neighbouring states to promote lifelong learning and strengthen and expand community learning centre as its vehicle (see Ahmed, 2009; UIL, 2009 and 2013; UNESCO, 2011 and 2012).

The emerging principles and strategies derived from the recent review and analysis of the Asia Pacific region can be grouped under the headings of policy development and commitment, institutional and governance concerns, ensuring quality with equity, learning and content relevancy, and resource adequacy.

6.1 *Commitment to Lifelong Learning and the Creation of Learning Societies and Communities as a Policy Imperative*

The task at hand requires the creation and implementation of an overarching vision of diverse and widespread youth and adult learning as the core of the lifelong learning approach, leading to a rich network of opportunities throughout life informed by learners' needs and aspirations. A wide spectrum

3 The UIL was established as the UNESCO Institute of Education in 1952 in Hamburg. It was renamed the UNESCO Institute of Lifelong Learning in 2006.

of learning objectives and groups of learners are to be served by formal, non-formal and continuing education programmes and an enriched informal learning environment, all of which are components of lifelong learning. The logical corollary to the idea of lifelong learning is that as all citizens benefit from, and contribute to, learning and society, they create a learning environment and communities become learning-friendly. The community learning centre, as a general concept, may act as the institutional base for this learning network. The content of programmes and learning objectives, of course, must be relevant and meaningful to learners, and address the critical concerns of society.

6.2 *Governance and Legal Framework*

Related to policy development is the formulation of the legal framework required to give effect to the policy. The legal provisions and associated rules, regulations and procedures derived from the adopted laws must help develop a systemic approach to lifelong learning and strengthen the governance and management of lifelong learning activities. China and several East and South Asian countries have either put in place or are in the process of refining a comprehensive legal framework.

If supported by such a legal framework, the network of community learning centres could become the vehicle for creating lifelong learning opportunities. These are most effective when they directly disseminate knowledge, provide relevant training and connect learners with ancillary support. community learning centres, brought together into national or regional networks for technical support, have the potential to act as a conduit for the education and learning opportunities necessary to reduce poverty and improve overall quality of life. Building effective partnerships among the concerned government agencies, non-governmental organisations, communities, and academic and research institutions is equally important to leveraging community learning centres to serve these goals. The legal and policy framework, therefore, has to support and promote this partnership-building. Only then can community learning centres be the essential building blocks for lifelong learning in the learning society.

6.3 *Relevance of Learning Content*

The objectives and content of lifelong learning must be relevant to the critical concerns of society. The *raison d'être* of lifelong learning is its links and direct relevance to both the identified needs and problems of individual learners and the collective priorities of society. This theoretical position, however, is not automatically translated into practice unless it is systemically integrated into the conceptualisation and design of strategies and programmes. The urgent task of establishing the relevance of lifelong learning to the goal of enhancing people's capabilities, knowledge, understanding and skills for sustainable development is a case in point. One of the key messages of CONFINTEA VI was that the planet will not survive unless it becomes a learning planet (Walters cited in UIL, 2010, 11).

To be effective, poverty reduction programmes must link literacy skills, employment skills, quality of life components and ancillary support. It is only in conjunction with ancillary support and other necessary factors, such as access to credit, management advice, market information and links with potential employers that skills training may result in an improved earning ability. Moreover, poverty is not just a matter of income. Fighting poverty through adult learning also, for instance, entails improvements in health and nutrition, protection from disease, and the knowledge and practice of family planning. Correspondingly, to be relevant and successful, high on the list of learning priorities must be issues such as parents' and care-givers' role and skills in early development of children, the status of women in the family and community, women's participation in economic activities outside the home, and the dissemination of information and knowledge relating to government services and people's entitlement to access them. These are often the priorities of individual learners and communities (Ahmed, 2009).

6.4 *Ensuring Quality with Equity*

An equivalency framework for assessing learning and competencies has to be established. A national qualifications framework helps deal with issues of access, mobility, quality and programme development in lifelong learning activities in an integrated way. In situations where credentials and certifications are important, the establishment of equivalency among them is obviously crucial. Equivalency may also serve as a measure of quality enhancement measure for all kinds of programmes (Walters cited in UIL, 2010, 10). Of course, this mechanism can only function effectively when adequate arrangements for coordination, communication and cooperation amongst key stakeholders are in place. Contestation and debate is to be expected, but if stakeholders share a vision of core objectives, and rely upon research-based evidence, these can be resolved (see UIL, 2013, chapter 6). In Bangladesh, the National Skill Development Council and Bureau of Non-Formal Education are currently at work developing a qualifications framework to guide the establishment of equivalency amongst competencies acquired in different ways.

Advances in information and communication technologies have opened new frontiers in creative content delivery and reaching and serving new groups of learners. The potential, however, is far from realised. In adult and lifelong learning, given their broad scope and mandate, information and communication technologies can help bridge the prevailing digital divide by severing the 'insidious link between quality and exclusivity' in education and promoting wider access, higher quality and lower costs, 'all at the same time' (Daniel cited in UIL, 2010,11).

6.5 *The Imperative of Significantly Increasing Public Resources*

The adult learning components of lifelong learning make up less than a fraction of one per cent of the government education budget in developing countries, and a microscopic share of Gross Domestic Product (GDP). With an expected increase in total government education spending in most countries in the coming years, it is reasonable to aim to raise the share of adult and non-formal learning components of lifelong learning to three to five per cent of the education budget in the medium term, and even higher in the longer term. Such an increase would certainly be consistent with the proclaimed role of adult learning and non-formal education as essential components of lifelong learning. As such, a strategy to ensure balanced support for different components of lifelong learning, including formal education, should be developed. A vigorous effort to raise greater financial resources from diverse sources—including the private sector, communities and external assistance—is also essential (see UIL, 2013, chapter 4).

To conclude, a wide spectrum of learning objectives and learners must be served by formal, non-formal and continuing education programmes within an enriched informal learning environment, all of which are components of lifelong learning. The logical corollary to the idea of lifelong learning is that as all citizens benefit from, and contribute to, learning; societies are empowered; and communities become learning friendly. As argued in this chapter, based on an assessment of the available empirical evidence, an institutional mechanism for making the provisions required for diverse and multifaceted learning is indispensable. The community learning centres, if they did not exist, would have to be invented, to make the grand vision of lifelong learning in the learning society a reality.

References

Ahmed, M. (2013) *The Post-2015 MDG and EFA Agenda and the National Discourse about Goals and Targets—A Case Study of Bangladesh* (Geneva: Graduate Institute of International and Development Studies).

——— (2009) *The State and Development of Adult Learning and Education in Asia and the Pacific Regional Synthesis Report* (Hamburg: UIL).

BRAC (Bangladesh Rural Advancement Committee) (2012) *Multi-purpose Community Learning Centres (Gonokendros)*, http://education.brac.net/multi-purpose-community-learning-centres (accessed on 10 March 2014).

CUE (Centre for Universal Education at Brookings) (2013a) *Toward Universal Learning: What Every Child Should Learn*, LMTF Report, No. 1, http://www.brookings.edu/research/reports/2013/02/learning-metrics (accessed on 10 March 2014).

——— (2013b), *Toward Universal Learning: A Global Framework for Measuring*, LMTF Report, No. 2, http://www.brookings.edu/research/reports/2013/07/global-framework-measuring-learning (accessed on 10 March 2014).

Cisco Systems (2010) *The Learning Society* (San Jose, CA: The Cisco Systems Inc.), http://www.cisco.com/web/about/citizenship/socio-economic/docs/LearningSociety_WhitePaper.pdf (accessed on 10 March 2014).

Coombs, P. and M. Ahmed (1974) *Attacking Rural Poverty: How Non-formal Education Can Help* (Baltimore: Johns Hopkins University Press).

Delors, J. (Chair) (1996) *Learning: The Treasure Within*, Report to UNESCO of the International Commission on Education for the Twenty-first Century (Highlights) (Paris: UNESCO), http://unesdoc.unesco.org/images/0010/001095/109590eo.pdf (accessed on 1 April 2014).

Derbyshire, J. (2013) 'Prospect Interviews with Amartya Sen', *Prospect Magazine*, 18 July 2013, https://www.prospectmagazine.co.uk/magazine/prospect-interviews-amartya-sen-the-full-transcript-jonathan-derbyshire/#.Ux8INryWRz8 (accessed on 11 March 2014).

Dreze, J. and A. Sen (2013) *An Uncertain Glory—India and Its Contradictions* (London: Allen Lane).

Faure, E. et al. (1972) *Learning to Be: The World of Education Today and Tomorrow*. Report of the Edgar Faure Commission (Paris: UNESCO).

Hasan, A. (2012) 'Lifelong Learning in OECD and Developing Countries: An Interpretation and Assessment' in Aspin, D.N. (ed.) *Second Springer International Handbook of Education* (Portland, OR: Powell Books), vol. 26, chapter 29, pp. 471–497.

Husén, T. (1986) *The Learning Society Revisited* (Oxford: Pergamon).

Hutchins, R.M. (1970) *The Learning Society* (Harmondsworth: Penguin).

Oyasu, K. and D. Riewpituk (2013) 'CLCs in the Asia Pacific Region', in Okayama ESD Promotion Commission, *Education for Sustainable Development and Kminkan/Community Learning Centre* (Okayama: Okayama University Press).

Peterson, G. (1997) *The Power of Words: Literacy and Revolution in South China, 1949–95* (Vancouver: University of British Columbia Press).

UIL (UNESCO Institute for Lifelong Learning) (2013) *Second Global Report on Adult Learning and Education—Rethinking Literacy* (Hamburg: UIL).

UIL (2010) *Shanghai International Forum on Lifelong Learning: Summary Report of General Rapporteur*, Shanghai, 19–21 May (Hamburg: UIL), http://uil.unesco.org/fileadmin/keydocuments/LifelongLearning/en/Summary%20of%20General%20Rapporteur.pdf (accessed on 17 April 2014).

——— (2009) *The Belém Framework for Action*, Sixth International Conference on Adult Education (CONFINTEA VI), Belem, Brazil, 1–4 December (Hamburg: UIL).

UNESCO (2012) *Community Learning Centres: Asia Pacific Regional Conference Report* (Bangkok: UNESCO Regional Office).

——— (2011) 'Sustainability of Community Learning Centres: Community Ownership and Support', *Asia-Pacific Regional Action Research Studies* (Bangkok: UNESCO Regional Office).

——— (2000) 'Expanded Commentary' in *Dakar Framework for Action* (Paris: UNESCO).

Walker, M. and E. Unterhalter (2010) *Amartya Sen's Capability Approach and Social Justice in Education* (New York and Basingstoke: Palgrave Macmillan).

CHAPTER 7

Exploring the Value of the Capability Approach for Vocational Education and Training Evaluation: Reflections from South Africa

Lesley Powell and Simon McGrath

Abstract

In the late 1990s, South Africa faced the three-fold challenge of reforming the apartheid-divided institutional landscape of vocational education and training (VET) institutions; ensuring equitable access to skills; and reorienting its skills development system in line with the nation's reinsertion into the global economy. A wave of institutional reforms was enacted which was followed by a large programme of evaluative research. While this body of work was both valuable and necessary, it nonetheless had several limitations. As part of efforts to overcome these, the authors suggest an alternative evaluation method that draws on insights from the 'capability approach'. By putting the needs of people first—rather than the needs of the economy—the capability approach emphasises social justice, human rights and poverty alleviation in VET evaluation. This approach is more focused on the values and goals of individuals and institutions, while retaining the economic rationale as a key analytical tool and emphasising the continued importance of evaluation for the improvement of delivery and outcomes.

1 Introduction

How we evaluate vocational education and training (VET) and the corresponding information sets we use is of considerable importance, as VET has moved to the centre of political reform targeted at unemployment, poverty alleviation and economic growth (McGrath, 2012a). As a result, VET systems are under constant and persistent political pressure to transform, and to do so in such a way that expands participation and raises its parity of esteem (Nieuwenhuis and Shapiro, 2004).

Evaluation research is seen as central to advancing the transformation of these systems. It generates evidence regarding what does and does not work, maintains accountability and evaluates the effectiveness of interventions. A

 | DOI 10.1163/9789004281158_008

range of questions can be raised about evaluation itself, including its effectiveness and efficiency. In this chapter, we will highlight two main issues regarding VET evaluation. First, we examine the 'information basis' of evaluative research undertaken on the sector and the assumptions that are made as to the role and purpose of the sector in selecting these, as opposed to other, information sets. Second, we consider the processes of inclusion and exclusion that take place during evaluation research that lead to both the privileging and silencing of certain voices.

The primary purpose of this chapter is to explore the potential of the capability approach for VET evaluation. We do so by situating our discussion in our experiences of carrying out more traditional evaluations in the context of the South African public Further Education and Training (FET) college sector. Between 1999 and 2002, Powell was research manager of the College Collaboration Fund (CCF), a business-funded project worth more than EUR 10 million aimed at supporting the Department of Education (DoE) in transforming the then-technical colleges into a FET college sector. Between 2002 and 2004, McGrath was a research director at the Human Sciences Research Council of South Africa, overseeing the research, monitoring and evaluation component of the Danish-funded Support to Education and Skills Development (SESD) Programme—the largest ever donor-funded project in the sector. While recognising the benefit of these programmes, however, we are both motivated to now move beyond the core assumptions that underpinned evaluation in these programmes. Broadly speaking, we seek to link to our wider attempts to develop alternate theoretical accounts regarding the purposes of VET and its role in development thinking (e.g. McGrath, 2012b; Powell, 2012). In so doing, we engage closely with the United Nations Educational, Scientific and Cultural Organization's (UNESCO) call for a transformative approach to vocational education and training and improved evaluation approaches to support them (UNESCO, 2014). The significance of this chapter lies in its attempt to point towards a new approach to the *practice* of evaluating VET research, informed by the latest theoretical and policy developments in the field.

The chapter is proceeds as follows. In the next section, we provide a brief history of research on the FET college sector in South Africa since 1994, before focusing specifically on the approach to evaluation that dominated in this era. We then turn to a discussion of the central concepts of the capability approach as they apply to both the challenge of evaluation generally and its potential contribution to VET evaluation more specifically. The subsequent section considers the operational implications of the capability approach. This is followed by a discussion of the potential challenges of such an approach. The chapter concludes with a summary of our main points.

2 A Brief History of Research on South African FET Colleges[1]

South Africa's public FET colleges are relatively new institutions that exist at the crossroads between school, higher education and the world of work (Fisher et al., 2004). This positioning results in multiple, overlapping remits, including the challenges associated with being a major source of intermediate skills and the mandate to help address mass youth unemployment and its highly racialised distribution.

The 50 new FET colleges were established between 1998 and 2002, largely by merging previously racially segregated-technical colleges. Although the primary drive was deracialisation, there was also a recognition that the previous institutions had serious issues of quality, relevance, staffing and leadership. These concerns spurred several studies on the FET colleges, undertaken between 1994 and 2004. Given a very weak existing research base, the major focus of these studies was on developing indicators and an information set upon which the size and shape of the sector could be built and against which the transformation of the sector could be measured (Powell and Hall, 2000, 2002 and 2004).

The period from 2004 to 2009 saw the consolidation of the sector: the FET Colleges Act was passed; college principals appointed; common management systems developed; college councils trained; a EUR c. 200 million Recapitalisation Fund implemented; and a new FET curriculum introduced. As many of the policy frameworks formulated and implementation began, research shifted to an increasingly critical engagement with the policies' coherence and initial outcomes (McGrath et al., 2004; Papier, 2006).

Much of the research undertaken between 1994 and 2009 was funded either by the government directly, or by donors and businesses working in partnership with government (Wedekind, 2009). With few exceptions, this research privileged quantitative methodologies, and when qualitative methods were used, these eschewed interpretivist approaches in favour of descriptive 'hard data' upon which policy could be built and revised (see Fisher et al. 2003). At the institutional level, research pragmatically adopted a new public

1 This section draws substantially from Powell's (2013) critical review of South African FET college literature.

management view of the colleges, and focused on aspects of institutional development such as governance and management systems (Geel, 2005), marketing strategies (Akoojee and McGrath, 2008) and the quality of teaching staff (Jaff et al., 2004). In contrast, theoretical work was seen as being of little value (McGrath, 2008).

The 2009 election of President Zuma, at least rhetorically, saw a shift away from neoliberalism and towards a 'developmental state' with a strong emphasis on South Africa's poor and marginalised. South Africa's new economic policy is committed to creating decent work and promoting a more inclusive economy. As part of the significant changes to government structures, a new Department of Higher Education and Training (DHET) was established, bringing the responsibility for higher education, further education and work-based skills together, with the latter repositioned from the Department of Labour. The establishment of the DHET is intended to build a 'single, coherent, differentiated and highly articulated post-school education and training system' (DHET, 2011, 4), and reflects, in part, an apparent response to researcher critiques of the disarticulation of the previous system (e.g. McGrath et al., 2004; Kraak et al., 2006). The advent of DHET has prompted a renewed debate on South Africa's skills sector and the FET colleges, characterised by three areas of concern:

1. The size of youth unemployment. South Africa has imported the British concept of NEET (not in employment, education or training), which accounts for an estimated 42 per cent of youth aged 18–24, or nearly 3 million people (Cloete, 2009).
2. The pervasive and persistent patterns of inequality in race, gender and class, which are reflected in access to, and success in, education and training.
3. The continued disjuncture between education and training and the skill needs of the economy, illustrated by the failure of FET colleges to produce 'the productive citizens' hoped for in South Africa's 'skills revolution'.

In response to these concerns, the DHET has decided to expand access to education and training by increasing participation in FET colleges (and other proposed post-school institutions) to 4 million learners by 2030 (DHET, 2011, xi). The shift in policy discourse towards an integrated and expanded post-school system focusing on 'the needs of the poor' emphasises dimensions that were previously largely absent. By highlighting the role colleges are to play in poverty alleviation, the DHET seeks to shift the traditional discourse regarding colleges away from solely meeting the needs of industry to incorporate a focus on the needs of learners and communities. Equally, the conceptualisation of the colleges as part of an integrated and differentiated post-school system reflects an awareness of the need to create institutions with a sensitivity to very different contexts, rather than attempting to make 'one size fit all'.

This ambitious new vision provides a unique opportunity to step beyond the productivist accounts that have dominated VET policy and research internationally.[2] It was not surprising, therefore, that Minister Nzimande was a keynote speaker at the Third International Congress on Technical and Vocational Education and Training in Shanghai (May 2012), where UNESCO launched its new vision for a transformative approach. Ambitious policy statements and new theoretical accounts, however, are only part of the answer. It is clear that evaluation research is positioned as pivotal to the next stage of FET college transformation, due to is perceived ability 'differentiate between stronger and weaker institutions in order to provide appropriate support and leadership to both' (DHET, 2011, 20) and mark progress in this new and expanded remit. For these efforts to succeed, however, there must be a new evaluation for the new transformation. Prior to explicating to our vision for a new evaluative approach, it is necessary to reflect in some detail upon the VET evaluation orthodoxy.

3 Evaluative Research on South African FET Colleges

Whilst there have been major innovations in evaluation methodology internationally (discussed below), VET evaluation in developing countries has been slow to progress. Four standard metrics form the standard information set of systemic and institutional VET evaluation internationally:

1. Measures of participation provided through Gross and Net Participation Rates, which aim to determine student enrolment patterns and are analysed by student, programme and institutional type.
2. Measures of institutional efficiency and effectiveness, determined through academic efficiency indicators such as pass and throughput

2 See McGrath (2012b) and McGrath and Lugg (2012) for further discussion of productivist accounts of VET and their implications for VET research.

rates, and resource efficiency indicators such as unit learner costs and lecturer to student ratios.

3. Measures of graduate employment, determined through graduate destination studies, which aim to verify the employment destinations of graduates.
4. Measures of employer and student satisfaction, generally determined quantitatively through student and employer surveys.

The first two of these metrics have been applied to the South African FET college sector in some detail, but the third remains underdeveloped and the fourth almost entirely absent.

3.1 *Measures of Participation*

Policy ambitions to expand VET enrolments in South Africa and many other countries of the world have made measures of participation a high priority for governments. This data is, however, fraught with problems stemming from the multimodal and programmatic complexities of VET systems (McGrath and Lugg, 2012). In South Africa, initial transformation focused on changing the student and staff demographics in terms of race and gender, and transforming the racially-segregated institutional landscape through institutional mergers (Powell, 2013). By 2000, the most significant progress in the sector was the change in the racial and (to a lesser extent) gender composition of the student body, with black enrolment increasing from 32 per cent in 1990 to 75 per cent in 1998, and female students increasing from 38 to 41 per cent of total learners (Cosser et al., 2011). The early 2000s policy goal of achieving equity in racial participation has been largely achieved in the student and staff body, although some concerns regarding the racial composition of senior management staff remain. The participation of women females, however, continues to be skewed towards certain programme areas.

3.2 *Measures of Institutional Efficiency and Effectiveness*

The new skills development system created in the first post-apartheid decade outlined the key objectives of a transformed education and training, which, in turn, shaped the institutional objectives of the transformed landscape. In each of the two main intervention programmes (CCF and SESD), these objectives were translated into performance dimensions, with corresponding indicators, against which the efficiency and effectiveness of FET colleges were to be determined. Although the details of the CCF and SESD approaches differ, they are each characterised by five key performance dimensions, as summarised in Table 7.1.

TABLE 7.1 *Performance dimensions and related indicators*

Dimension	*Goal*	*Indicators*
Leadership and management effectiveness	To manage and lead a transformed FET college in line with FET college legislation, to ensure the college meets the standards of an efficient, high-quality education and training institution that is responsive to the needs of the labour market	• Existing vision and mission • Governance systems are in line with the FET legislation • Establishment of effective management teams • Functioning and updated information systems • Effective knowledge sharing and communication within the institution • Practice of responsible and sustainable financial management • Existence of adequate infrastructure for teaching and learning • Existence of adequate infrastructure for management • Effective human resource capacity management
Marketing and communication	To effectively market the college to employers and prospective students	• Existence of a marketing strategy • Existence of a marketing office or personnel dedicated to the task of marketing
Learner support	To provide learners with the support required to learn effectively, make career decisions and manage personal crises through student counselling	• Implementation of academic support programmes • Implementation of learner support programmes

TABLE 7.1 (*cont.*)

Dimension	*Goal*	*Indicators*
Responsiveness	To achieve the employability of learners	• Existence of good partnerships with public/private sector • Existence of good relationships with communities • Existence of good relationships with other state bodies • Possession of institutional capacity to exercise leadership and develop skills programmes • Learner employment tracking exists • Learners are employable
Teaching and learning	To provide high quality teaching and learning	• Existence of a functioning curriculum development process • Lecturers are suitably qualified • Well-functioning staff development processes are in place • Development of a quality assurance system

SOURCE: AUTHORS.

In the context of contemporary policy plans to expand the FET colleges, measures of institutional effectiveness and efficiency have taken on additional importance, as DHET is aware of the 'danger that quality will be compromised' (DHET, 2011, 28) by the rapid growth.

Together, these studies painted a picture of a FET college sector beset with institutional problems, including the poor capacity of governing councils, college management and lecturing staff, and unacceptably low throughput and pass rates.

3.3 *Measures of Employability*

Following on from measures of efficiency and effectiveness, the third metric of conventional assessment, as mentioned above, is employability, a key element of current international policy discourses on post-school education. Typically, employability is captured through graduate destination studies, and tracer studies more specifically. Currently, very few institutions have reliable data in this area. The data that is available is often either out-dated or so limited it fails to capture information regarding the nature of the work, the extent to which work relates to the field of study, or the nature of the employment contract. As a result, only a limited number of employment tracer studies have been undertaken in South Africa, notably by Cosser et al. (2003) and Gewer (2009), who argue that a low percentage of graduates are successful in the labour market and even fewer in an area of work related to the programme they studied.

Employability is central to the move to expand participation. The hope is that expanding access to education and training will ensure that 'those entering the labour market are qualified and competent to take up the employment and income generating opportunities that exist and that will exist as the economy grows and changes in the future' (DHET, 2011, viii). The aim is that this will then 'contribute to fundamentally reducing unemployment and poverty' (DHET, 2011, viii). Within this context, the need and demand for employment tracking studies able to monitor (ideally, increased) employment is likely to grow.

3.4 *Measures of Employer and Student Satisfaction*

The fourth, and remaining, area of measurement relates to employer and student satisfaction. Employer and student satisfaction studies have not been a serious part of the evaluation research undertaken in South Africa. Select interviews were undertaken as components of larger projects, but these were small in scale and not systematic in nature. The employer satisfaction studies that were undertaken, however, indicate that employers find it difficult to determine their skill needs and are unsure about what the FET colleges can do to meet them (Mercorio and Powell, 1999). In many cases, unless a partnership existed between the employer and the college, employers were unsure as to what percentage of their employees were trained at an FET college.

3.5 *The Limitations of the Orthodox Approach to VET Evaluation in South Africa (and Beyond)*

As key actors in delivering this first wave of South African VET evaluation research, we still believe it made an important contribution to the establishment and reform of South Africa's FET colleges and that many of its ambitious should continue to inform future approaches. Upon reflection, however, we believe it was insufficient, in six regards, for what must be done in the next phase. First, it reflected a narrow VET understanding of evaluation that was poorly attuned to developments elsewhere in evaluation methodologies, a point we will return to below. Second, it drew on a new public management view of institutional development, which, though grounded in the wider assumptions of South African policy reform, provides an inadequate account of institutional change and quality, both generally and in the South African context.[3] Third, it underplayed the wider economic and labour market contexts in which providers operate, focusing on the 'failings' of learners and colleges rather than those of employers or government. Fourth, it displayed a methodological deafness to the voices of learners, lecturers and communities, instead assuming that employability was the only goal of FET. Fifth, as the traditional approach is not designed to evaluate or address the new policy concerns with social justice or human development, it is not fit-for-purpose for the new phase of transformation being envisaged in South African FET policy. Sixth, it does not engage sufficiently with the emerging UNESCO account of VET and human development, which appears better attuned both to trends in development theory and South Africa's increasing official emphasis on human development. Taken together, these weaknesses have led us to envision an alternative way of thinking about VET evaluation, outlined below, which draws on the insights of the capability approach.

4 The Capability Approach

By emphasising the quality of life and well-being of individuals, the capability approach offers a normative framework in alternative to the output and efficiency measures usually applied to social evaluation. A central commitment of this approach, informed by the principles of social justice and, more recently, by what Sen (2009) has termed 'comparative justice', is to the dignity of each person. At its core, the capability approach is about providing individuals with the opportunities to live lives they value, enabling them to become agents in their own life (Deneulin and Shahani, 2009). By putting the needs of people first, rather than the needs of the economy, the capability approach brings social justice, human rights and poverty alleviation to the forefront of the VET and skills development discourse.

The concepts of capabilities, functionings and freedom are central to the capability approach and, according to Sen, provide the best metric for interpersonal evaluations. Capabilities comprise 'what a person is able to do or be' and represent both 'the opportunity to achieve valuable combinations of

3 See McGrath (2010) for an exploration of the use of new public management logic in the South African FET college sector.

human functionings' (Sen, 2005, 153) and the freedom to choose among them. Freedom, in the capability approach, has not only instrumental importance in providing a greater range of alternatives, but, as 'acting freely' and 'being able to choose are [...] directly conducive to well-being' (Sen, 1992, 50), it is also intrinsically important to individual fulfilment. Functionings, on the other hand, represent what a person actually does and the life that a person actually lives, as well as person's state of well- (or ill-)being.

While it might appear that attempting to distinguish between 'capabilities' (opportunities) and 'functionings' (doings) is a matter of splitting hairs, the distinction is crucial for social justice and identifying inequality of opportunity—both of which are elided in conventional approaches to VET evaluation. In this regard, the distinction between capabilities and functionings offers three advantages to the evaluation of VET. First, the distinction highlights the importance of human freedom by differentiating between what people *actually* do (functionings) and what they *can* do (capabilities). This thus allows for the consideration of the possibility that individuals might achieve the same functioning (for example, an FET qualification) but have significantly different opportunities from which to select. This differs markedly from conventional resource input-output approaches to VET evaluation, which tend to focus purely on functionings. The distinction highlights the choices that an individual has regarding what to achieve in a particular area and the array of opportunities from which they are able to choose. The key difference lies between choosing to do and doing, i.e. between *choosing* to have a particular functioning (or achievement) and *having* a particular functioning (Sen, 1992).

Second, the distinction enables VET evaluations to identify differences in individual ability to convert the characteristics of an ability (such as commodities or skills) into functionings (such as employment). Interpersonal variations in this conversion ability could be due to either individual or social factors (Robeyns, 2000). Hence, limiting analysis to functionings (be they resources, qualifications or abilities)—as done by conventional VET evaluations—does not provide sufficient leverage on individual well-being.

Third, the distinction between capabilities and functionings is crucial is the approach's key conceptualisation of poverty as consisting of capability deprivation across multiple dimensions. In the context where large numbers of FET students come from what Gewer (2009) describes as 'poverty-stricken family environments' (2009, 145) and policymakers are committed to positioning an expanded FET college sector as a central instrument in poverty alleviation, the importance of the above conceptualisation of poverty for the evaluation of

FET colleges becomes clear. In this context, measures of participation, while instrumental to monitoring increased individual access to education and training, apply what Qizilbash and Clark (2002) describe as a 'vague' definition of poverty that fails to adequately capture its multiple dimensions. As a result, these approaches also fail to consider both the critical threshold that must be surpassed in each of the multiple dimensions of poverty for an individual to move beyond poverty and the ways in which FET colleges can contribute to this achievement. The result is that measures of participation tell us little about the ways in which colleges contribute (and could potentially contribute more) to poverty alleviation.

Fourth, the capability approach allows differential risks and costs to individuals to be identified by VET evaluations. It also allows for the recognition of the potential contradictions in capabilities individuals may encounter. This is critical for ensuring policy success, as without an understanding of the potential costs or risks of attending VET institutions, policies for expanded participation face the risk of failure. For instance, consider the contrast between a student who risks his family's financial well-being by leaving employment to enrol for full-time study at a FET college and a student who attends college with no financial risk to his family at all. Both students are enrolled for study, but they experience very different stresses over the course of their programme. Such nuanced differentials, the recognition of which is crucial to the fulfilment of FET colleges' mandate to alleviate poverty, are discounted and rendered invisible by the conventional VET evaluations which dominate contemporary research on South African FET colleges.

The capability approach stresses the analytical distinction between means and ends. In essence, it argues that we should be clear when attributing value to something (or somebody) whether we value it (or s/he) for its own sake, or because it makes something else that we truly value possible. For the capability approach, the purpose (or 'ends') of interpersonal evaluation is the expansion of capabilities (opportunities), and the freedoms to elect from these capabilities. As such, institutions and structures—including VET institutions—should be evaluated in terms of the 'causal importance that they have for individuals' well-being' (Alkire, 2008, 33). In other words, 'it is people's capabilities that must guide the evaluation rather than how much money, educational resources, or qualifications they are able to command' (Walker and Unterhalter, 2010, 4). Correspondingly, the analytical focus rests on the capabilities that matter to individuals and the extent to which institutional and socio-economic arrangements expand or constrict individuals' capabilities, rather than on the institutional structures themselves.

Through its focus on human well-being, the application of the capability approach to education and training in South Africa suggests a new set of questions for VET evaluation that asks, 'Do they [the social policies] really improve [people's] prospects in terms of capabilities?' (Bonvin and Farvaque, 2006, 3). Or, in the terms of the FET colleges specifically, do these institutions serve to expand or to constrict the capabilities, functionings and freedom of FET college students? South Africa's policy ambition is to create increased participation in an expanded FET college sector, but what valuable opportunities will these larger colleges offer, and how do we identify which opportunities matter to these students? This chapter argues that current approaches to evaluation, while useful for political and institutional accountability, are silent on these important matters. The capability approach, in contrast, raises a number of questions pertinent to the well-being of FET college students that differ to those considered by conventional approaches and that cannot easily be answered by the information sets generated by past VET evaluations. These questions include the following:

- Which dimensions of institutional functioning enable individuals to expand the capabilities they value and which serve to limit and constrict the expansion of capabilities and functionings?
- Which capabilities and functionings matter to students and to what extent are these being addressed by existing institutional arrangements, cultures and the pedagogic approach of VET?
- How does expanding the capabilities and functionings of an individual VET student contribute to the development of their families and communities?
- Given the existing institutional arrangements and pedagogic design of VET, do all students in the sector have the same opportunities to participate in and to succeed in VET?

The practical value of the capability approach is that it goes beyond providing an abstract, theoretical notion of social justice to provide a practical framework through which social justice can be enacted, monitored and evaluated through the lived lives of human beings (Walker, 2005). Reflecting on the contribution the capability approach makes to higher education, Walker notes that 'these are attractive ideas for higher education' but, she asks, 'how might they be applied for more practical evaluation purposes?' (2008, 477). The capability approach is similarly attractive, if not more so, for VET, than for higher education, as through its commitment to human well-being, it challenges the neoliberal underpinnings of VET policy that prioritise human resource development (McGrath, 2012b; Powell, 2012). The tricky question of how to operationalise the capability approach for practical purposes, however, remains. As Alkire writes: 'proof must be in the pudding' (2008, 1).

A first step in operationalising the capability approach is provided by Bonvin and Farvaque (2006), who argue that it affects evaluation on two levels: the *substantial* and the *procedural*. The *substantial* level involves the actual information sets upon which we base our evaluations, which are in turn driven by the kinds of questions asked above. The *procedural* level relates to the processes involved in deciding on the information sets and gathering the information required. With respect to the *substantial* level, Bonvin and Farvaque (2005) argue that the information upon which we base our evaluations 'is not neutral', as decisions are made during evaluations as to what to measure, which information sets are to applied to these measures and, conversely, what will not be measured and which information sets will not to be included. Core to the 'substantial level' of evaluation, as discussed above, is the importance of human flourishing, as conceptualised by the notions of 'capabilities', 'functionings' and 'freedom'. Tikly explains that 'from a human capabilities perspective', this suggests that 'evaluation of VET systems whilst important needs to be evaluated against a more holistic set of criteria' (2012, 19).

But how are we to develop this more 'holistic set of criteria', to which Tikly refers? Bonvin and Farvaque (2006) suggest that this can only be achieved by paying attention to the *procedural* levels of evaluation which, according to Sen (1999), must involve a process of democratic participation that provides opportunities for this 'set of criteria' to be publicly scrutinised and debated. This participation is central to evaluation for two distinct reasons. The first, the 'evaluative reason', lies in the importance of evaluating developmental (or institutional) interventions in light of whether they have enhanced the capabilities that matter (1999, 4). The second, relevant to Bonvin and Farvaque's (2006) *procedural* levels, is the 'effectiveness reason', which derives from Sen's argument that the 'achievement of development is thoroughly dependent on the free agency of people' (Sen, 1999, 4), wherein development is understood as constitutive of freedom, and the 'expansion of freedom is viewed as both the primary end and the principal means of development' (Sen, 1999, 36). In other words, he argues that people are to be envisaged as agents capable of acting, and desiring to do so, in the world, rather than as 'motionless patients' (Sen, 1999, 137) standing in a line waiting patiently (or impatiently) to be developed. Correspondingly, failing to include people in the process of development might result in 'targeting-achievements [being] quite different from targeting-attempts' (Sen, 1999, 137).

Contrary to the emphasis placed on participation in the capability approach, current approaches to FET college evaluation have largely ignored the voices and experiences of students. Like conventional approaches to VET evaluation internationally, these evaluations tell us nothing about why these students elected to enrol, the costs to themselves and their family of said enrolment, or the extent to which the college has or has not met their expectations. The reason for this is that it is assumed that learners' voices are irrelevant, as it is 'obvious' what they want—jobs now. As Wedekind argues:

> [M]uch of the reform process [for FET colleges] cares little about understanding the people in the system [...] as long as more staff and students are black and enrolments are increasing there is little more that needs to be considered. (2009, 17)

Recent discussions on the operationalisation of the capability approach have centred on the development of capability lists that identify the capabilities that matter to individuals and define a set of corresponding measurement dimensions or indicators (Alkire, 2002).[4] Democratic participation and public debate are emphasised as essential to developing these capability lists, as the selection of capabilities to be promoted through policy and institutional interventions and the information sets used for evaluation is not neutral, but involves expediently trading the benefits of one capability, and therefore one information set, against another. As Alkire argues, 'the capability approach can be likened to a sophisticated balance upon which two states of affairs or alternative courses of action can be analysed and compared' (2008, 28). From this perspective, the first step towards resolving these complex decisions and the contradictions underpinning them lies in public deliberation and participation. This must be matched by expanding the 'capability of voice' through the establishment of procedures for social choice and provid-

4 It is important to note that the capabilities approach is not homogeneous. While all who work within its framework share a common commitment to social justice and the distinction between capabilities and functionings, there are a diversity of perspectives and developments. An important distinction must be drawn between the interpretations of Amartya Sen and Martha Nussbaum, who have very different approaches to the definition of capabilities and freedom, and to the development of capabilities lists. Sen believes in deliberately leaving capability lists unspecified in favour of public deliberation, while Nussbaum argues for the development of basic capabilities which governments should then constitutionally guarantee their citizens.

ing individuals with the abilities and spaces to meaningfully express their opinions (Bonvin and Thelon, 2003).

An important motive for the development of capability lists, their role in the expansion of voice, is that enables researchers to determine whether a particular social initiative (in this case, VET institutions) has expanded or contracted capabilities that matter by developing a 'set of criteria', selected during the process of social evaluation, against which progress can be evaluated. Another benefit of capabilities lists lies in their ability to act as 'devices to focus attention' (Kamsler, 2006, 199). Highlighting Mark and Rock's (1998) work on 'inattentional blindness', Kamsler argues that what we pay attention to 'profoundly affects both our personal evaluations of well-being and our formulation of focused goals, such as political agendas' (2006, 200). By focusing attention on human well-being, capability lists correct for 'inattention blindness' to human flourishing.

5 The Contribution of the Capability Approach to VET Evaluation

On the surface, the 'procedural aspects' might appear quite similar to newer, more participatory approaches to VET evaluation, such as that put forward by Nieuwenhuis and Shapiro (2004), which have been developed in response to positivistic assumptions of the neutrality of evaluation. This literature argues for the importance, in '*high-quality* evaluations', of 'acceptance and credibility of evaluations amongst programme participants' (Beywl and Speer, 2004, 55). The difference, then, lies in the underlying paradigm, with many of these 'new' approaches emphasising the importance of evaluation as a 'steering mechanism' in the context of 'deregulation and decentralisation' (Beywl and Speer, 2004, 55) and/or the importance of systemic interaction within the skills development system (Nieuwenhuis and Shapiro, 2004). The distinction drawn in the capability approach between means and ends, and corresponding focus on human well-being, thus diverges from the human capital and productivist approaches underpinning much of contemporary evaluation research. As a result, job readiness is privileged above all other educational values. This is particularly so in VET, where the 'singular emphasis on a narrow "initiative" version of employability (Gazier and Houneman, 1999) has left little room for the role that education and training plays in preparing young people for the challenges and opportunities that they will face in their families, their communities and their workplaces' (Powell and McGrath, 2013, 9).

In contrast to the dominant, often productivist approaches to VET evaluation (Anderson, 2003), including the newer, participatory approaches discussed above, the capability approach provides a revised normative framework for the evaluation of VET. In general, 'productivist' approaches emphasise economic growth and income generation as key development objectives, understanding employability and the creation of human capital solely as a means to that end. Conversely, the capability approach prioritises human flourishing, with economic growth seen as a necessary but not sufficient means of achieving development. Understood in these terms, the evaluation of employability must be seen in a new light. For the capability approach, employability is more than the ability to access work; it is about 'the real freedom to choose the job one has reason to value' (Bonvin and Galster, 2010, 72). From this perspective, employability requires not only valuable opportunities to access the skills and abilities necessary for work, but also the existence of valuable opportunities that contribute to human flourishing within the labour market.

Conventional evaluation of VET's affect on learners focuses on achieving objective targets in key policy areas, such as participation, institutional effectiveness and employability, rather than on the capabilities that matter to the lives of students. As with the evaluations of the South African FET colleges discussed above, many of these new and participatory approaches to VET evaluation are guilty of 'inattention blindness' to human well-being. They fail to consider the well-being of students or the extent to which VET systems are providing real opportunities for learners to expand their options and life achievements. This is due, as argued by Grubb and Ryan, to the fact that these 'evaluations of VET programmes often fail to describe with any precision what particular programmes do; what a programme is, and why it should have any positive effects at all' (Grubb and Ryan, 1999, 8). We agree with Grubb and Ryan when they insist that 'the purpose of a particular programme should influence the kind of evaluation undertaken' (1999, 8). Moreover, as Sen argues, 'if freedom is what development advances, then there is a major argument for concentrating on the overarching objective, rather than on a particular means, or some chosen list of instruments' (1999, 3).

Conventional VET evaluation, while instrumental in maintaining the political and institutional accountability necessary for creating the conditions required for capability expansion, is paradigmatically limited as an approach for evaluating the contribution of VET to poverty and social inclusion. Paradoxically, however, both are key goals of South Africa's FET college policy. The orthodoxy is unable to identify the capabilities (or opportunities) that are of value to students; the extent to which VET institutions expand or restrict these valued capabilities; and the future policies and institutional trajectories required to achieve such capability expansion. As such, the emphasis on human well-being in the capability approach marks a major departure from productivist conceptions of VET (McGrath, 2012b; Powell, 2012; López-Fogués, 2012). Its insistence on the centrality of agency differs markedly from the dominant paradigm applied to much of VET evaluation research, which is primarily concerned with structure—the institution, the skills development system and the relationship with the economy being foremost—at the expense of students' agency and experiences (Powell, 2013).

6 Challenges with Applying the Capability Approach

It is beyond the scope of this chapter to survey the critiques of the capability approach, particularly as Robeyns (2005) and Alkire (2002) have already produced excellent work on the subject. There are obviously many limitations to the approach; here, we will focus on concerns regarding the operationalisation of the capability approach in social evaluations.

The use of the capability approach as a tool for the evaluation of social policy is still in its infancy (Alkire, 2008). Sen's highly philosophical approach does not lend itself easily to operationalisation. Indeed, Robeyns notes that 'some critics' frustration with Sen's capability approach seem[s] to stem in part from uncertainty as to whether or not they have "done it right"' (Robeyns, 2002, 122). The realisation that conventional evaluation approaches are inadequate may be of little value if, 'after scrutiny, we must concede that the capability approach in practice can do no better' (Alkire, 2008, 26).

Evaluation is necessarily a pragmatic exercise; it must be timely and cost-effective. As such, many are rightly concerned that the capability approach may be poor value for money. At this point in time, the data to clearly address this issue simply does not exist. What we do know, however, is that the fair comparators, in terms of cost, are past VET evaluation programmes. Once such recent evaluation cost nearly EUR 400,000, which leads us to believe there is some hope for better value for money from a capability approach. Equally, having experienced week-long conventional evaluation visits to institutions, our expectation is that the time required for a capabilities-based evaluation is unlikely to be excessive in comparison.

That said, an important argument of this chapter is that, as yet, we do not know whether a capability approach to VET evaluation is viable. What we do know is that, more important than cost and time considerations, the current approach is too limited to serve the social inclusion goals of South Africa's new FET college policy framework. In this context, though it remains to be tested in practice, the capability approach provides a promising alternative. We believe that even if it proves limited in practice, the capability may be invaluable in highlighting the well-being of students, which justifies the need for experimentation in and of itself.

7 Conclusion

We will conclude this chapter with five key propositions.

First, whilst past evaluation research has made an important contribution to the establishment and reform of South Africa's FET colleges, the approach is inadequate to address the new challenges faced by the sector.

Second, a deep-held belief regarding the central importance of employability to the sector's mission lies at the heart of the current approach to determining VET's success. This narrow, Anglophone model of employability, however, neglects the roles played by policies, labour markets and employers' decisions and tends to produce an insufficient account of individual learners. We argue, moreover, that said learners are not simply empty slates enrolling at colleges in the hope of acquiring employability skills.

Third, the above arguments are linked to a wider insistence in contemporary development theory, driven by the human development and capability approach, on the multifaceted nature of development. A narrow, economistic view of development, therefore, is far too narrow to generate an adequate understanding of the role FET colleges can play in poverty alleviation, unemployment reduction and well-being enhancement.

Fourth, we believe that the sweeping assumptions frequently made as to what learners, staff and communities value from their VET experiences are fundamentally flawed. We instead agree with Cook-Sather, that there is 'something fundamentally amiss about building and rebuilding an entire system without consulting at any point those it is ostensibly designed to serve' (2002, 3).

Fifth, in the light of the previous four propositions, we suggest that there is a strong case for exploring the suitability of a new approach to VET evaluation that draws on the human development and capability approach.

This chapter constitutes an initial step into complex territory. It suggests there are merits in a shift in VET evaluation from the narrow areas of concentration outlined above to a broader and more humanistic vision targeted at the well-being of VET students. It must be recognised, however, as Alkire (2008) notes, that 'to operationalise an alternative approach [...] which is what the capability approach is—is not a modest task, nor is it very nearly accomplished' (2008, 130). Our next task is to offer some proposals for operationalising this approach. But that task remains for another paper.

References

Akoojee, S. and S. McGrath (2008) 'The Marketing of Public FET Colleges', *Journal of Education*, 45, pp. 131–153.

Alkire, S. (2008) 'Using the Capability Approach: Prospective and Evaluative Analyses' in Comim, F., M. Qizilbash and S. Alkire (eds.), *The Capability Approach: Concepts, Measures and Applications* (Cambridge: Cambridge University Press).

——— (2002) *Valuing Freedoms: Sen's Capability Approach and Poverty Reduction* (Oxford: Oxford University Press).

Anderson, D. (2003) 'From Productivism to Ecologism: Dilemmas, Issues and Strategies for VET', *Australian Vocational Education Review*, 10(1), pp. 1–14.

Beywl, W. and S. Speer (2004) 'Developing Standards to Evaluate Vocational Education and Training' in Descy, P. and M. Tessaring (eds.) *The Foundations of Evaluation and Impact Research* (Luxembourg: Office for Official Publications of the European Communities).

Bonvin, J. and N. Farvaque (2006) 'Promoting Capability for Work: The Role of Local Actors' in Deneulin, S. et al., (eds.), *Transforming Unjust Structures: The Capability Approach* (Dordrecht: Springer).

——— (2005) 'What Informational Basis for Assessing Job-Seekers? Capabilities vs. Preferences', *Review of Social Economy*, 63(2), pp. 269–289.

Bonvin, J. and L. Thelon (2003) *Deliberative Democracy and Capabilities: The Impact and Significance of Capability for Voice*, paper presented at the 3rd Conference on the Capability Approach, Pavia.

Cloete, N. (2009) *Responding to the Education Needs of Post-school Youth* (Cape Town: Centre for Higher Education Transformation).

Cook-Sather, A. (2002) 'Authorizing Students' Perspectives: Toward Trust, Dialogue, and Change in Education', *Educational Researcher*, 31(4), pp. 3–14.

Cosser, M., et al. (2011) *Further Education and Training (FET) Colleges at a Glance in 2010 FET Colleges Audit* (Cape Town: Human Sciences Research Council).

——— (2003) *Technical College Responsiveness* (Cape Town: HSRC Press).

Deneulin, S. and L. Shahani (2009) *An Introduction to the Human Development and Capability Approach* (London: Earthscan).

DHET (Department of Higher Education and Training) (2011) *Green Paper for Post School Education and Training* (Pretoria: Department of Higher Education and Training).

Fisher, G., et al. (2004) 'Public Further Education and Training Colleges' in Kraak, A. and K. Press (eds.), *Human Resources Development Review 2003* (Cape Town: HSRC Press).

Gazier, B. and S. Houneman (1999) 'Employability: An Evolutionary Notion, an Interactive Concept' in Gazier, B. (ed.), *Employability: Concepts and Policies* (Berlin: European Employment Observatory Research Network).

Geel, P. (2005) *The Management of Staff Development Programmes at FET Colleges in the Gauteng Province*, unpublished PhD thesis, University of South Africa.

Gewer, A. (2009) *Features of Social Capital that Enhance the Employment Outcomes of FET College Learners*, unpublished PhD thesis, University of the Witwatersrand.

Grubb, W. and P. Ryan (1999) *The Roles of Evaluation for Vocational Education and Training* (Geneva: International Labour Organization).

Jaff, R., et al. (2004) *The Challenge of Staffing Responsiveness in FET Colleges* (Pretoria: Department of Education).

Kamsler, V. (2006) 'Attending to Nature: Capabilities and the Environment' in Kaufman, A. (ed.) *Capabilities Equality: Basic Issues and Problems* (London: Routledge).

Kraak, A., et al. (2006) *Debating High Skills and Joined-Up Policy* (Cape Town: HSRC Press).

López-Fogués, A. (2012) *Theorising Further Education through a Capability Lens: Vulnerability and Freedoms*, Jubilee Working Papers (Nottingham: School of Education, University of Nottingham).

Mark, A. and I. Rock (1998) *Inattentional Blindness* (Cambridge, MA: MIT Press).

McGrath, S. (2012a) 'Building New Approaches to Thinking about Vocational Education and Training and Development: Policy, Theory and Evidence', *International Journal of Educational Development*, 32(5), pp. 619–622.

——— (2012b) 'Vocational Education and Training for Development: A Policy in Need of a Theory?', *International Journal of Educational Development*, 32(5), pp. 623–631.

——— (2010) 'Beyond Aid Effectiveness: The Development of the South African Further Education and Training College Sector, 1994–2009', *International Journal of Educational Development*, 30(5), pp. 525–534.

——— (2008) 'FET Needs Research', *Mail and Guardian*, 30 June, http://mg.co.za/article/2008-06-30-fet-needs-research (accessed on 4 March 2014).

McGrath, S. and R. Lugg (2012) 'Knowing and Doing Vocational Education and Training Reform: Evidence, Learning and the Policy Process', *International Journal of Educational Development*, 32(5), pp. 696–708.

McGrath, S., et al. (eds.) (2004) *Shifting Understandings of Skills in South Africa* (Cape Town: HSRC Press).

Mercorio, G. and L. Powell (1999) *A Report on Work Conducted amongst Stakeholders within the Western Cape: Partnerships and Linkages* (Johannesburg: The Colleges Collaboration Fund, National Business Initiative).

Nieuwenhuis, L. and H. Shapiro (2004) 'Evaluating Systems Reform in Vocational Education and Training: Learning from Danish and Dutch Cases' in Descy, P. and M. Tessaring (eds.), *Evaluation of Systems and Programmes. Third Report on Vocational Training Research in Europe: Background Report* (Luxembourg: Office for the Official Publications of the European Communities).

Papier, J. (2006) *All Further Education and Training Colleges (FETCs) Are Equal, but Some Are More Equal Than Others (with Apologies to Orwell)*, Harold Wolpe Memorial Trust Open Dialogue, 2 February, Cape Town.

Powell, L. (2013) 'A Critical Assessment of Research on South African FET Colleges', *South African Review of Education*, 19(1), pp. 59–81.

——— (2012) 'Reimagining the Purpose of VET: Expanding the Capability to Aspire in South African Further Education and Training Students', *International Journal of Educational Development*, 32(5), pp. 643–653.

Powell, L. and G. Hall (2004) *Quantitative Overview of the Further Education and Training College Sector* (Pretoria: Department of Education).

——— (2002) *Quantitative Overview of the Further Education and Training College Sector* (Pretoria: Department of Education).

——— (2000) *Quantitative Overview of the South African Technical Colleges* (Pretoria: Department of Education).

Powell, L. and S. McGrath (2013) *Advancing Life Projects: South African Students Explain Why They Come to FET Colleges*, Presented at the Journal Vocational Education and Training Conference, Researching Vocational Education and Training, Worcestor College, Oxford, 5–7 July.

Qizilbash, M. and D. Clark (2002) *Core Poverty and Extreme Vulnerability in South Africa*, Economics Research Centre Discussion Paper, No. 2002–3, University of East Anglia.

Robeyns, I. (2005) 'The Capability Approach: A Theoretical Survey', *Journal of Human Development*, 6(1), pp. 93–117.

——— (2003) 'Sen's Capability Approach and Gender Inequality: Selecting Relevant Capabilities', *Feminist Economics*, 9(2–3), pp. 61–92.

Sen, A. (2009) *The Idea of Justice* (London: Belknap Press).

——— (2005) 'Human Rights and Capabilities', *Journal of Human Development*, 6(2), pp. 151–166.

——— (1999) *Development as Freedom* (Oxford: Oxford University Press).

——— (1992) *Inequality Reexamined* (Oxford: Oxford University Press).

Tikly, L. (2012) *Reconceptualising TVET and Development: Towards a Capabilities and Social Justice Approach*, background paper for the World Report on TVET (Paris: UNESCO).

UNESCO (2014) *Transforming Technical and Vocational Education and Training* (Paris: UNESCO).

Walker, M. (2008) 'A Human Capabilities Framework for Evaluating Student Learning', *Teaching in Higher Education*, 13(4), pp. 477–487.

——— (2005) 'Amartya Sen's Capability Approach and Education', *Educational Action Research*, 13(1), pp. 103–110.

Walker, M. and E. Unterhalter (2010) *Amartya Sen's Capability Approach and Social Justice in Education* (Basingstoke: Palgrave Macmillan).

Wedekind, V. (2009) *Report on the Research on Further Education and Training (FET) Colleges in South Africa*, EAP project working paper 2, University of Nottingham.

PART 3

China, Migration, MOOCs: What's in It for Higher Education in Africa?

CHAPTER 8

China's Higher Education Engagement with Africa: A Different Partnership and Cooperation Model?

Kenneth King

Abstract

What is the nature of China's educational partnerships with Africa? This chapter examines China's investment in human resource development in Africa, especially in higher education, through several programmes including long- and short-term training of Africans in China, Confucius Institutes, stand-alone projects, and the 20+20 scheme for higher education cooperation between China and Africa. It investigates several apparent differences between China's aid discourse and practice and those of traditional Organisation for Economic Co-operation and Development (OECD) donors. It asks how the enduring continuity of China's discourse on mutual benefit and common good in educational aid can be explained. Can what looks like a one-way partnership in terms of financing really, in fact, be symmetrical?

Author's Note

The research from which this paper is primarily derived was funded by the Hong Kong Research Grants Council (RGC/UGC 750008). The views expressed here are the author's alone, and may not be attributed to the Hong Kong Research Grants Council.

1 Introduction

To date, China has paid very little attention to giving a full or detailed presentation of its aid or development cooperation in education or training with Africa, or, indeed, in any other areas.[1] It does not produce glossy accounts of its education development projects, such as those of the Korea International Cooperation

1 The first full-length account of China's education cooperation with Africa is provided in King (2013a).

 | DOI 10.1163/9789004281158_009

Agency (KOICA, South Korea), the Japan International Cooperation Agency (JICA, Japan) and the Department for International Development (DFID, UK), at the global, regional or the country level.[2] Nor does it produce regular sector policy statements about education. Of course, unlike the above-mentioned bilateral donors, China does not have a designated development agency, just a small Department of Foreign Aid within the very large Ministry of Commerce.[3]

The lack of detailed accounts of China's education, training or capacity building programmes for Africa makes it harder to pinpoint key differences with traditional donors. Additionally, unlike neighbouring East Asian states, such as South Korea or Japan, where the rationale and scale of their training policies is outlined and readily accessible on their respective websites,[4] it is challenging to tease out the culture of China's education and training aid. In the absence of the training and/or education policy papers common to most Development Assistance Committee (DAC) donors,[5] it is necessary to sift through the more general discourse of China's cooperation for references to educational aid.

It is fortunate, however, that in April 2011 China's State Council issued a White Paper on *China's Foreign Aid* (China, 2011). This illustrates that China provides foreign aid related to education and skills development under several different headings, notably 'technical cooperation', 'human resource development cooperation', as well as 'education' and 'training'. Human resource development (also 'HRD') is perhaps the most general of these terms:[6]

> Human resource development cooperation means that China, through multilateral or bilateral channels, runs different kinds of research and training programmes for government officials, education programmes, and other personnel exchange programmes for developing countries. (China, 2011, 8)

2 See, for example, DFID (2013), JICA (2010 and 2013), or KOICA (2011, 192–206).

3 That said, there have been some very recent indications that China is moving towards a dedicated development agency, possibly entitled the 'International Development Agency of China'.

4 See, for instance, the detail on KOICA's website, http://www.koica.go.kr/english/aid/education/index.html (accessed on 26 November 2013) and the JICA site, www.jica.go.jp/english/ (accessed on 26 November 2013).

5 Not all DAC donors have habitually produced education policy papers; Germany, for instance, just launched its first ever education policy in 2011 (BMZ, 2011).

6 Though the 2011 White Paper notes that 'human resource training is an important part of capacity building' (China, 2011, 23), these two terms are used interchangeably with 'training'.

Similarly, in its 2013 White Paper on *China-Africa Economic and Trade Cooperation* (China, 2013, 23), 'human resources development and educational cooperation with Africa' are treated almost as a single concept.

Occasionally, China distinguishes support to education and culture from more general human resources development, but, for instance, in *China's African Policy* (China, 2006, 7), 'Cooperation in Human Resources Development and Education' is discussed under the heading of 'Education, Science, Culture, Health and Social Aspects'. More important than these changing descriptors, however, is the fact that the key elements of this educational capacity building in Africa (and other areas), principally involving tertiary level training, goes back to the 1950s. The foreign aid White Paper puts it nicely: 'Educational aid from China has helped recipient countries train a large number of qualified personnel in the fields of education, management, and science and technology, and rendered intellectual support for their social and economic development' (China, 2011, 14).

The range and diversity of these cooperation activities between China and Africa in the area of higher education and research have grown markedly in the eight years following the Forum on China-Africa Cooperation (FOCAC) summit of November 2006, as new forms of exchange have been established by the triennial FOCAC conferences. We shall not, in the space of this chapter, be able to review more than a selection of these modalities of 'intellectual support', but we shall seek to draw out some of the common features of this engagement. In particular, we shall explore the extent to which the character of China's aid policy in general can be illustrated by its education and training policies and practice.

China claims to present what is essentially an ethical aid policy, based on principles of mutuality, complementarity, political equality and common development. Even though the overall politics of the Maoist era were very different from those of Deng Xiaoping, Zhou Enlai, for example, in the mid-60s, frequently characterised China's solidarity with Africa and Asia in the following terms: '[M]utual economic assistance among the Asian and African countries was the kind of assistance between poor friends who were in the same boat pulling oars together' (China, 2000). This emphasis on reciprocity is reproduced, several decades later, in the closing remarks of the 2010 aid exhibition: 'This is a road of sincere and selfless friendship [...] This is a road of win-win for all on an equal and reciprocal basis. During these 60 years [...] China has stepped up mutual trust with the developing countries, explored complementarities and realised common development' (China, 2014).

Interestingly, the terms 'mutual respect', 'mutual trust', 'mutual understanding' and 'mutual learning', which are so widespread in China's formal discussions of its relations with Africa, are seldom connected to age-old Confucian doctrines of relationship. In a recent work, however, Stephen Chan suggests that not only is this 'horizontal reciprocation' derived from Confucius, but it is also 'natural, desirable, and inescapable' (Chan, 2013, 16). He argues that '[...] when Chinese officials begin their perorations on Africa with sermonesque reiterations of peace and friendship and assistance, they really mean it' (Chan, 2013, 16).

Clearly, if there is such a thing as a 'Chinese brand' of development aid, it is one that revolves around the principles we have just mentioned: friendship, mutual trust, mutual respect, mutual support and benefit, common development, and win-win economic cooperation. It is these elements, presumably, that China would regard as 'overseas aid with its own characteristics' (China, Ministry of Commerce, 2014). Bearing this wider ethics of overseas aid in mind, in this chapter we shall review China's primary modalities for cooperation in education and training, with a particular focus on higher education partnerships.

We shall argue, firstly, that since 2000 China, along with Japan, India and South Korea, has developed[7] a Pan-African mechanism, the Forum on China-Africa Cooperation, to address Africa as a whole. Several interesting issues surround the status and nature of these Pan-African mechanisms on aid or cooperation. Clearly, documents with specific pledges to Africa such as the FOCAC 2009 Declaration (China, 2009), the India-Africa Forum Summit of 2008 (Government of India, 2008), or the Seoul Declaration of the Second Korea-Africa Forum (Ministry of Foreign Affairs, South Korea, 2009) are not owned solely by specific countries in Africa; they are continent-wide. But are they also owned by the African Union, in additional to particular states? In this regard, there may be an interesting contrast between India's reliance, after its India-Africa Forum Summit, upon the African Union in deciding on the precise location of its various 'human resource development' institutional commitments, and China's continued practice of bilateralism in allocating its 'aid' hospitals, schools and training provision.

Secondly, China, along with India, Japan, Germany and South Korea, pays considerable attention to training and/or capacity building in the host country. Arguably, Japan, China, India and Germany run the largest short-term training schemes in the world.[8] South Korea, in turn, has pledged to raise the number of African trainees in South Korea to 5,000 by 2012. It should be noted, however, that most forms of short and long-term training, with the possible exception

7 In the 1960s and 70s, China maintained political and diplomatic relations with a small number of African nations, such as Ghana, Tanzania, Zambia, Ethiopia and Egypt.

8 See NORRAG (2011) for a detailed analysis of both the long- and short-term training aid provided by these and other countries.

of third country training, are tied aid. It is important to underline the fact that, in the view of the donor countries, such training is justified on the grounds of the benefits of exposure to specific, relevant development experience of each state. For instance, both South Korea and Japan make clear that in-country training is vital in order to profit from the unique development experience of the host nation. A similar case is made by China, for example, with respect to its International Poverty Reduction Centre, which seeks to demonstrate the strategies used by China to move millions out of poverty to international policymakers. Equally, China's success in providing nine-year compulsory education even before the 2001 creation of the Millennium Development Goals (MDGs) is frequently referenced (King, 2013b).

Thirdly, many countries, including Japan, China and South Korea, place great store in the role of their own experts, sent overseas as technical assistance. Arguably, their experts and volunteers are an absolutely crucial part of bilateral aid. In this regard, it is significant to note that as of November 2009, South Korea had decided to send as many as 1,000 aid volunteers to Africa alone. China's volunteer numbers are growing slowly, with the exception of language volunteers, but its contingent of doctors, nurses and teachers in Africa remains large (China, 2011, 10).

These are just a few examples of instances where these three major Asian countries, China, Japan and South Korea, have followed rather similar paths.[9] There are, of course, other dimensions of their aid history that stand apart, such as China's involvement with the non-aligned movement. Equally distinct is the very substantial historic migration of Chinese to different parts of Africa for trade and enterprise development.

As we turn now to examine briefly the main modalities used by China in providing higher education cooperation to Africa, we should note that mutual learning is one of the key emphases of the collaboration.[10] Indeed, one of the first themes highlighted out in *China's African Policy* is two-way learning, expressed as follows:

> Learning from each other and seeking common development. China and Africa will learn from and draw upon each other's experience in governance and development, strengthen exchange and cooperation in education, science, culture and health. (China, 2006, 3)

9 For a comparison of the similarities of Chinese and Japanese cooperation approaches, see King (2007).

10 There are of course substantial disagreements regarding the very idea of lesson learning and 'best practice'. These have been reviewed in *NORRAG News*, 2007.

Of course, it is one thing to claim and another to translate into practice. The task at hand thus invokes the age-old challenge of analysing policy-and-practice. Mawdsley (2011), for example, persuasively draws the landscape of South-South cooperation, including China's key role, but notes that there is a lack of empirical study of the claims regarding mutual benefit.

Intriguingly, the final draft of the Busan Outcome Declaration makes some reference to mutual learning, focusing, significantly, on South-South learning:

> Encouraging the development of networks for knowledge exchange, peer learning and co-ordination among South-South co-operation actors as a means of facilitating access to important knowledge pools by developing countries. (OECD/DAC, 2011, para. 30)

In this context, the appearance of the term 'triangular co-operation' in the Declaration is worth noting. This term is frequently bracketed by South-South co-operation in the document, arguably implying that South-South co-operation may be enriched by triangulation with a Northern partner.[11]

We shall now analyse in more detail the modalities used by China in its general human resource cooperation with Africa. We shall cover 1) the human resource dimensions of the FOCAC pledges, paying particular attention to the latest commitments from the November 2009 and July 2012 Ministerial Conferences in Egypt and Beijing; 2) the short- and long-term capacity building of African personnel in China; 3) the role of the Confucius Institutes (also 'CIs') in Africa; 4) stand-alone education or training projects outside the FOCAC framework; 5) and, finally, the 20+20 higher education co-operation between China and Africa. We pay particular attention to the theme of partnership running through a good deal of this interaction between China and Africa in education and training, particularly the 20+20 project. We should note, however, that while some of these items are concerned with the formal education system of either China or various African countries, others are related to training beyond the formal education sector, in agriculture, health, infrastructure, etc.

2 The Latest Human Resource FOCAC Commitments to Africa for 2010–2012

As mentioned above, China has a mechanism, the FOCAC, which seeks to engage with virtually the whole of Africa. Unlike many traditional donors, such

11 We shall note an initiative in trilateral cooperation in our subsequent, brief review of the China-Africa 20+20 cooperation, and its link to UNESCO.

as France and Britain, China does not now, as it once did, cooperate principally with a special sub-set of countries with political, historic, linguistic, geographic or economic ties with the donor country. Also, China has historically sought to avoid giving these FOCAC pledges the appearance of aid or development assistance. Instead, these pledges are presented as elements of a joint agreement between two partners, 'featuring political equality and mutual trust, economic win-win cooperation and cultural exchanges' (China, 2009, para. 1.2). China would also argue, like Japan, that its cooperation is primarily responsive. Both countries have substantial bilateral discussions at the country level, which correspondingly lead to country agreements, but also have continent-wide agreements negotiated through the Tokyo International Conference on African Development (TICAD) and FOCAC. Indeed, it could be claimed that the very clear three-year target orientation of the FOCAC process has influenced the TICAD, spurring it to similarly adopt highly active follow-up measures upon the implementation of pledges. The same may be true of the Korea-Africa Forum, which has met at three-year intervals in 2006, 2009 and again in 2012.

Be that as it may, the FOCAC action plan for Africa is not an accumulation of individual country plans, but rather a freestanding framework that has manifest a fairly stable pattern in its declarations over five FOCAC triennia since its inception in 2000. First of all, FOCAC emphasises political cooperation, then cooperation in international affairs and economic cooperation, followed by 'social development' (China, 2003, para. 5) and, within this 'human resources development and educational cooperation' (China, 2003, para. 5.1). 'Cultural exchange and cooperation' also falls under social development (para. 5.3), and finally there is 'people to people exchange' within the same major section (5.4). The precise allocation of education and training to different categories differs a little in the different triennial FOCAC action plans. It is also worth noting from FOCAC IV in 2009, however, that items such as the training of 2,000 agricultural technicians and the deployment of 50 agricultural technology teams to Africa are categorised as Economic Cooperation (China, 2009, para. 4.14). Equally, the 'China-Africa joint research and exchange plan to strengthen cooperation and exchanges between scholars and think tanks' actually falls under the people to people exchanges and cooperation (China, 2009, para. 6.3.2).[12] The diffuse nature of the development portfolio is probably best understood as the coordination and collection of the many different plans of various sectoral ministries in China by the FOCAC process.

12 The first meeting of the China-Africa Think Tank Forum took place in Hangzhou on 23 November 2011, between China and 27 African countries. See FOCAC website, www.focac.org/eng/xsjl/zflhyjjljh/t880276.htm (accessed on 27 March 2014).

The education-specific pledges build on the format of previous FOCAC commitments,[13] and include an increase in long-term Chinese government scholarships per annum to 5,500 by 2012 and 6,000 by 2015; a pledge to support teacher and head teacher training for 1,500 participants; and a new 20+20 cooperation plan for intensive one-to-one cooperation between 20 Chinese universities or vocational colleges and 20 African counterparts. FOCAC IV, in contrast, pledges to provide Masters in Publication Administration (MPA) training to 200 middle- and high-level administrative personnel in programmes in China. Finally, the 'education' section contains a strong commitment to continue to develop Confucius Institutes, increase scholarships for African Chinese language and cultural teachers, and a redoubling of efforts to raise the capacity of African Chinese studies instructors.[14] Under the category of human resources development, moreover, there is a continued commitment to the massive, short-term training of what the FOCAC calls 'African professionals in various sectors', with numbers reaching 20,000 in the 2012 triennium and 30,000 in the triennium ending in 2015.

One of the biggest additions to the FOCAC pledges in the 2010–12 agenda is the strengthened commitment to science and technology cooperation. This now includes the launch of a China-Africa science and technology partnership plan, China's execution of 100 joint research and demonstration projects, and the invitation of 100 African postdoctoral researchers to conduct scientific research in China. The FOCAC V commits to support the development of Chinese studies centres in African universities, and makes a generous contribution to the United Nations Educational, Scientific and Cultural Organization (UNESCO) for higher education in Africa.

Similarly, in the field of medical cooperation, where, under the 2006–2009 triennium, China built 30 hospitals and 30 malaria treatment centres, they were now, under FOCAC IV, proposing the provision of medical equipment, the training of 3,000 doctors, nurses and administrative personnel, and the

13 Interestingly, the FOCAC first proposal for education and training aid in 2000 did not contain numerical targets, but rather stated the following: 'The Chinese side pledges to: grant more scholarships to African students to study in China, continue to send teachers to Africa to help local institutions of higher learning improve their disciplines and specialties, and set up channels of communications between universities of the two sides for the study of the Chinese and African civilisations; and establish an African Human Resources Development Fund and gradually increase financial contribution to the Fund for the training of professionals of different disciplines for African countries'(China, 2000, para. 15.1).

14 China is particularly eager to increase the numbers of African teachers of Chinese in Confucius Institutes and Confucius Classrooms.

contribution of USD 1.5 million to support the New Partnership for Africa's Development's (NEPAD's) nurse training and maternity projects.

How are we to understand these highly varied pledges with respect to China's aid modalities and approaches, potential differences from the practices of traditional DAC donors, or the leverage these offers might have on recipient countries? First, we can say that in addition to the continuation of its long-term historical support for student exchange and despatch of Chinese teachers, China's current commitments demonstrate much greater diversity than those of the past. Second, there is little doubt that China's educational aid agenda does not mirror the Education for All (EFA) priorities of the World Conference on EFA at Jomtien in 1990 or the World Forum on EFA at Dakar in 2000. Though the 2009 FOCAC notes the urgency of achieving the MDGs, it sees this more as the obligation of developed states in particular to deliver on their earlier pledges. Third, although FOCAC pledges are not bilateral but pan-African, they will very clearly be executed by Chinese universities or vocational colleges, Chinese think tanks, scientists, agricultural technologists or language teachers, and medical personnel. In other words, as mentioned above, Chinese expertise is central to the execution of these elements of the FOCAC agenda, just as elsewhere on the agenda, Chinese firms and entrepreneurs are seen as critical to the delivery of the China-Africa investment commitments.

The question, therefore, arises as to whether FOCAC's priority is basic or post-basic education and training. In terms of numbers, up to 50,000 short-term trainees are anticipated over the two triennia from 2009–2015; 34,500 Chinese governmental scholarships are allocated for the same period; and 4,500 spaces for doctors and nurses, with another 2,000 for agricultural technicians, have been created, not to mention those for postdocs, NEPAD trainees and others. In other words, from 2009–2015, well over 90,000 African personnel are intended to receive training at the post-basic level. These figures would seem to demonstrate that China focuses primarily on post-secondary and vocational training in practical applications of technology.

How precisely these very specific categories are decided at both the FOCAC and bilateral level when there are 50 African partner countries, and one non-African partner, China, involved, is not well-known, or much researched,[15] but, as stated above, it is complicated by the fact that the FOCAC agenda also includes the priorities of the multiple Chinese ministries of Commerce, Foreign Affairs, Culture, Education, Science and Technology, Agriculture, Health and several others. As mentioned earlier, these are not yet coordinated by a single development agency in China.

15 See available information in King (2009b) and Taylor (2011).

In light of this, the ability to set priorities and translate them into a single document adopted in consensus with African countries for FOCAC is a substantial diplomatic achievement. The allocative challenge of distributing all these varied offers across an enormous variety of African contexts, however, must be huge, and involve staff in many Chinese and African ministries, host universities in China, as well as both the political and economic and commercial branches of China's African embassies. Some sense of the sheer scale of the activities associated with the FOCAC process can be gathered from a brief look at the FOCAC summary document on 'Implementation of the Follow-up Actions of the Beijing Summit of the Forum on China-Africa Cooperation' presented at the end of the three-year period from 2007–2009 (FOCAC, 2009a).

Again, in terms of comparing this goal-setting with that of traditional donors, it does appear that these 'human resource development' and other targets are taken very seriously by China. While aware of the dangers of the 'targetisation' of development—or what Jansen (2005) has called the 'politics of performance'—in which the very target numbers actually become a substitute for policy, many traditional donors would do well to consider China's determination to deliver on its target pledges, and compare that with the failure of several major countries to deliver on their 2005 Group of Eight (G8) commitments.[16] At the same time, however, it is arguable that China itself is somehow caught in these target numbers, as there is clearly pressure to ensure that each set of FOCAC human resource development targets goes beyond those of the previous triennium.

It should be remembered also that unlike many of the more established agencies, such as DFID and the United States Agency for International Development (USAID), which have professional cadres associated with gender, environment, health, education, social development and governance, China has not developed these groups of aid professionals. Indeed, across the whole of Africa, China only has two Education Counsellors and two Science and Technology Counsellors, and their responsibilities have been limited to just two countries, South Africa and Egypt. In this area, Japan, again, has been more like China, relying on generalists and a very small number of professionals until an attempt, in the early 2000s, to develop more professional communities of practice within JICA.[17]

16 For instance, most G8 countries have not met the 2005 G8 Gleneagles target of doubling aid to Africa. See also the threats of reduced education aid financing in EFA/GMR (2011). The UK's DFID, in contrast, has successfully held to its overall aid target of reaching 0.7 per cent of its gross domestic product (GDP) by 2013.

17 See King and McGrath (2004) for an account of this process in JICA.

3 Short- and Long-Term Capacity Building of Africans in China

We have already mentioned the rise in target numbers for short-term trainees to 30,000 and long-term students to 18,000 over the 2012–2015 triennium. We have also noted that two DAC donors, Japan and Germany, pay serious attention to short-term training, while others such as the United Kingdom (UK) have cut back on this overseas training element. China, like Japan, Germany and, also, India, continues to believe that the direct exposure of students and trainees to their own development experience is vital. Moreover, serious students from Africa find it easier, in terms of visas etc., to access universities in China and India than those in many European countries, most notably the UK. The apparent ease and speed with which China still appears to be able to organise access for this diverse range of short and long-term training is noteworthy.[18]

4 Locating and Categorising the Unique and Dramatic Case of the Confucius Institutes[19]

The rise of the Confucius Institutes over the last nine years is commonly understood as something akin to the British Council, Goethe Institute or Alliance Française—another form of cultural diplomacy.[20] There are, however, very significant differences between these institutions and the Confucius Institutes, not least among which is China's insistence the spread of Confucius Institutes should be demand-driven, and not the object of a particular FOCAC numerical target. This is expressed as 'the principle of the foreign party taking precedence whilst the Chinese party plays the role of providing assistance'.[21] In other words, unlike other training modalities, China does not have a target for Confucius Institutes expansion in Africa.

18 Much more detail on these two very large modalities of training in China is available in King (2013a).

19 None of the other obvious BRICS (Brazil, Russia, India, China, South Africa) nations, such as India, Brazil or Russia, have expended such efforts in promoting their major national language.

20 There are also an even large number of Confucius Classrooms that operate principally at the school level.

21 See the Hanban/Confucius Institute Headquarters website, http://english.hanban.org/ (accessed on 3 March 2014).

As a result of this policy, there are some 100 Confucius Institutes in the United States of America (USA) and just 33 in all of Africa. The global diffusion of Confucius Institutes does appear, in a small way, to parallel the British Council and other cultural bodies, which are often associated as much with their countries' foreign offices as they are with development aid. What distinguishes the Confucius Institutes as a mechanism and an approach, however, is that they are not located on the main streets of the world's national and regional capitals, but rather in the heart of their major universities. Thus, they are found in the University of Nairobi, Rhodes University, the University of Cairo and a further thirty African sites. As their principal focus is the promotion of Mandarin and Chinese culture, it is unsurprising that their parent body, *Hanban*, the Chinese Language Council and Confucius Institute Headquarters, is a public body affiliated with the Ministry of Education.

There are several varieties of scholarships linked to Chinese language instruction from *Hanban*; these can be both long- and short-term, and, since 2010, the organisation has run a three-week summer 'camp' which brings groups of Chinese language learners from different universities and secondary schools to spend time in China. The sheer range of opportunities to study in China, from Confucius Institute scholarships to short-term language exposure, is considerable.

A further distinguishing modality of the Confucius Institutes and Confucius Classrooms is that while all of these institutions are located outside the Chinese Mainland, each of them is formally linked to a university or secondary school in China. The Chinese institutions thus comprise the source of the Chinese co-directors of the various Confucius Institutes as well as regular and volunteer Chinese teachers sent to partner universities in Africa. The Chinese partner may host the different scholarship and language visitors to China from Africa. This crucial school and university partnership arrangement provides an attractive and versatile aid modality in a world that is increasingly keen to develop sustainable links with Chinese educational institutions.

As to locating the Confucius Institute as a particular aid modality, there are clearly problems with identifying it as a form of official development assistance, as more than 50 per cent of the support from China is going to Confucius Institutes and Confucius Classrooms in so-called developed countries. Yet almost all Confucius Institutes currently receive a generous annual subsidy from China for their work, in addition to receiving language teachers and volunteers. Furthermore, it is clear that there is scope for the Confucius Institutes to become a mechanism for broadening inter-university cooperation beyond language to include Centres of Chinese studies, as encouraged by FOCAC V in 2012.

This raises the further question as to the character of the partnership associated with the Confucius Institute. There are broadly two modalities: in cases where the Confucius Institute arrives at a university, such as Rhodes or Nairobi, with no previous instruction in Chinese language or culture, the Confucius Institute is responsible for introducing the study of Chinese at the degree level into the university system. On the other hand, when the Confucius Institute is invited to a university that already grants degrees in Chinese language and culture, though the Confucius Institute may supplement that instruction, it principally offers a range of non-credit activities for both regular and extramural students. It may also be responsible for organising seminars and special lectures relating to China.

Clearly, the Confucius Institute initiative may be classified as a form of soft power, or cultural diplomacy, but those terms do not do justice to the demand side of the Confucius Institute equation. The Confucius Institutes are not so much creating the demand for Chinese language learning as they are responding to a widespread vocational interest, evident in many countries, in acquiring Chinese linguistic and cultural expertise. This demand is of course inseparable from the very visible presence of Chinese enterprise, industry and commerce in so many different countries, especially in Africa, and their appreciation of workers with Chinese language skills.

Over the last nine years, this huge language initiative has continued to be basically demand-driven and responsive. Firstly, host institutions have taken the initiative in terms of starting up Confucius Institutes and Confucius Classrooms. Secondly, there is considerable evidence of *Hanban*'s openness to local institutional proposals generated by the Confucius Institutes. Different programmes and projects have been associated with different Confucius Institutes, including those in Africa. There is no evidence of a single, common curriculum and/or agenda for the Confucius Institutes and Confucius Classrooms being promoted by Beijing. Instead, there appear to be some several hundred flowers blooming in different contexts and economic environments.

5 China's Stand-Alone Education and Training Projects in Africa

Thus far, we have briefly examined two large-scale frameworks within African countries that are supported by China. The FOCAC framework operates as a pan-African modality for relating to the continent, encompassing a series of human resource development, cultural, education and training commitments offered to, and negotiated with, the whole of Africa (with the exception of the three countries maintaining diplomatic relations with Taiwan). Depending upon their economic status, and the visibility and impact of China's wider presence in their state, countries may differ in the extent to which they are able to profit from these FOCAC offers.

In contrast, the Confucius Institute framework, though mentioned in the later FOCAC agreements, extends far beyond Africa; the continent hosts only a 12th of global Confucius Institutes and a handful of Confucius Classrooms.

Independent of these frameworks, China has continued to give considerable attention to its bilateral commitments to African countries, as evidenced by the long-standing tradition of very senior politicians visiting Africa annually for more than 20 years. Often, these visits end in both sides signing off on a series of bilateral agreements. Of course, these non-FOCAC bilateral commitments cover a wide range of areas, including education and training, but they tend to be driven by the priorities of the African partners as much as by China's. The official rhetoric frames these interactions as win-win agreements amongst partners rather than donor-recipient agreements.

It should, therefore, not be surprising that African partner governments have tended to prioritise development projects that have proved difficult to secure from traditional sources, such as infrastructure, with a particular emphasis on roads, dams, power projects, stadia, etc. In contrast, many OECD donors are more prepared to support projects central to the delivery of the MDGs, including basic education and health care. This is not to say that human resource development projects, including formal education, have not figured in China's cooperation agenda with Africa. But unlike DFID's commitments to several African countries, for instance, China is certainly not allocating millions of renminbi (RMB) a year to basic education in sector budget support. Rather, it is responding to countries that have made specific higher education initiatives a priority. Hence, China has been responsible for building, equipping and staffing the large Ethio-China Polytechnic College in Addis Ababa. Similarly, in Malawi, China recently constructed a new Science University. In a further project supporting NEPAD's education and training programme, China has agreed to fund the development of a clinical master's degree in nursing in five African countries. Liberia also hosts several completed university projects, and several others are planned for the Democratic Republic of the Congo.

For many African countries, their priorities for bilateral projects with China lie outside formal education. Other donors, such as the UK and Japan, have very much larger formal education support programmes than does China. It is perhaps for this reason that China does not significantly participate in the various country-level arrangements for education aid donors to meet and coordinate their activities. This is also attributable, however, to the fact that China remains very hesitant about being seen as an aid donor as opposed to a partner in South-South cooperation.

6 The 20+20 Higher Education Collaboration between China and Africa

China claims partnership is at the heart of its higher education cooperation with Africa. It is perhaps most obvious in the Confucius Institute partnerships, but several of other modalities also rely upon a Chinese partner to deliver staffing, local or overseas training, and/or administration. University partnerships between China and Africa go back to at least the 1980s and 1990s. Several of these long-standing examples of twinning have been reinforced by the addition of a Confucius Institute on the African side of the partnership. On the Chinese side, many domestic universities now have multiple Confucius Institute staffing obligations, not just to Africa, but also to the USA, Europe and other regions. The Confucius Institute framework has thus acted as an agent in the multi-dimensional internationalisation of Chinese universities. That said, it is by no means the only mechanism, as a series of competitive schemes in China exist to support the further internationalisation of its own higher education.

One such initiative with substantial connections to Africa is the 20+20 scheme linking twenty universities or colleges in Africa with counterparts in China, announced at the November 2009 FOCAC IV ministerial conference. Universities in China competed to recruit appropriate African partners and to be selected by the Chinese Ministry of Education. One of the key selection criteria was evidence that the Chinese partner has considerable experience of working in and with Africa.

Although it might be thought that Chinese universities would prefer to partner and work with high-ranking European and North American universities—and many such collaborations do exist—the final twenty Chinese universities selected for the 20+20 project included several eminent institutions, such as Peking University, Jilin, East China Normal, Shanghai Normal, Hunan, and Beijing Language and Culture Universities.[22] On the African side, most of the selected higher education institutions (HEIs) were in the top 100 African HEIs;

22 In terms of China's different schemes for encouraging the development of world-class universities, no less than five of the twenty selected Chinese universities were in the prestigious 985 scheme, ten were in the similarly prestigious 211 scheme, and ten in China's top 100 universities.

these included some of the continent's most prestigious universities, such as Pretoria, Stellenbosch, Makerere, Lagos, Dar es Salaam, Nairobi and Cairo.

Certainly, as just mentioned, the 20+20 scheme is an attractive opportunity for the internationalisation of Chinese universities. The same attraction, however, likely also exists for many of the African HEIs, as they have diversified their academic links beyond their historical European partners.[23] The funding for 20+20 is provided by China's Ministry of Education and remains with the Chinese partner, in contrast to the Confucius Institute framework, wherein Chinese funding is actually transferred to the African or other overseas partner. As with the Confucius Institutes, there is the expectation that the host university, be it African or Chinese, would support the accommodation and expenses of delegations, staff or students coming from the other university. Better-off African universities are intended to support the costs of their own staff travelling to China, but, otherwise, travel for African university staff or students are dependent on the Chinese partner.

What are some of the research issues around this particular example of China-Africa higher education partnership? In the all-important area of symmetry in South-South cooperation, there is evidence that some Chinese professors perceive their 20+20 partnership as a form of capacity building for their African partners. In this sense, the 20+20 is seen as 'an aid project'. Equally, however, many—perhaps most—Chinese staff see the relationship as potentially symmetrical, even if most of the funding comes from the Chinese side. It is in this spirit that a senior Chinese international office staff member stated:

> There is learning on both sides; we have learnt on the research side. So we see it as equal. There is an old saying: '*Qu Chang Bu Duan*—To enhance each other we learn from each other'. We have weaknesses and advantages and vice versa for our partners in Africa. We compensate for and take advantage of each other. (Chinese University, International Office, interview by the author, 31 May 2013)

The partnership thus seems to be at least as much about widening the horizons of Chinese professors as the other way round.

The other important dimension of China's higher education partnerships is that they are seen as long-term. Several of the university partnerships initiated

23 Other organisations and institutions, beyond the two immediate partners of China and Africa, have expressed interest in the 20+20 scheme. UNESCO has organised, with funding from China, two meetings which have sought to develop a trilateral cooperation initiative from this originally bilateral project. See, for example: 'UNESCO-China-Africa Tripartite Initiative for University Cooperation', 24–25 October 2013, UNESCO, Paris.

by China in the 1990s are still running and being supported by Chinese staff, many of whom have been in Africa for twenty years. There is therefore a strong understanding amongst Chinese staff both in the Confucius Institutes and 20+20 partnerships that they are engaged in a long-term commitment to their partner university in Africa. Given this time scale, it would be difficult to exaggerate the importance of attitudes towards Africa held by individual Chinese professors. For instance:

> I would say that Africa has a good feeling about China. Africa is not as advanced as China, but a beautiful continent and friendly people. No disease except malaria. I tell my staff that Africa is the place to go to in your lives.
>
> There are challenges of course. But the Chinese are ready to offer something. And in China we don't have so many politicians running around. We have a long and positive relationship with Africa. We don't have the baggage of colonialism. We did a lot in Africa for infrastructure. People appreciate our help. We never saw ourselves as world leaders. We have a low-key approach and are modest. We make progress. Great. And we learn from our mistakes. (Interview, senior Chinese professor, 5 June 2013)

Equally, if not more important, are the attitudes of the African partners involved in the many academic and research collaborations with China. It is likely many share the position of this senior academic in Kenya:

> China's success will be determined by its ability to persuade Kenya and other African countries that it is not going to be an exploiter, but a dependable development partner operating under mutual respect. (Amutabi, 2013, 26)

Many more accounts are available from the diverse characters involved in these partnerships, from the Chinese Mainland and African universities, as well as from both 20+20 universities and the CIs. The discourse around partnership is of course hugely varied, but academics and administrations on both sides frequently use terms such as 'mutual benefit' and 'mutual respect'.[24] Both Chinese and African students are exposed to very different environments through these schemes, and something of the resulting changes in

24 For more detail, see King and King (2014).

their assumptions and perceptions has already been captured in King (2013a, chapter 3, passim).[25]

7 Conclusion

Having briefly examined some of the modalities of China's higher education cooperation, the issue of whether these mechanisms actually illustrate the explicitly ethical discourse of mutuality, friendship, common development and 'a road of overseas aid with its own characteristics' remains to be discussed.[26] Can the ordinary world of university partnerships, language teaching and government scholarships to study in China really demonstrate 'a road of sincere and selfless friendship'? Can such educational aid point to a 'road of win-win for all on an equal and reciprocal basis'?

Determining the extent to which a particular aid discourse or rhetoric translates into specific aid practices is hugely demanding. Mawdsley's review of the aid discourses of non-DAC donors touches on this key issue of performance on the ground, claiming for instance, that at the micro-level 'China's development assistance is conducted in ways that are often strikingly different from much Western aid work' (Mawdsley, 2012, 157). Intriguingly, the observation that 'the modesty of the Chinese as a donor government was truly exemplary' is actually taken from a novel—*Gifts*, by Nuruddin Farah—(Mawdsley, *op. cit.*), but reflects the sentiment of many other comments regarding the relative modesty or humility of both Chinese and Japanese 'aid' workers or 'experts' in the field (King, 2013a, xi).[27]

It is difficult to draw firm conclusions from this brief discussion of some of the current modalities of Chinese aid to human resources development in Africa. We have, however, outlined both some preliminary insights and some continuing research challenges. For instance, amongst both Chinese academics and the Chinese policy community, there is a genuine hesitation to 'beat

25 For more information on the Confucius Institute as offering an insight into 'the real China' without the media overlay, see the Chinese co-director of a Confucius Institute (King, 2013a, 178).

26 '60 Years of China's Overseas Aid' website, http://yuanwaizhan.mofcom.gov.cn/images/zhuantiting_en.shtml (accessed on 3 March 2014).

27 Additional data, particularly on the African side of the 20+20 partnerships, will shortly be available through the research project on China-Africa university partnerships in education and training, supported by the Hong Kong Research Grants Council and based in the Chinese University of Hong Kong (CUHK). The project is led by Li Jun of CUHK in partnership with Kenneth King (Edinburgh) and Bjorn Nordtveit (Amherst).

the drum' and boast about what can be learnt from China. Hence, on the one hand, there is pride in the achievements of the China-Africa cooperation, and a readiness to show tens of thousands of African and Asian professionals, through the short-term training programme, just a little of China's own (successful) experience as a developing country.[28] On the other hand, there is very little 'preaching', or specific articulation of development 'lessons' for Africa. Part of the culture of non-interference is the belief that countries should make up their own minds about what can be learnt from elsewhere; they do not need to be told. In the discourse of policy analysis, this would be described as the crucial importance of policy learning by the country concerned, as opposed to top-down policy transfer from China.

In the human resource development domain, however, one of the principal difficulties in performing policy learning is that the Chinese do not openly discuss options for the allocation and use of educational aid. An accessible account of the trade-offs of investing in basic education versus secondary or higher, as has been produced in the West for decades, does not exist. As we said at the outset, China does not articulate an aid policy for the education sector of the kind that has been widespread in the West for 50 years. The importance of this point cannot be understated. As education cooperation is seen as just one among several vectors contributing to development, it is not perceived as a stand-alone sector. Correspondingly, though we have sought to comment on whether the human resource development elements of the FOCAC agreements are, on balance, tilted more towards higher education than basic, this is ultimately a somewhat artificial exercise. The FOCAC agreements should probably not be broken down into the conventional sectors or sub-sectors associated with DAC donors, any more than should *China's African Policy* of 2006 (China, 2006) be mined for its mere two-paragraph comment on cooperation in human resources development and education. Ultimately, the many elements of China's education and aid cooperation with Africa are inseparable from its political, economic and trade engagements on the continent. Discussions of the kind found in the aid and financing chapter of the EFA Global Monitoring Reports, which deal primarily with allocation *within* the education sector, are a world away from China's view of human resource development as a completely integral element of development policy and politics, whether in Africa or the West of China.

---

28 See, for example, Liu Hongwu, the director of China's largest Institute of African Studies: 'Today's China-Africa cultural exchange and cooperation, in particular, has become a shining scene shedding a spotlight on the changing global scene' (Liu, 2009, 17).

Consequently, it should not be surprising that China, though it was present and active at the 4th High Level Forum on Aid Effectiveness in Busan, South Korea, does not spend much time considering whether its educational aid could be better harmonised with, and more complementary to, that of other education donors. Indeed, China, along with India and Brazil, decided not to be part of the Busan notion of a Global Partnership for Effective Development Cooperation. This is doubtless in part a reflection of their hesitations about appearing to be part of the donor 'club'.

It may still be useful to sort out, as we have tried to do, what, if anything, constitutes the specificity of human resource development in China's engagement with Africa. This brings us back to the issue of the ethical discourse regarding development aid with which we started this paper. The claims about mutuality, reciprocity, trust, respect and common development are far from constituting aid modalities or mechanisms. They cannot be evaluated like the other FOCAC targets. These ethical assertions do, however, set the context in which the FOCAC targets are deliberately placed. China seeks to avoid positioning the FOCAC engagements to appear as aid or development assistance. Instead, they are presented, as mentioned above, as elements of a joint agreement between two partners, 'featuring political equality and mutual trust, economic win-win cooperation and cultural exchanges' (China, 2009, para. 1.2).

The final challenge, therefore, is to interrogate the particularity of the politics of higher education partnerships in practice, on the ground, whether between China and South Africa, China and Kenya, or China and Ethiopia (see NORRAG, 2008). We have highlighted some distinct aspects of the discourse surrounding this cooperation, as well as some of the distinctive modalities of China-Africa higher education partnerships. We have commented on the characteristics of China's engagement with African universities through Confucius Institutes and the 20+20 initiative. These comments, however, by their nature, are principally suggestive and preliminary. We look forward to a much richer vein of analysis on China's aid-in-practice once the full detail of both the Chinese and African sides of the 20+20 project becomes available over the course of 2014.

References

Amutabi, M.N. (2013) 'Home Truths', *ChinAfrica* (Beijing), vol. 5, October, p. 26.

BMZ (Federal Ministry for Economic Cooperation and Development) (2012) *Ten Objectives for More Education—BMZ Education Strategy 2010–2013* (Bonn: Federal Ministry for Economic Cooperation and Development).

CCS (Centre for Chinese Studies) (2010) *Evaluating China's FOCAC Commitments to Africa, and Capping the Way Ahead*, Centre for Chinese Studies (Stellenbosch: University of Stellenbosch).

Chan, S. (2013) *The Morality of China in Africa: The Moral Kingdom and the Dark Continent* (London: Zed Books).

China, Ministry of Commerce (2014) *60 Years of China's Overseas Aid*, http://yuanwaizhan.mofcom.gov.cn/index_en.shtml (accessed on 3 March 2014).

China, Ministry of Foreign Affairs (2009) *Forum on China-Africa Cooperation Sharm El Sheikh Action Plan (2010–2012)*, 8–9 November, Sharm El Sheikh, www.focac.org/eng/ltda/dsjbzjhy/hywj/t626387.htm (accessed on 7 April 2014).

——— (2003) *Forum on China-Africa Cooperation-Addis Ababa Action Plan (2004–2006)*, 15–16 December, Addis Ababa. www.focac.org/eng/ltda/dsjbzjhy/hywj/t626387.htm (accessed on 7 April 2014).

——— (2000) 'Premier Zhou Enlai's Three Tours of Asian and African Countries' (Beijing: Ministry of Foreign Affairs), http://www.fmprc.gov.cn/eng/ziliao/3602/3604/t18001.htm (accessed on 3 March 2014).

China, People's Republic of (2013) *China-Africa Economic and Trade Cooperation* (Beijing: State Council).

——— (2011) *China's Foreign Aid* (Beijing: State Council).

——— (2006) *China's African Policy*, 12 January (Beijing: State Council), http://gov.cn/misc/2006–01/12/content_156490.htm (accessed on 3 March 2014).

DFID (Department for International Development) (2013) *Education Position Paper: Improving Learning, Expanding Opportunities* (London: DFID), https://www.gov.uk/government/uploads/system/uploads/attachment_data/file/225715/Education_Position_Paper_July_2013.pdf (accessed on 15 April 2014).

EFA GMR (Education for All Global Monitoring Report) (2011) *Trends in Aid to Education, 2002–2009: Despite Increases, Aid is Still Vastly Insufficient and Fragile*, Policy Paper, 1 November (Paris: UNESCO), http://www.unesco.org/new/fileadmin/MULTIMEDIA/HQ/ED/pdf/gmr2011-pp01-trends-in-aid-to-education.pdf (accessed on 15 April 2014).

FOCAC (Forum on China-Africa Cooperation) (2009) *Implementation of the Follow-up Actions of the Beijing Summit of the Forum on China-Africa Cooperation, FOCAC*, 10 November, http://www.focac.org/eng/dsjbzjhy/hywj/t627504 (accessed on 15 June 2010).

FOCAC (2000) *Programme for China-Africa Cooperation in Economic and Social Development*, 10–12 October, http://www.focac.org/eng/ltda/dyjbzjhy/DOC 12009/t606797.htm (accessed on 3 March 2014).

GOI (Government of India) (2008) *India Africa Forum Summit* (New Delhi: Ministry of External Affairs).

Jansen, J. (2005) 'Targeting Education: The Politics of Performance and the Prospects of Education for All', *International Journal of Educational Development*, 25, pp. 368–380.

JICA (Japan International Cooperation Agency) (2013) 'Africa: A Brighter Future', *JICA's World*, vol. 20, no. 2, May, http://www.jica.go.jp/english/publications/j-world/1305_vol20.html (accessed on 3 March 2014).

——— (2010) *JICA Basic Education Cooperation in Africa: The Joy of Learning for All Children* (Tokyo: JICA).

King, K. and S. McGrath (2004) *Knowledge for Development? Analysing British, Japanese, Swedish and World Bank Aid* (London: Zed Books).

King, K. (2013a) *China's Aid and Soft Power in Africa: The Case of Education and Training* (Woodbridge: James Currey).

——— (2013b) *China's Engagement with the Post-2015 Development Agenda: The Case of Education And Training*, UKFIET International Conference on Education and Development, 10–12 September, http://www.ukfiet.org/cop/2013-conference-papers/ (accessed on 3 March 2014).

——— (2011a) 'China's Cooperation with Ethiopia—With a Focus on Human Resources', *OSSREA Bulletin*, vol. 8, no. 1, pp. 88–113, http://www.ossrea.net/images/stories/ossrea/bulletin-feb-2011.pdf (accessed on 3 March 2014).

——— (2011b) *China's Human Resource Engagement with Africa: A New Voice, New Values, and a New Partnership?*, General Conference of European Association of Development Research and Training Institutes (EADI) and Development Studies Association of the UK, 19–22 September, University of York.

——— (2010) 'China's Cooperation in Education and Training with Kenya: A Different Model?', *International Journal of Educational Development*, 30(5), pp. 488–496.

——— (2009a) 'China's Cooperation with Ethiopia. A New Approach to Development with a Focus on Human Resources?' *OSSREA Bulletin*, vol. 6, no. 2, June 2009, pp. 45–51, http://ossrea.net/images/fbfiles/files/publications/bulletin_june_2009.pdf (accessed on 15 April 2014).

——— (2009b) *China's Cooperation with Africa: Meeting the FOCAC Targets*, Africa Day Workshop, African Studies Programme, 25 May 2009, University of Hong Kong.

——— (2007) *China's Aid to Africa: A View from China and Japan*, IFIC-JICA Seminar on China's Aid to Africa, 29 January (Tokyo: JICA).

King, K. and P. King (2014) *China's Higher Education Partnerships with Africa: The Rhetoric and the Reality in the Case of the 20+20 Universities*, Presentation at Comparative International Education Society (CIES) Conference, 10–15 March, Toronto.

KOICA (Korean International Cooperation Agency) (2011) *20 years of KOICA, 1991–2010* (Seoul: KOICA).

Liu, H. (2009) 'African Studies and "New Frontiers" of China's Academic Domain' in Liu, H. and J. Yang (eds.) *Fifty Years of Sino-African Cooperation: Background, Progress, and Significance. Chinese Perspectives on Sino-African Relations* (Yunnan: University Press).

Mawdsley, E. (2012) *From Recipients to Donors: Emerging Powers and the Changing Development Landscape* (London: Zed Books).

——— (2011) 'The Changing Geographies of Foreign Aid and Development Cooperation: Contributions from Gift Theory', *Transactions of the Institute of British Geographers, NS 2011* (London: The Royal Geographical Society).

Ministry of Foreign Affairs, South Korea (2009) *Seoul Declaration of the Second Korea-Africa Forum*, 24 November (Seoul: MOFA).

Mutambo, A. (2013) 'Cultural Fusion', *ChinAfrica* (Beijing), 5, no. 16.

Nordtveit, B.H. (2010) 'An Emerging Donor in Education and Development: A Case Study of China in Cameroon', *International Journal of Educational Development*, 31(2), pp. 99–108.

NORRAG News (2011) *The Geopolitics of Overseas Scholarships and Awards*, vol. 45, April, http://www.norrag.org/fileadmin/Full%20Versions/NN45.pdf (accessed on 3 March 2014).

——— (2008) *The Politics of Partnership: Peril or Promise?*, vol. 41, December, http://www.norrag.org/en/publications/norrag-news/online-version/the-new-politics-of-partnership-peril-or-promise.html (accessed on 3 March 2014).

——— (2007) *Best Practice in Education and Training: Hype or Hope?*, vol. 39, October, http://www.norrag.org/fileadmin/Full%20Versions/NN39.pdf (accessed on 3 March 2014).

OECD/DAC (Organisation for Economic Co-operation and Development / Development Assistance Committee) (2011) *Sixth Draft Outcome Document for the Fourth High-Level Forum on Aid Effectiveness*, Busan, 28 November, Working Party on Aid Effectiveness, DAC (Paris: OECD).

Taylor, I. (2011) *The Forum on China-Africa Cooperation (FOCAC)* (Abingdon: Routledge).

UNESCO (United Nations Educational, Scientific and Cultural Organization) (2010) *Education for All Global Monitoring Report: Reaching the Marginalized* (Oxford: UNESCO, OUP), http://www.unesco.org/new/en/education/themes/leading-the-international-agenda/efareport/reports/2010-marginalization/ (accessed on 14 April 2014).

CHAPTER 9

Western African Student Migration: A Response to the Globalisation of Knowledge

Denise Efionayi and Etienne Piguet

Abstract

While European countries have devoted considerable resources to efforts to block the flow of irregular migration, they have at the same time been vying with one another to attract the best minds and solve the problem of demographic ageing. How do African students navigate through such contradictory policies? This chapter discusses the plans for international migration as expressed by university students from three West African countries (Senegal, Côte d'Ivoire, and Niger). Based in particular on a questionnaire distributed to around 4,000 students, the study identifies a series of factors contributing to students' intention to migrate: family networks abroad, level of educational attainment, lack of confidence in their country's future, supportive attitude of family members, etc. Contrary to the widespread assumptions expressed in the media and in policy debates in industrialised countries, 'migration intentions' appear to be carefully pondered and proactive in nature, rather than impulsive headlong rushes. Students are relatively well informed, and their intentions to undertake what is mostly temporary migration are based on a weighing of their interests in terms of education and professional experience. This article therefore calls for improved coordination of mobility and development policies to unlock the potential of migration while satisfying the thirst for knowledge identified in the three countries concerned.

1 Introduction

Images of shipwrecked migrants off the small Italian island of Lampedusa were broadcast all over the world in October 2013. Apart from their direct emotional impact, these images also reinforced the prevailing narrative maintained by the media and politicians: that of an African continent mired in poverty, instability, and armed conflict. This narrative, reflected in the comments of observers who were both fascinated and horrified by the unfolding drama,

 | DOI 10.1163/9789004281158_010

has become deeply ingrained in the minds of Europeans. From the perspective of those living north of the Mediterranean, these migrants must be utterly desperate to embark on such a perilous journey, which only a few daring reporters are willing to share.

While more and more resources are being directed towards curbing apparently poverty-driven migration, European countries are vying with one another for the best brains to tackle the problems of an ageing population and the future needs of a globalised labour market. This strategy includes, or even hinges upon, attracting the world's best researchers to the European Higher Education Area. However, it largely disregards Africa, despite close geographic and economic ties, and the continent's young population, markedly increasing school attendance rates, and similar education systems, which are largely modelled on those of former colonial powers. The European Union's mobility partnerships—or 'migration partnerships' as they are referred to in Switzerland—are more concerned with matters of return and cooperation in the countries of the South than they are with developing educational or employment prospects for young people from 'partner countries'. When decision-makers mention shortages of qualified workers in IT, engineering, or even health care, their gaze usually turns to Asia or North America as potential sources of skilled workers.

Grants and other programmes facilitating mobility in globalised higher education are mostly directed at the major emerging economies, which present significant economic growth prospects. African student mobility, in contrast, is mostly associated with poverty-driven migration. Student migration to former colonial countries, and later to North America, has nevertheless been commonplace ever since African nations gained their independence. Many of the parents and teachers of today's African students were educated in Britain, France, Germany, or Switzerland. The available data from some African countries show that university students are more likely to emigrate on a temporary basis than their less well-educated compatriots. Even prior to the introduction of the Bologna process in Europe, and subsequently in Africa, international mobility ratios[1] for African students were among the highest in the world. And yet, this group remains one of the least studied categories of migrants (Piguet, 2013b).

Given the above, it would be interesting to know how young university students from sub-Saharan Africa feel about mobility issues and how they view their futures in terms of education and employment. These questions are at the

1 International mobility ratio: the number of students enrolled abroad compared with those studying at higher education institutions in their own countries.

heart of a study conducted among several thousand students in West Africa on behalf of the Swiss Network for International Studies (SNIS). The main aim of the study was to understand how the migration option—whether temporary or long-term—forms part of the life plan of individuals and families and how those wishing to emigrate differ from those who do not intend to leave their own countries. In order to achieve this objective, the following research questions were addressed:

- Which socio-demographic, economic, biographical, and geographical factors play a role in students' aspirations to migrate? What factors discourage mobility?
- What is the geographical distribution of the destinations considered? What reasoning can be derived from this geographical distribution?
- More generally, what lessons may be retained for development, education, and migration policies in both the South and the North?

The question of why people choose to migrate and how they migrate has been of concern to social scientists for over a century. The determinant factors include geography, psychology, economics, sociology, anthropology, and demographics. As Babacar Ndione explains (2007, 326),

> It is now acknowledged that a prospective migrant's willingness and ability to migrate abroad depend on their personality and socioeconomic trajectory, their domestic and community environment, the flows of information to which they are exposed, migration networks and the political and economic context of the receiving country.

In the present study, we focus on the initial stages of migration, namely the forming of an intention to migrate and the initial steps that follow. Our hypotheses are based on a pluralist model that aggregates migration flows at the macro level and considers decision-making theories centred on the immediate surroundings and motivations of individuals (Piguet, 2013a).

Our system of hypotheses was partly inspired by the work of Gordon De Jong (2000), who analysed the determinant factors of decisions for or against migration, as well as the factors allowing migration to take place. De Jong highlighted five significant factors that came out of the literature: (1) transnational networks, (2) values and concrete expectations of migration, (3) family norms, (4) gender roles, and (5) satisfaction with living conditions. Also taken into account were direct opportunities and constraints, which are viewed as facilitating or discouraging factors rather than catalysts per se: financial means, prior experience of migration, professional contacts, etc. In order to complete and adapt this list to the specific situation of students, we have identified the following groups of determinant factors, which combine three analytical dimensions relating to students' individual situations, social dynamics (e.g. the role of families), and the political and sociocultural contexts of the countries concerned:[2]

1. Educational context (discipline studied, level of attainment, satisfaction, etc.).
2. Social, demographic, and psychological factors (gender, age, childhood home).
3. Family context (civil status, siblings, family background).
4. Transnational networks and connections (friends and family abroad, experience of migration).
5. Social and cultural context (country, religion, ethnic group).
6. Political context (perception of institutions, gender equality).
7. Economic and material factors (resources, confidence in economic prospects).
8. Quality of life (housing, environment, health-care system).

It goes without saying that these dimensions must be considered as interacting with one another, rather than being mutually exclusive.

This study is mainly interested in students' intentions, aspirations, and motivations in their decisions on whether to stay or go. It also takes into account the preliminary steps taken towards the implementation of migration plans, such as information gathering. It has not sought to establish, however, whether the person actually migrated at a later time. Here, the intention to migrate is considered separately from the act of doing so, which depends on specific opportunities to put plans into action and, especially in the case of young students, on the family's decision to support an individual's plans. However, several research studies show, as far as migration is concerned, that people's intentions and actions are frequently linked and respond to similar explanatory factors (Lu, 1999; Dalen et al., 2005).

2 The latter aspect has been investigated in national studies, although space constraints have made it impossible to discuss it in this article. Cf. *Leave or stay? Migration in the life plans of students in West Africa (2011): Report on Côte d'Ivoire* by Raffaele Poli and Désiré Nassa; *Report on Niger* by Patrick Gilliard and Amadou Oumarou; *Report on Senegal* by Jérôme Chenal and Yves Pedrazzini, http://www.migration-population.ch/sfm/publications (accessed on 19 May 2014).

The research plan was based on both a quantitative and qualitative approach to students from three West African universities, in Côte d'Ivoire (Abidjan), Niger (Niamey), and Senegal (Saint-Louis). These three contexts, despite differences between the countries, have many points in common. The research consisted of three successive empirical stages:

- A series of exploratory, semi-structured interviews with students and specialists in the three cities. This enabled an almost identical semi-standardised questionnaire to be developed for all three case studies.
- A questionnaire survey among more than 4,000 students. Respondents were selected on a random basis from various faculties on the three campuses.
- Around 50 semi-structured follow-up interviews with students to elaborate on specific survey results.

The exploratory interviews were thematic (attitudes to migration, local opportunities and alternatives, knowledge of various destinations, etc.), methodological (expected progression of survey), and organisational (local partners, authorisations, selection of locations, etc.). These questions were discussed with 18 experts—researchers, university staff, and representatives of the relevant authorities, NGOs, and international organisations—and with 29 students. Conducted by Swiss and/or local staff from October to December 2008, these interviews also shed light on the situation of each university and on the numbers of people who were studying there or who had emigrated, as well as on the characteristics of students. A series of exchange workshops and on-site work assignments allowed a common approach to be developed while taking specific local factors into account.

The quantitative data were gathered between 20 April and 15 May 2009, in direct collaboration between the project managers at the universities of Neuchâtel and Lausanne (Switzerland) and the research teams at the three West African universities. Despite a number of setbacks including a strike at Gaston Berger University, Saint-Louis, all the surveys were carried out in favourable conditions and drew considerable interest from respondents. This undoubtedly helped to increase the reliability of responses. There were relatively few refusals to participate—the response rate was 90 per cent in Niger and Senegal, and 47 per cent in Côte d'Ivoire.[3] Generally speaking, the profile

---

3 This difference may be explained by campus configurations. In Côte d'Ivoire, due to the size of the university, questionnaires were distributed at the front entrance of the campus, where there was a large flow of students. Many students chose not to respond due to a lack of time.

of students who responded to the questionnaire matched that of the student population as a whole in terms of age, gender, and faculties or branches of study, etc.[4] In Saint-Louis, a small minority of students expressed concern regarding the anonymity of the results, but the follow-up interviews and discussions with students show that, on the whole, they had responded sincerely and the results were highly reliable.

The results were taken from a total of 4,106 valid questionnaires.[5] In order to gauge the individual impact of the various explanatory factors identified in our system of hypotheses, we used logistic regressions to explain a binary variable, 'migration intention', which is defined below. This is a multivariate analysis because it simultaneously considers all potential explanatory variables. For example, it allows us to determine, *ceteris paribus* (i.e. same gender, same age, etc.), whether people who judge their financial means to be insufficient express a stronger intention to leave their country. It also allows us to determine the extent to which financial considerations play a role in shaping migration intention.[6]

Once questionnaire responses had been fully analysed, a total of 47 follow-up interviews were held with students of various disciplines to discuss the results. Conducted between February and July 2010, this third stage of the study allowed the quantitative results to be elaborated further and helped to clarify uncertainties. Although carried out slightly differently in each context,

---

In Senegal, where questionnaires were distributed at on-campus dormitories and where respondents were given the option of returning the questionnaire to interviewers on the following day, most students agreed to respond.

4 Just over a quarter of the respondents were female. While this matches the proportion of enrolments in Niger, female students were overrepresented among respondents in Senegal (38 per cent) and slightly underrepresented in Côte d'Ivoire. At each university, the distribution of studies represented by respondents was relatively close to the actual distribution of studies for the student body as a whole, reflecting a very wide range of disciplines—leaving medicine aside as it is only taught in Niamey. Most students held upper-secondary level qualifications (38 per cent) or a Bachelor's degree (52 per cent); only 10 per cent had a Master's degree. More Senegalese students (20 per cent) had already attained a Master's degree. Although the sample was widely representative of the student body, it seemed to contain a bias towards those in the early stages of their studies, which may be explained by their greater availability or presence on campus when the questionnaire was being distributed.

5 The largest sample, with 1,757 questionnaires, was from the biggest of the universities, the Université Félix Houphouët-Boigny in Abidjan. This was followed by the sample from the Abdou Moumouni University in Niamey (1,501 questionnaires), and the sample from the Gaston Berger University of Saint-Louis (848 questionnaires).

6 The coefficients for the different models used were explained in detail in the working paper that followed the study (Piguet, 2013b, 19–20).

the interviews mainly focussed on interpreting and verifying the available data with the help of students who were already far advanced in their studies in various disciplines and who were familiar with the situation at the university.

In the following paragraphs, we will briefly set out the contexts of the universities in the three countries studied (2). We will then cover the indicators used to analyse migration intentions and the main relevant results (3). The various explanatory factors behind these intentions and the choice of destinations will be discussed after this (4) before giving an assessment of the policy implications of our findings (5).

2 University Contexts

Although this research consists of three case studies, the aim is not to compare the countries concerned to each other. Most of the analysis relating to individual decision-making processes and attitudes towards migration apply to all those interviewed. However, specific features of the university settings in the three countries should be noted to better understand the situations and university careers of the students.

With around 54,000 students, the Université Félix Houphouët-Boigny (formerly the University of Cocody-Abidjan) is by far the largest of the three universities. Its student numbers have steadily increased, which presents challenges in terms of infrastructure and quality of teaching. Many students perceive it to be the 'university for the poor', since there are several private universities in Côte d'Ivoire that attract students who are able to pay their high registration fees. Foreigners and inhabitants of the north of the country are underrepresented in the student body for both political and economic reasons. It should also be noted that the deterioration in the political and economic situation in Côte d'Ivoire from 2002 onwards had repercussions in the university sector. University dormitories are full, which obliges many students to live in other parts of Abidjan. Only a small minority of those who enrol receive a state grant and when the survey was conducted fewer than half the students interviewed (44 per cent) said they were satisfied with the quality of teaching (compared with around 66 per cent in Niger and Senegal).

In Niger, few disciplines are taught in private universities, and Abdou Moumouni University in Niamey is the only public university in the country. It has 10,000 students, and enjoys a good reputation. Around a quarter of these students receive grants. Like in Abidjan, university accommodation is completely full, which forces some students to live on the outskirts of Niamey. Ranked as the world's poorest country in the Human Development Index of the United Nations Development Programme (UNDP), Niger has the lowest higher education attendance rates for the continent after Malawi (Findlay et al., 2012; Mounkaila et al., 2009). Unlike at the two other universities considered in this study, it is not possible to obtain a PhD or doctorate in Niger for most disciplines; students are therefore forced to go abroad to complete their education (Tabapssi, 2010).

With its 5,000 students, Gaston Berger University, Saint-Louis, Senegal, is considered one of the best in the country. Senegal has long played a pioneering role in establishing higher education in French-speaking sub-Saharan Africa. It also has several private universities, but Gaston Berger University holds second place after Dakar's Cheikh Anta Diop University in several international ranking lists. Since it was founded in 1990, Gaston Berger has operated a selective quota system, limiting entry to the best students in the country, many of whom benefit from a state grant (Goudiaby, 2009).

Student assessments of their own financial means tally with the economic situation of their respective universities and, more generally, their countries of residence. These indicators are less favourable for students from Côte d'Ivoire compared with those from Niger and even worse compared with those from Senegal.[7] The crisis that struck Côte d'Ivoire in 2009 should be borne in mind in this regard. Despite local conditions, the economic situation of students should not be conflated with that of other groups within the population. In the three countries studied, university students tend to be from a relatively privileged fringe of society, often from families within the political, economic, or intellectual elite of the middle classes.

Most students have a relatively damning opinion of study conditions in terms of resources (computers, textbooks, rooms, etc.) and, to some extent, the quality of teaching. These assessments are hardly surprising given the deterioration in the university situation as documented by specialists in the field (Khelfaoui, 2009), who also highlight significant political interference in academic affairs. This interference was bemoaned in comments from several students, many of whom, particularly in Côte d'Ivoire, have had whole years written off ('blank years') because of strikes or political developments.

Even if opinions differ between campuses, with students from Niger tending to be less critical, one is left with an image of general dissatisfaction with study conditions. To what extent can this be linked to the migration intentions of individuals? Do other factors come into play? It is precisely these questions that lie at the heart of our research.

---

7 Means at one's disposal (average), perception, and development of financial situation over previous five years.

3 Attitudes Towards Migration

When asked whether they would like to live abroad in the relatively near future either to work, to study, or for any other reason, around 38 per cent of students responded fairly categorically in the negative, although practically the same proportion of them had a 'strong desire' or 'very strong desire' to live in another country (Figure 9.1). In total, over 60 per cent of students were considering spending some time abroad. Unfortunately, we do not have comparable data for other student populations of a similar average age (24.5). For indicative purposes, one could cite the Eurobarometer survey that estimates that a little over half of Europeans aged between 15 and 35 are prepared to consider working in another European country (European Commission, 2011).

The vast majority of students who wanted to leave (83 per cent) also said that they had a specific migration plan in mind. However, since respondents tended to be in the early stages of their degree programmes, most (52 per cent) intended to migrate after they had obtained their next qualification or once their studies were complete. A non-negligible proportion (40 per cent) remained uncertain regarding the best time to leave. The varying stages of preparation no doubt account for the fact that only 27 per cent of respondents had already taken specific steps to implement a migration plan, even if it was

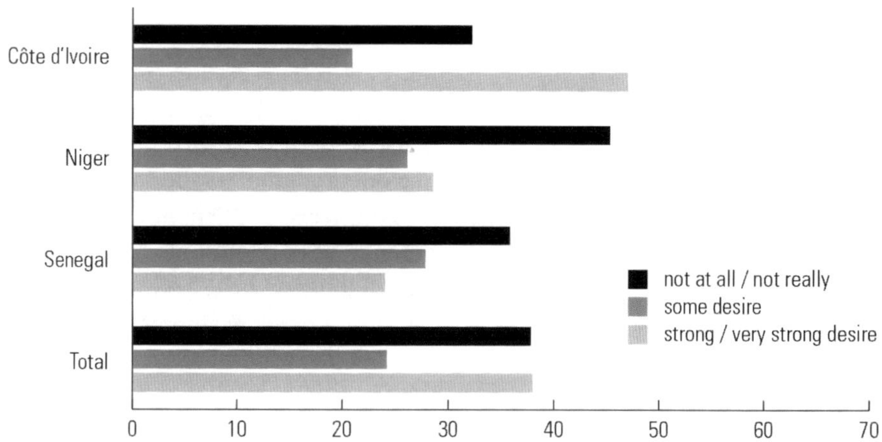

FIGURE 9.1 *Desire among students to live abroad, by country.*
Note: Students responded to the following question—'If you had the chance, would you want to live abroad in the relatively near future?'
SOURCE: AUTHORS.

only to consult the Internet[8] or to seek information from an embassy. When such measures prove unsuccessful, they can result in a student abandoning the idea of leaving: 23 per cent of respondents who had already taken such a step no longer wished, at the time of the survey, to live abroad. As other researchers have pointed out (Armitage and Conner, 2001; Lu, 1999; van Dalen et al., 2005), there are multiple interdependencies between wanting to leave, having a specific plan, and actually implementing it. The personal interviews showed that a concrete migration plan is sometimes more of a reaction to the decisions of the people around students than the result of students' own desire to leave. The abandonment of such plans despite having already taken some steps may also be a response to administrative barriers, or it could reflect the dispelling of certain misconceptions.

In order to identify the determinant factors behind a relatively strong desire to migrate, a cumulative indicator comprised of three criteria was used: expressed desire to leave, the existence of a precise plan, and at least one step already taken towards implementation.[9] On this basis, the proportion of students declaring an intention to migrate falls to 17 per cent of respondents as a whole, albeit with marked differences between the three countries. The figure for Senegalese students is twice as high (32 per cent) as that of Côte d'Ivoire (16 per cent) and three times higher than that of Niger (11 per cent). The differences are accentuated even further in terms of concrete steps taken, these being more common in Senegal. At Gaston Berger University, competitions are arranged to award mobility scholarships to the best baccalaureate pupils as well as to students enrolled in the second and third cycle of university studies.[10] Magatte Fall (2010) described 'the recruitment of whole squads of successful candidates thanks to a system of grants for specialisation in specific fields'.

8 An information search of this sort might at first appear trivial, but the interviews put this into perspective: making the effort to carry out such a search already implies an intention to leave. First, students do not necessarily know how to get the information or what site to consult; second, reliable Internet access is far from guaranteed for all.

9 The decision to simplify the analysis by considering a binary choice was reinforced by results obtained from alternative models using either other binary re-coding or ordered multivariate variables (multinomial logistic regression). The gain in goodness of fit turned out to be negative or marginal, and the list of significantly correlated independent variables was shown to be relatively stable between models.

10 This opportunity to study abroad exists thanks to agreements signed within the framework of dynamic partnerships with organisations in countries such as France, the United States, Canada, and Japan.

Whereas, on the whole, there is only a marginal distinction between men and women in terms of their desire and firm intention to migrate, gender differences are of central importance in some contexts. A much higher proportion of Senegalese women intended to emigrate compared with their male compatriots (42 per cent as opposed to 27 per cent). The reverse was the case in Côte d'Ivoire (11 per cent compared with 17 per cent). In principle, patriarchal structures tend to encourage male emigration, although it is possible that the symbolic value of emigrating might prove more 'profitable' for women—and their families—by allowing them to overcome the specific difficulties that they encounter in the labour market. It emerged from the interviews that female students in Senegal were highly confident about their chances of securing high-level jobs following a period abroad. A number of examples of women securing managerial positions within public administration may have had a ripple effect. Other research suggests that female students tend to come from more privileged social backgrounds (Biraimah, 1987; Kunzler, 2008; Lebeau, 1997). For the upper-middle class, studying abroad could be a springboard and a way of overcoming certain barriers to women's social mobility in their countries of origin, barriers which the wealthiest people in society do not face.

A further element of the gender dimension arises from the fact that female students are more careful about ensuring that their university career does not come at the expense of family life. During personal interviews, several female respondents stressed that long courses of study were likely to reduce their chances of getting married. Beyond a certain age, being single is not an option that is freely tolerated in societies that favour family traditions. While the degree of importance accorded to family life over individual aspirations varies in the three countries considered, family life takes precedence in all cases.

The influence of family considerations in forming the intention to migrate has been confirmed by a series of other results. The desire to leave tends to diminish with age and following marriage, especially for women. The attitude of one's partner—or indeed, the impossibility of migrating as a couple or a family (Geddie, 2013)—seems to play a crucial role. More generally, multivariate analysis emphasises the decisive influence that family support exerts, in a broad sense, on the intention to leave. Whereas, in all countries, the family's support for emigration is marked (Figure 9.2), students who lack such support are far less likely to make concrete plans to leave. Along with networks of contacts abroad, family support is one of the most important factors determining the decisions to leave or stay for both men and women at the three universities.

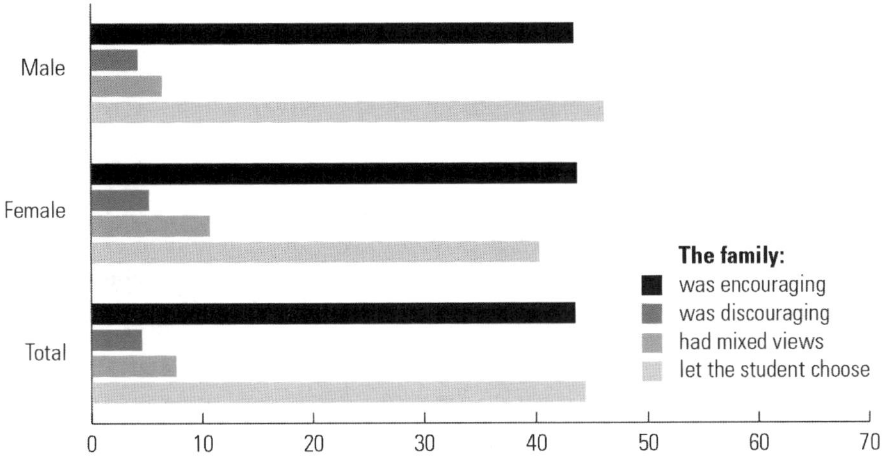

FIGURE 9.2 *Attitude of family to departure of student, by student's gender.*
Note: Students answered the following question—'Has your family encouraged or urged you to live or study abroad?' Those respondents who had not raised the matter with their families (30 per cent) were not included.
SOURCE: AUTHORS.

The importance of the family's role in the various types of migration and its impact at different stages of the migration process have been confirmed by many empirical and theoretical studies (De Jong, 2000; Harbinson, 1981; Palloni et al., 2001), including those in the new economics of migration (NEM) field. Among those students who had spoken with their families about the possibility of living abroad, 44 per cent were encouraged to do so, and a similar number reported that their family had left them free to choose. Only a small minority (5 per cent) had been dissuaded. However, Nigerien families, and in general the families of female students in all three countries, were more likely to have mixed views. This favourable inclination towards mobility is reinforced by the social prestige that university study abroad brings not only to the students themselves, but to their extended families as mentioned in qualitative interviews. Whereas the symbolic distinction of this sort of international experience is not unique to the African context, it is particularly significant with regard to upward social mobility in developing countries (Pinto, 2013).

Despite the numerous arguments in favour of migration, there is a fringe group comprising around one-fifth of the students interviewed who said that they were resolutely opposed to going abroad, with neither the inclination nor any plans to go away—and who had not taken any steps in this regard. Multivariate analysis shows that the likelihood of falling into this group increases if one is: a woman, older, has children, has confidence in the future of the country, and is satisfied with the resources available at the home university. A discouraging attitude on the part of family members is also influential in this regard.

These initial results allow us to construct a general outline of the factors that contribute to the migration intentions of students (Figure 9.3). They also reveal the coherent, considered nature of attitudes to migration and how they are affected by the level of satisfaction with the university and political climate. We will revisit these themes in the next section.

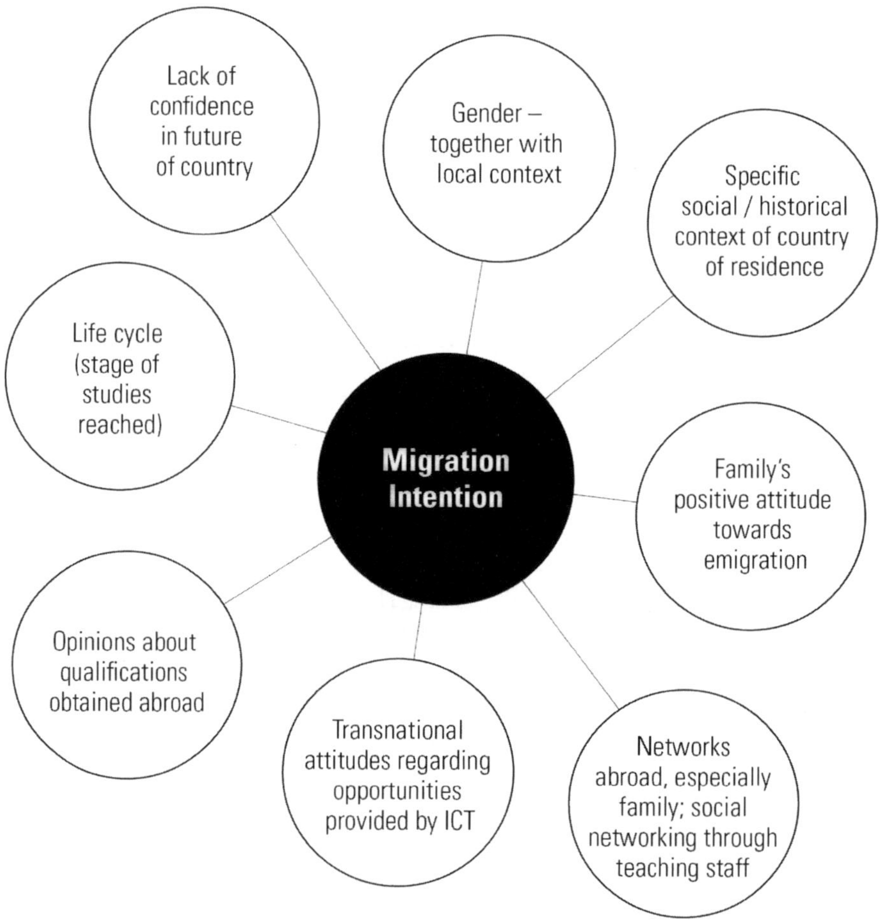

FIGURE 9.3 *General explanatory framework of students' migration intentions.*
SOURCE: AUTHORS.

4 Migration: Determinant Factors and Objectives

Contrary to prevailing views—which tend to skew policy and media debate in developed countries—potential African migrants do not behave reactively when it comes to migration; they adopt a reflective, forward-looking attitude. This is demonstrated by a proper weighing of their interests in terms of educational, professional, and life experience. This was clear from the results of our questionnaires, and was corroborated by the interviews. A large majority of those interviewed (84 per cent) only had a temporary stay outside their country in mind. Their goal was to complete their education and, if possible, obtain a foreign qualification, or just gain new life experience. This matches the main reason mentioned by European students (Terrier, 2009), and also Tanzanian students (Prinz, 2006), and has been confirmed by other studies (Flahaux et al., 2011). The desire to pursue studies was a very frequently mentioned motivation in Niger and Senegal—indicated by over two-thirds of respondents. Similarly, it is only following an initial period of education at home that migration plans become more concrete.

Students who already hold a Master's degree are generally more inclined to consider leaving than those who find themselves at a less advanced stage. As mentioned earlier, it is not always possible for students to take their studies to a higher level at a home institution. However, there are agreements on the recognition of qualifications between some faculties and universities in member states of the Organisation for Economic Co-operation and Development (OECD) and among African universities, sometimes accompanied by the opportunity to obtain a grant. A number of the students who took part in this study also explained that their professors maintained or had established privileged contacts with universities overseas, which could help with their enrolment (Babo, 2009). Generally, the argument put forward by neoclassical migration theories (Piguet, 2013a), which contend that the desire to migrate arises mostly from economic dissatisfaction, has not been confirmed. The most disadvantaged university students are fully aware of the fact that they lack the necessary means to go abroad. They also understand that living conditions are more favourable abroad, but this does not make them more inclined to leave. Similarly, while unsatisfactory study and living conditions are certainly fertile ground for migration plans to take root, they are only rarely the main trigger. A lack of confidence in the home country's political future, on the other hand, has a clear influence on the intention to leave. On the whole, students' intention to emigrate does not appear to be an aim in itself or a sudden imperative. Instead, it is pondered as a stage of their career, with the objective of improving their education or leveraging their studies to improve their employment prospects.

When it comes to the choice of destination countries, both the interviews and the questionnaire results show that students from Niger and Côte d'Ivoire more often consider migration within Africa (e.g. South Africa, Senegal, and Ghana) whereas Senegalese students look to destinations further afield. Generally speaking, only 11.3 per cent of students cited France (a former colonial power) as their preferred destination. France has been largely supplanted by Canada and the United States as the destination of choice. A wide range of countries was also mentioned, including some of the new hubs in the globalisation of knowledge such as South Africa, Saudi Arabia, and Japan (Figure 9.4) that offer attractive grants to African students, Saudi Arabia being especially keen to attract Muslim students.

Taking a closer look, student comments contain no shortage of arguments in favour of migration, mainly to the countries of the North. Aside from the more extensive educational opportunities, a large majority of respondents to the questionnaire felt that the quality of teaching was better outside their own countries, that a higher value was placed on competences, and also that those who have lived abroad receive more recognition once they return. Above all, most students (almost 80 per cent of respondents) consider that qualifications acquired abroad offer a distinct advantage both in terms of employment in the local labour market and for an academic career. This conviction is clearly confirmed by the relevant literature (Pinto, 2013; Prinz, 2006). The personal interviews also show that the marked interest in going to North America can be

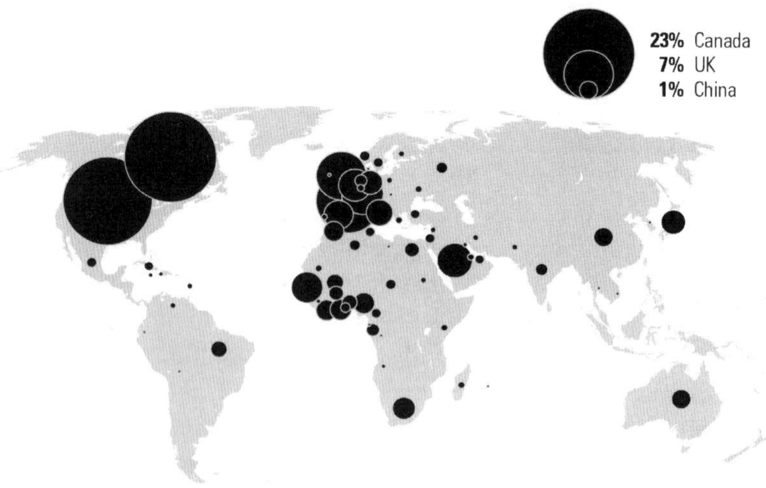

FIGURE 9.4 *Destinations of choice for students from West Africa.*
SOURCE: AUTHORS.

explained by a positive perception of an English-language education—English tends to be considered more as an opportunity than as a barrier—due to the simpler enrolment formalities and a less restrictive policy towards migrants than is considered to be the case in France and elsewhere in Europe.

Against this backdrop, investing in one's education abroad may be seen by potential migrants as a means of using the symbolic prestige of their course of study and the resultant degree to gain upward social mobility after completion of their studies (Waters, 2006). Thus, a class of local, foreign-educated elite develops in the country of origin. This is true for the public sector in particular, a throwback to the colonial period when native executives were educated in the *Grandes Écoles* of metropolitan France. In the private sector, these elites can contribute to the emergence of a transnational capitalist class (Findlay et al., 2012). Beyond considerations directly relating to the value of an academic degree, many students believe that the conditions for studying abroad, particularly in the countries of the North, are more satisfactory: better quality, delivery, and structure of teaching, and more advanced technologies. Students also feel that there are fewer 'disruptions', political interference, or 'deceit' within universities outside their home country. These considerations are certainly not without merit, given the shortage of resources and the lack of autonomy among the universities analysed. Following various structural adjustments, African higher education entered a critical phase in the 1980s. The problem of inadequate means, infrastructure, and human resources has grown even more acute now that African universities have to contend with burgeoning student populations resulting from demographic changes and rising school enrolment rates—albeit modest by international standards (Khelfaoui, 2009).

This starting position places African universities at a clear disadvantage in the globalised higher education market, which forms part of the global drive to recruit the best talents. Attendance at a university that is highly regarded in international rankings, along with transnational mobility, can confer a certain prestige to any student, irrespective of his or her country of residence. For students of West Africa, there is a further distinction, given the unequal progression of higher education institutions in developing countries compared to those in industrialised countries. This hiatus effectively encourages South-North—or North-North—mobility, which is hardly favourable for the development of African universities, cut off as they are from other social spaces and from the economic world, and being subject to political interference. The *Times Higher Education World University Rankings* only included two African universities, both in South Africa, among the world's top 300 universities in 2012. According to Hocine Khelfaoui (2009), the reforms stemming from the

Bologna process, which are essentially tailored to the needs of the European Union, only reinforce this unequal development. It is therefore hardly surprising that the reasons for the departure of staff and students—whether temporary or long term—are far from purely economic. It also explains why the rate of mobility abroad remains high, despite the admission restrictions put in place by countries of the North.

5 Policy Implications

One of the main findings from our research is that education-driven migration offers considerable potential for the furthering of development aims. The evidence suggests that people are highly motivated to acquire the best possible education and training. This will continue to fuel transnational mobility in sub-Saharan Africa provided that it is not constrained by 'migration fears'. Obtaining a foreign qualification is certainly a strategy for acquiring symbolic capital. At the same time, it can also contribute to upward social mobility, which helps countries of origin by way of knowledge transfer. Our results show that, on the whole, migration intentions continue to be temporary as long as institutions remain stable and at least a minimum level of personal development is assured. This observation puts fears of a brain drain into perspective and makes the suggestion of a true circulation of competences more plausible.

These observations should prompt a shift in political focus away from purely migration-based considerations towards more general objectives of cooperation and development. They also raise the issue of African participation in the new European and global geography of education (Charlier and Croché, 2009). They argue in favour of greater coherence between policy sectors in both the North and South in order, for example, to tackle the paradox of restrictive entry policies for African students on the one hand and efforts by development agencies to foster access to higher education in the South on the other; a stance that Switzerland has started to adopt with its 'whole-of-government' approach to dialogue on migration and development. Promoting the voluntary mobility of African students and, more generally, working together to improve university courses is a positive way of reconciling migration and development objectives. The students whom we encountered were highly in favour of cooperation programmes to improve education in their countries of origin and offer opportunities to pursue additional studies abroad. Such programmes could potentially be included in mobility or migration partnerships. Despite their stated intentions, such partnerships have thus far failed to include this dimension to any meaningful extent, as immigration issues are always given priority over development issues in policy agendas.

6 Conclusion

A quick interpretation of our results could be that a dichotomy exists between African migrants who risk their lives to cross the Mediterranean and the students who agreed to take part in our survey. Apart from a potential desire to leave their continent, these two categories of people seem to have very little in common, as illustrated by the answer that students gave to the question of whether they would be prepared to migrate illegally: only 6 per cent of the students said that they would. The unpredictable actions of young, irregular migrants seem to be diametrically opposed to the reasoned career plans made by university students. While there certainly are differences between these two categories of potential migrants (e.g. different profiles, socioeconomic background, and resources at their disposal, and risk-taking capacity), the sociological reality of irregular migration may not be as clear-cut as humanitarian and security rhetoric would have us believe. These young Africans, who make sporadic appearances in the media, are motivated by a profound desire to do something with their lives, to seek opportunities and to make a name for themselves. This desire is at least as strong as their wish to flee conflicts or poverty. In this, the aspirations of irregular migrants do not seem so different from those of students. However, it is the students that are more likely to migrate to Europe (MAFE Project, 2013). Studies that have closely examined the lives of irregular migrants, rather than limiting themselves to a few quotes from survivors, lend credence to the idea that most of them, far from being naive or ill informed, also make highly conscious decisions within the realm of what is possible for them. They do so even if they lack sufficient means or transnational networks to implement their plans legally (Alpes, 2012; Bredeloup and Pliez, 2006; Bredeloup, 2013).

These observations also allow us to re-examine another dichotomy, this time engendered by the specialist literature that all too often considers student mobility as fundamentally distinct from other forms of migration and as only responding to the imperatives of education and careers. This production-centred, 'non-family' vision is called into question by our results and by other recent research (Geddie, 2013; King and Raghuram, 2013), which underscores the importance of the role of the family, of transnational networks, and of partners in education-driven migration. It is therefore necessary to develop current theories further in order to better understand student mobility and certainly all forms of migration within the context of globalisation.

References

Alpes, M.J. (2012) 'Bushfalling at All Cost: The Economy of Migratory Knowledge in Anglophone Cameroon', *African Diaspora*, 5(1), pp. 90–115.

Armitage, C.J. and M. Conner (2001) 'Efficacy of the theory of planned behavior: A meta-analytic review', *British Journal of Social Psychology*, 40, pp. 471–499.

Babo, A. (2009) 'Quels partenariats scientifiques pour des universités africaines en crise? Le cas de la Côte d'Ivoire', in Droz, Y. and A. Mayor (eds.) *Partenariats scientifiques avec l'Afrique: réflexions critiques de Suisse et d'ailleurs* (Paris: Karthala), pp. 103–128.

Biraimah, K.L. (1987) 'Class, Gender and Life Chances: A Nigerian Case Study', *Comparative Education Revue*, 31(4), pp. 570–582.

Bredeloup, S. (2013) 'The Figure of the Adventurer as an African Migrant', *Journal of African Cultural Studies*, 25(2), pp. 170–182.

Bredeloup, S. and O. Pliez (2006) 'Migrations entre les deux rives du Sahara', *Autrepart*, 36, pp. 3–20.

Charlier, J.-E. and S. Croché (2009) 'Can the Bologna Process Make the Move Faster towards the Development of an International Space for Higher Education Where Africa Would Find Its Place?', *Revue de l'enseignement supérieur en Afrique*, 7(1–2), pp. 39–59.

Dalen, H.P. van, G. Groenewold and J.J. Schoorl (2005) 'Out of Africa: What Drives the Pressure to Emigrate?', *Journal of Population Economics*, 18(4), pp. 741–778.

De Jong, G.F. (2000) 'Expectations, Gender, and Norms in Migration Decision-Making', *Population Studies*, 54(3), pp. 307–319.

European Commission (2011) *Youth on the move: Analytical report*, Flash Eurobarometer Series 319b, http://ec.europa.eu/public_opinion/flash/fl_319b_en.pdf (accessed on 19 May 2014).

Fall, M. (2010) 'Migration des étudiants sénégalais', *Hommes et Migrations*, 1286–1287, pp. 222–233.

Fall, P.D. (2008) *Les migrations africaines vers l'Europe: de l'appel de main-d'œuvre aux migrations clandestines vers les îles Canaries*, text presented at the conference 'Migraciones internacionales e integración cultural en los espacios insulares: una perspectiva histórica', Universidad de La Laguna et Academia Canaria de la Historia, 2–4 June, Las Palmas de Gran Canaria.

Findlay, A.M., R. King, F.M. Smith, A. Geddes and R. Skeldon (2012) 'World Class? An Investigation of Globalisation, Difference and International Student Mobility', *Transactions of the Institute of British Geographers*, 37(1), pp. 118–131.

Flahaux, M.-L., C. Mezger and P. Sakho (2011) *La migration circulaire des Sénégalais*, CARIM-AS 2011/62, Robert Schuman Centre for Advanced Studies (San Domenico di Fiesole [FI]: European University Institute).

Geddie, K. (2013) 'The Transnational Ties That Bind: Relationship Considerations for Graduating International Science and Engineering Research Students', *Population, Space and Place*, 19(2), pp. 196–208.

Goudiaby, J.-A. (2009) 'Le Sénégal dans son appropriation de la Réforme LMD: déclinaison locale d'une réforme "globale"', *Revue de l'enseignement supérieur en Afrique*, 7(1–2), pp. 79–93.

Harbinson, S. (1981) 'Family Structure and Family Strategy in Migration Decision Making', in De Jong, G.F and R.W. Gardner (eds.), *Migration Decision Making: Multidisciplinary Approaches to Microlevel Studies in Developed and Developing Countries* (New York: Pergamon Press), pp. 225–251.

Khelfaoui, H. (2009) 'Le Processus de Bologne en Afrique: globalisation ou retour à la "situation coloniale"?', *Revue de l'enseignement supérieur en Afrique*, 7(1–2), pp. 1–20.

King, R. and P. Raghuram (2013) 'International Student Migration: Mapping the Field and New Research Agendas', *Population, Space and Place*, 19(2), pp. 127–137.

Kunzler, D. (2008) *L'éducation pour quelques-uns?: Enseignement et mobilité sociale en Afrique au temps de la privatisation: le cas du Bénin* (Paris: Editions L'Harmattan).

Lebeau, Y. (1997) 'The daughters of evil! Images de l'étudiante sur les campus nigérians', *Politique africaine*, 65, pp. 21–34.

Lu, M. (1999) 'Do People Move When They Say They Will? Inconsistencies in Individual Migration Behavior', *Population and Environment*, 20(5), pp. 467–488.

MAFE Project (2013) 'Factors of Migration between Africa and Europe: Assessing the Role of Education, Family and Policy', *MAFE Project Briefing Paper*, No. 3 (Paris: Institut national d'études démographiques).

Mounkaila, H., B. Amadou and F. Boyer (2009) 'Le Niger, espace d'émigration et de transit vers le sud et le nord du Sahara: rôle et comportements des acteurs, recompositions spatiales et transformations socio-économiques', *Document de synthèse des projets du programme FSP 2003–74: migrations internationales, recompositions territoriales et développement* (Paris: Institut de recherche pour le développement), pp. 109–120.

Ndione, B. (2007) 'Contexte local et migration: l'exemple des dynamiques migratoires internationales de quartiers dans la ville sénégalaise de Kaolack', *Revue européenne de démographie*, 25(3), pp. 325–354.

Palloni, A., et al. (2001) 'Social Capital and International Migration: A Test Using Information on Family Networks', *American Journal of Sociology*, 106(5), pp. 1262–1298.

Piguet, E. (2013a) 'Les théories des migrations: synthèse de la prise de décision individuelle', *Revue européenne des migrations internationales*, 29(3), pp. 141–161.

——— (2013b) *The Move to Move: What Motivates West African University Students to Consider Leaving Their Countries*, working paper (Geneva: Swiss Network for International Studies), http://www.snis.ch/system/files/movetomove_0.pdf (accessed on 3 April 2014).

Pinto, C. (2013) *Mobilité sociale et mobilité internationale d'étudiants étrangers: trajectoires de jeunes professionnels chiliens et colombiens à Paris, New York et Boston*, doctoral thesis, Université Paris-Est.

Prinz, V. (2006) *Imagine Migration: The Migration Process and Its Destination Europe in the Eyes of Tanzanian Students* (Vienna: Südwind-Verlag).

Tabapssi, T. (2010) *La migration hautement qualifiée au Niger*, CARIM-AS 2010/16, Robert Schuman Centre for Advanced Studies (San Domenico di Fiesole [FI]: European University Institute).

Terrier, E. (2009) 'Les migrations internationales pour études: facteurs de mobilité et inégalités Nord-Sud', *L'Information géographique*, 73(4), pp. 69–75.

van Dalen, H.P., G. Groenewold and J.J. Schoorl (2005) 'Out of Africa: What Drives the Pressure to Emigrate?', *Journal of Population Economy*, 18, pp. 741–778.

Waters, J.L. (2006) 'Geographies of Cultural Capital: Education, International Migration and Family Strategies between Hong Kong and Canada', *Transactions of the Institute of British Geographers*, 31(2), pp. 179–192.

CHAPTER 10

Boosting Higher Education in Africa through Shared Massive Open Online Courses (MOOCs)

Gérard Escher, Dimitrios Noukakis, and Patrick Aebischer

Abstract

Massive open online courses (MOOCs) have taken the world of higher education by storm. Ubiquitous use of tablets and smartphones, rapid increase of broadband penetration, and the coming-of-college-age of the 'digital native' generation have led many top universities to offer some of their courses to a wider audience online, free of charge. Millions of students are actively engaging. We present lessons learned after two years of experience with these new educational platforms and explore the opportunities and challenges of delivering MOOCs to students in Africa (and other developing regions) through a North-South partnership involving universities and teaching staff.

Acknowledgements

The authors would like to thank Patrick Jerman, Executive Director, and Pierre Dillenbourg, Academic Director of the Centre for Digital Education (CEDE) at *École polytechnique fédérale de Lausanne* (EPFL) for their helpful insights into the world of MOOCs and for providing EPFL data. We thank Sanna Fowler for help with editing the manuscript.

1 Introduction

Higher education in its present form is falling short of worldwide demand, currently estimated at 100 million potential students annually, primarily from emerging economies (Laurillard, 2014). By 2020 the population aged between 18 and 22 is expected to number 474 million (Lawton et al., 2013), with India and China accounting for 210 million of this cohort. Over the next decade, significant growth in enrolment in tertiary education is forecast,

 | DOI 10.1163/9789004281158_011

notably in China (37m), India (28m), the USA (20m), Brazil (9m), but also in Nigeria (1.4m), Turkey (0.7m) and Ethiopia (0.6m) (British Council, 2012). Given that only about 2 per cent of students in higher education globally study in countries other than their own (Lawton et al., 2014), current levels of student mobility across borders are not expected to meet the growing demand. Furthermore, building brick-and-mortar universities to satisfy demand is also likely to pose a major challenge for many countries. For instance, between 2009 and 2011 alone, China had to build 426 new higher education institutions, for a total of 2,049 universities. Access to higher education for all—in the words of former UK Prime Minister, Gordon Brown, 'the global ladder of opportunity for education'—is threatened by a huge increase in demand for higher education.

Globalisation of the education sector is being driven by the rapid spread of Internet access. As of 2013, 77 per cent of the industrialised world and 31 per cent of the global South had Internet access. The growth of mobile connectivity, particularly in the developing world, has brought online content and interaction to a global audience (UNESCO, 2013). By January 2014, the global population had risen to just over 7 billion, of whom 2.5 billion (35 per cent) were Internet users, and 1.9 billion were active social network users (26 per cent penetration). Across the world, current mobile subscription penetration is 93 per cent (with 6.6 billion mobile subscriptions) (We Are Social, 2014). Africa has an Internet penetration of 18 per cent, and a social network penetration of 7 per cent. However, mobile phone penetration is currently an impressive 67 per cent. The most important regional differences today are found in levels of broadband penetration: 55 per cent in Europe, 7 per cent in Africa (primarily mobile 'smartphone' broadband subscriptions), and 4 per cent in India (We Are Social, 2014).

Online education is driven by both student demographics and Internet penetration. Although 'distance learning' has been a feature of higher education since the 1960s (starting with the Open University in the UK), the path of online education is littered with corpses (Lawton and Katsomitros, 2012). For instance, investments of tens of millions of dollars were unable to prevent the collapse of NYOnline (New York University platform for continuing education) in 2001. Similarly, Fathom, a 2003 joint for-profit e-learning portal of Columbia University, the London School of Economics and others failed to survive, as did AllLearn, a not-for-profit collaboration between Yale, Oxford and Stanford, in 2006 (Haggard et al., 2013). Yet, despite these successive failures, MOOCs emerged.

2 Massive Open Online Courses

Two sets of factors have contributed to the rapid rise of MOOCs (Aebischer and Escher, 2013). First, technology has matured with widespread use of notebooks, tablets and smartphones, massive broadband penetration and easy cloud storage of data. Second, social factors too have been decisive: notably the coming-of-age of the 'digital native' generation that has now reached university age and with it the all-pervasive use of digital social networks for personal communication. Added to this, MOOCs saw the light of day within an entrepreneurial context, the 'Silicon Valley mentality'; finally, world-class universities were involved from the start. Unlike their online educational predecessors, the costs of MOOCs are borne not by students, but rather by institutions. MOOCs are open to everyone, they are synchronised—they follow a set timetable and deadlines, which enables social learning and interaction (crowd sourcing,[1] peer grading and discussion forums)—and are personalised (Aebischer and Escher, 2013).

Several world-class universities, including *École polytechnique fédérale de Lausanne* (EPFL), have recognised the benefits of MOOCs in terms of increased visibility and reputation and have rapidly begun to offer them. MOOCs shift the focus towards high-quality teaching, resulting in higher levels of motivation and ultimately enhanced teaching both on and off campus. MOOCs also enable outreach to partner institutions in Africa and elsewhere. MOOCs have truly taken on a life of their own: since September 2012, some 400,000 students have enrolled in the courses offered by EPFL.

'MOOCs hyped, humbled, but hardy' (Bacon, 2013), is an accurate description of the MOOCs phenomenon. Launched in April 2012, within just four months Coursera, the leading MOOCs platform, had over 1 million students. In 2013, this had risen to 5.2 million users. By February 2014, the three biggest MOOC providers had 7.1 million (Coursera), 2.2 million (edX) and 1.6 million (Udacity) students respectively.[2] The hype, however, has not gone unnoticed: only about 10 per cent of registrants complete a course. For this reason, perhaps, the number of courses and participating universities (numbers that are steadily

1 Crowdsourcing is the practice of obtaining services, goods, or content by soliciting contributions from a large group of people, and especially from an online community (see for instance Brabham, 2013).

2 The websites of the main MOOCs providers are https://www.coursera.org/, https://www.edx.org/ and https://www.udacity.com/ (accessed on 14 May 2014).

increasing) provides a better metric of the success of MOOCs than the number of registrants, which counts both one-time video-watchers and students who complete all exercises. As of February 2014, Coursera offered 603 courses from 108 universities, while edX offered 140 courses from 31 universities.

3 MOOCs Today

MOOCs have been scrutinised extensively (for a recent review of the literature, see Haggard et al., 2013). As early adopters of the platform, we at EPFL believe that 'MOOCs initiate a Copernican shift' (Pierre Dillenbourg,[3] personal communication, 2014). 'If students can watch the video of the course at their own pace before the exercise session, this session will progressively become the most important learning event.'

MOOCs were initially proposed as individualised learning tools, since each student could watch the videotaped courses and do the quizzes and exercises at leisure. Our students appreciate the quality of the courses and the flexibility to replay the course in their own time; however they have also stressed the importance of social interaction.

The motivations underlying a student's decision to take a MOOC are many and varied. About half of MOOC students surveyed reported that they had enrolled out of 'curiosity, just for fun', while 43.9 per cent said they had enrolled to 'gain skills to do my job better' (Christensen et al., 2013). Evidence from several universities suggests that well over 60 per cent of those who register for MOOCs already have university degrees (Christensen et al., 2013). At EPFL, the average age of MOOCs students was 26 years, 34 per cent had a Bachelor's degree, while 31 per cent had a Master's degree; about half of students wanted a certificate, and 80 per cent cited career advancement as a reason for enrolling in a MOOC (unpublished EPFL data).

Despite their popularity, MOOCs remain primarily the preserve of the privileged and are currently failing to reach the disadvantaged. A recent University of Pennsylvania survey of 35,000 students who had undertaken at least one assignment of a course showed that of participants from developing countries, 80 per cent already had a college degree (Emanuel, 2013). Based on Coursera numbers from April 2013, only 2 per cent of registrants were from Africa (UNESCO, 2013). Better access to technology globally will be necessary before

---

3 Academic director of the EPFL Centre for Digital Education and head of the CHILI (Computer-Human Interaction for Learning and Instruction Lab).

MOOCs can live up to their promise to reach underprivileged students, in and outside universities (Emanuel, 2013).

It has long been recognised (e.g. the Open University experience in UK) that students of distance-learning often struggle to complete a course if left to their own devices; MOOCs will have to pay close attention to this if they are to reach underprepared college students. Nevertheless, MOOCs have once again raised awareness among universities of the value of affordability and access, and have brought the conversation back to teaching and learning.

4 Future Directions

MOOCs allow faculty to 'flip the classroom', i.e. teach the usual *ex-cathedra* class online while concentrating on problems, exercises and discussions in class. This could conceivably be applied to universities across whole sectors (Lawton and Katsomitros, 2012): if introductory lectures were provided online *en masse* to a consortium of subscribing institutions, it would free up resources to focus on hands-on seminars and laboratory-based teaching and learning. In the future, MOOC technology could become widely used by faculty members to break down their existing residential courses into modules—the 'textbook function' of MOOCs. However, there is a risk that this 'unbundling' of courses could ultimately result in universities moving away from strict 3- or 4-year curricula (Harvard Magazine, 2013), with students building a personal education path by picking from a vast array of individual modules. The momentum created by MOOCs may also result in a new 'packaging': to date, MOOCs have been delivered as individual courses, however, they may in future aggregate into full and later, accredited programmes. For instance, Udacity has already created a USD 6,000 Master's degree in computer science in partnership with AT&T and Georgia Tech.[4] Finally, different universities using common lectures, complemented by seminars and exercises unique to each location, are certain to be part of the landscape in 2020 (Lawton et al., 2013); this will be of great relevance in the deployment of MOOCs in Africa since both partners from the North and the South will be able to contribute to the content of the course.

The number of MOOCs providers is likely to multiply. In addition to the 'Big Three', a number of providers or platforms have already been created. The most recent include *France Université Numérique* (FUN, financed by the French

4 On this partnership with Georgia Tech and AT&T, see the Udacity webpage 'Online Master of Science in Computer Science': https://www.udacity.com/georgia-tech (accessed on 7 May 2014).

Ministry of Education with EUR 20 million),[5] and the Queen Rania MOOC Portal of the Arab World, EDRAAK. Both FUN and EDRAAK are powered by the open edX platform. Others include FutureLearn (UK), Iversity (Germany), Miriade (Spain), Rwaq (Saudi Arabia) and Xuetang (China). Similarly, Pan European platforms have also been established (the OpenUpEd initiative), as have Francophone portals (Ocean).[6] Over the coming years, intense competition between different providers (or even countries) may drive the development of MOOCs, with important impacts on the MOOCs' economic model (will they remain cost-free to students?), university intellectual property (this is about student data and course content, with the interplay of the university, the professor and the MOOC provider).

Finally, while MOOCs have been developed with the typical 'can do' spirit of Silicon Valley, their sustainability will depend on the regulatory environment. In keeping with PCAST, the (US) President's Council of Advisers on Science and Technology (2013), we suggest three strategies: (1) let market forces decide which innovations in online teaching and learning are best; (2) encourage accrediting bodies to be flexible in response to educational innovation, and (3) support research and the sharing of results on effective teaching and learning.

5 Higher Education in Africa

Over a period of just 15 years, the number of higher education students in Africa increased by an average of 16 per cent per year, climbing from 2.7 million in 1991 to 9.3 million in 2006, while the level of public funding grew only at 6 per cent annually. Despite dramatic growth, only 6 per cent of college-age students in Africa are enrolled in higher education, compared to 20–40 per cent in most developing countries and 72 per cent in North America and Western Europe (World Bank, 2010).

A World Bank review of French-speaking Africa, meanwhile, suggests that expansion of higher education has been impressive, with enrolment rates doubling between 1991 and 2004 (Brossard and Foko, 2008). However, average higher education coverage remains low, as only an estimated 3 per cent of individuals in Francophone Africa currently have access to higher education

5 http://www.france-universite-numerique.fr/nouvelles-mesures-pour-developper-les-moocs.html (accessed on 14 May 2014).

6 See the websites of these platforms, amongst others, FUN: http://www.france-universite-numerique.fr/; EDRAAK: https://www.edraak.org/; FutureLearn: https://www.futurelearn.com/; OpenUpEd: http://www.openuped.eu/ (accessed on 7 May 2014).

(2008 figures). The World Bank study shows that public expenditure per student is high in most of the countries studied, with important social (student assistance services) expenditure, and high administrative costs. The student population in French-speaking Africa is expected to grow from 800,000 in 2004 to approximately 2 million in 2015, making the development of higher education financially unsustainable. In a sample containing 18 of the 21 countries in French-speaking Africa for which data are available, the funding gap for current expenditure on public higher education over the 2004–15 period was about USD 3.3 billion (in 2004 USD). Yet the expansion of higher education in Francophone Africa corresponds to rising social demand. The World Bank report suggests that this demand will continue to grow over the coming decade due to the expansion in secondary education, the increase in universal primary completion (UPC) rates, and high levels of private sector profitability—28 per cent for one year of higher studies in French-speaking Africa versus only 19 per cent worldwide (Brossard and Foko, 2008).

6 The Information and Communication Technologies Revolution in Africa

The International Telecommunication Union (ITU) estimates that 16 per cent of sub-Saharan Africans (about 140 million people) are using the Internet today and that only 6.7 per cent of households have access—mainly in urban centres. Even in Kenya, where an undersea cable from the United Arab Emirates (UAE) has been operating since 2009, 72 per cent of the population lack Internet access (yet only 11 per cent lack telephone access). Africa's unmet demand for telecoms, therefore, remains very high (Lawton and Burrows, 2013). Online and distance provision can reduce the cost of education while at the same time increasing access. Although there is limited ICT infrastructure in Africa, it is improving: the expanding undersea fibre optic cable network around the continent is rapidly increasing the number of living rooms from which MOOCs can be accessed (Lawton and Burrows, 2013).

As in many other developing countries, African states have relied heavily on foreign loans for their development, mainly from the International Monetary Fund (IMF) (Samoff and Caroll, 2003). As a result, in the 1980s most states adopted structural adjustment programmes and their agendas, with their emphasis on deregulation and privatisation of services to promote economic growth. Meanwhile, fiscal crises and budget constraints of the 1970s resulted in chronic underfunding of the public sector in general and the education sector in particular (Mkandawire, 2005). The resources available were targeted at the expansion of primary education, which was seen by the international development community as a better use of funds, yielding more beneficial returns for state development. Even the Poverty Reduction Strategy Papers (PRSP), which most African states have adopted in recent years, exclusively identify primary education as key to development (Samoff and Caroll, 2003). As a result, higher education has not been given priority in most states. According to David Bloom, 'the international development community has encouraged African governments' relative neglect of higher education. For example, from 1985 to 1989, 17 per cent of the World Bank's worldwide education-sector spending was on higher education. But from 1995 to 1999, the proportion allotted to higher education declined to just 7 per cent' (Bloom et al., 2006).

This failure to prioritise higher education in Africa has had a considerable impact on its current state. Lack of funds has directly affected institutional budgets, resulting in imposition of tuition fees and inadequate equipment (Varghese, 2004). As a result, only privileged groups are able to assume the financial burden and therefore benefit from higher education institutions, effectively limiting access to an exclusive section of the population. Another result of underfunding in higher education is the state of independent research and publication. Most institutions emphasise teaching and do not allocate sufficient resources to funding research (Varghese, 2004). This affects the academic discourse and the quality of lecturers. However, the neglect of educational services has also facilitated the emergence of private institutions to compensate for the absence of quality public education. This private sector is well funded and manages to provide an exclusive group with a good education (Mkandawire, 2005).

Private sector institutions charge higher tuition fees and are able to pay better salaries to their employees. Education therefore often becomes a two-speed system consisting of an underfunded, inadequate public sector on the one hand and a fragmented private sector of superior quality, on the other hand (Bloom et al., 2006).

7 MOOCs in Higher Education in Africa

In the developed world, MOOCs are expected to promote the idea of lifelong learning and encourage new interactive teaching methods and exchange of views among students (Lane, 2013). Whether MOOCs will revolutionise education entirely or turn out to be an improved kind of existing e-learning method remains to be seen; their potential for education in developing countries is in our view real, but must be carefully monitored. The most apparent advantage addresses the lack of resources at universities. Accommodating high-quality MOOCs from leading universities in the existing curricula of African institutions can greatly improve the quality of courses. Moreover, MOOCs not only educate students, but also help lecturers to update their knowledge (Liyanagunawardena et al., 2013). This is especially true in technical subjects such as engineering, where the lack of state-of-the-art equipment and highly skilled staff greatly affects the proficiency of students; here, MOOCs have the potential to improve higher education (World Bank, 2013). But MOOCs are educational tools created in a developed context. Their approach to teaching and learning might differ greatly from African forms of education, which are largely copied from older European models. As an example, *ex-cathedra* teaching still remains the dominant form of lecture in African universities. It remains to be seen how MOOCs, with their innovative, interactive structure will fit in the African context.

As MOOCs are accessible to anyone with a working Internet connection, they may reach a much greater pool of interested learners outside higher education institutions (Liyanagunawardena et al., 2013). MOOCs have the potential to overcome the financial and infrastructural barriers that deny many people access to higher education. However, there are serious questions about the implementation of MOOCs in developing countries. While MOOCs are theoretically available to everyone, they still require a certain level of familiarity with technology (Younous, 2012). This greatly limits the pool of potential users, as Internet connections and tech-savviness become rare as distance from urban areas increases (Liyanagunawardena et al., 2013).

For the African Virtual University (AVU),[7] the MOOC concept is appealing and has great potential. However, it is not without its limitations. In addition to technical challenges, MOOCs focus on courses, not on programmes and to date have no formal accreditation procedure. MOOCs should, according to AVU, morph into full and accredited massive open online programmes (MOOPs). AVU is currently conducting a feasibility study. MOOCs can offer a substitute for the textbook, especially for technical courses, and could therefore fit in with ongoing efforts by AVU to provide open education resources in which over 200 textbooks in English, French and Portuguese are available online free of charge.

7 Pan-African intergovernmental organisation, initially launched in Washington in 1997 as a World Bank project and later transferred to Kenya in 2002. Its mandate is to increase access to higher education and training through the use of information and communication technologies, see www.avu.org (accessed on 8 May 2014).

8 Ongoing MOOC Initiatives in Africa

A few projects have sought to implement MOOCs in Africa. The World Bank's New Economy Skills for Africa Program-Information and Communication Technologies (NESAP-ICT), launched in 2008, aims to improve the IT skills of Tanzanian graduates to meet the demand of emerging markets (World Bank, 2008). The NESAP-ICT programme offers a customised curriculum tailored to the needs of Tanzanian private sector employers. By combining existing courses and MOOCs from high-profile universities, NESAP-ICT guarantees the provision of top-quality education. Furthermore, private sector employers collaborate with the scheme to validate the relevance of its content as well as improve employment opportunities by offering internships to advanced students. In a way, the NESAP-ICT programme designs education according to the needs of the market and encourages closer collaboration between teaching institutions and employers.

The Kepler project in Rwanda, launched in 2013, takes an even more innovative approach. While pursuing similar goals to the NESAP-ICT programme, the Kepler scheme almost totally foregoes any kind of collaboration with existing educational institutions. Instead, the programme, built independently by a small community in Kigali, provides a campus-like environment in which students live together for the duration of the course and are assisted by qualified staff. Using MOOCs from leading universities, a customised degree course was developed to meet the needs of the Rwandan market (O'Neil, 2013). Just like the World Bank scheme, Kepler works in close consultation with the Rwandan private sector to identify the skills needed by graduates. During the four-year course, students have the opportunity to choose internships with potential employers and develop employment-specific skills (Kepler, 2013).

A few universities have embraced MOOCs' development as a way to enhance their own educational programmes, but also as a means to foster academic cooperation with other parts of the world and in particular with emerging economies. As an instigator of the RESCIF network,[8] EPFL was in an ideal position to launch a large-scale initiative on higher education in Africa and emerging economies. The programme dubbed 'MOOCs for Africa and future

8 RESCIF (*Réseau d'excellence des sciences de l'ingénieur de la Francophonie*) is a Francophone network of science and technology universities. See http://www.rescif.net (accessed on 7 May 2014).

emerging economies' was launched in spring 2013 and has since received support from the Swiss Agency for Development and Cooperation (SDC) as well as private donors.

In this programme, partners from the North develop MOOCs and work with faculty from African partners to integrate courses into local curricula. Alternatively, teaching staff from Northern and African universities work together to co-develop MOOCs. In both cases, faculty members from African universities spend a few weeks with their Northern counterparts to become acquainted with the technology, design the courses and subsequently record the lectures.

The EPFL-MOOCs collaboration in Africa seeks to create an alliance for higher education between institutions from the North and the South around a common MOOCs programme. In particular, it seeks to educate a generation of graduates so that they are able to make informed choices about technologies in Africa and emerging economies over the next decade; educate young professionals on technical disciplines in line with the needs of the local economy; work with universities from the South to build capacity to deliver up-to-date education; and reach a wider public, which traditionally does not have access to higher education courses (EPFL, 2012).

For MOOCs to reach their full potential in developing countries, several technological, cultural and administrative challenges will need to be addressed. One challenge rests with the fact that access to video-intensive online courses is dependent on IT hardware that comes with high acquisition costs. In addition, access to connected terminals is still limited in many universities, and insufficient connection bandwidth is frequent. These IT costs must be balanced with the expected economies of scale that MOOCs might bring to universities: no large lecture halls, lower course production costs from sharing among several partners. The often limited number of faculty members in African universities makes it difficult to allocate resources to new online education projects; MOOCs could be useful for building teaching capacity and increasing student numbers. Administrative hurdles, notably the necessary accreditation of courses at the national level and the validation of credits and universities, will hopefully be overcome by rectors and presidents of universities in the South, who see this project as an opportunity to build capacity and, at the same time, extend their academic ties with the North. Finally, even if access to courses from excellent universities is a powerful incentive for students, their acceptance of courses designed and delivered by instructors from the North may not be easy; the involvement of local teaching staff—something that is planned—will be important.

MOOCs could be targeted at all those citizens wishing to further educate themselves. Key stakeholders and groups targeted by the 'MOOCs in Africa' initiative might include, but are not limited to:

a) Universities: Institutions of higher education, and for EPFL and partners, particularly those using French as a teaching language.
b) Students: Students following undergraduate and graduate programmes at partner academic institutions.
c) Professionals: Those working in the secondary or tertiary sector, or as independents, wishing to acquire further knowledge and a certification of professional value (continuing technical education).
d) Citizens: All those wishing to gain advanced-level education for their own personal development, without necessarily seeking a professional certification.

Table 10.1 summarises the potential added value for the different categories of students enrolled in MOOCs.

TABLE 10.1 *Reaching African students and professionals who are using MOOCs*

Students	In university curriculum?	Rewards/Incentives	Expected outcome
Students with a first degree (BSc, MSc and Eng.) who could not pursue graduate studies	No	Access to scientific literature, internships in Western labs	Stimulate technology-oriented entrepreneurship
Enrolled undergraduate and graduate students	Yes	Better and more complete education	Diploma with greater prestige
Professionals seeking post-graduate or continuing education	Yes	Enhanced career prospects	Certificate, diploma with professional value

SOURCE: AUTHORS.

9 Potential Impacts of MOOCs in Africa

Universities in Africa and many emerging economies lack qualified instructors. Too often, teaching staff do not have PhDs. Offering well-structured online courses from leading academics (in the form of MOOCs) represents a unique opportunity to help local faculty update their courses and connect with researchers/instructors from the North. In addition, MOOCs will enable them to present students with courses that are on a par with those delivered by world-class universities.

There are not enough specialised courses at the Master and post-graduate levels that address technological, financial and cultural challenges in Africa, while existing ones are often outdated. By offering MOOCs co-developed by academics from the North and the South, EPFL aims to provide the necessary know-how and logistical support to design graduate courses of direct relevance to developing countries and to focus on themes that are in line with global issues (water, energy, health, urban planning) and that need to be addressed by the North and the South. Finally, MOOCs will provide a platform for long-term partnerships between academics from the North and the South.

'Massification' of higher education in emerging economies is a major issue. Booming demographics coupled with chronic underfunding create serious capacity problems. The advent of MOOCs is part of the solution as it has the potential to replace some of the *ex-cathedra* lectures and, as a consequence, increase the capacity of local instructors. Integrating MOOCs in the local curricula in emerging economies will, on the one hand, increase the teaching capacity of local universities, while freeing up local instructors for more and better face-to-face interactions with the students; on the other hand, it will avoid duplicating courses and the necessity to build real-estate capacity (large lecture halls), especially for undergraduate courses (1st and 2nd year) in basic, natural and computer sciences.

French-speaking MOOCs have the potential to reach a large population. As of 2010, 180 million people used French to communicate or as a teaching language; of these, over 115 million were in Africa. The number of universities using French (fully or partially) as a medium of instruction in Africa is estimated to be about 269 (the *Agence universitaire de la Francophonie* (AUF), the higher education and research network of Francophone universities, has 782 members). Among the RESCIF network, eight universities from developing countries represent a community of 72,000 students and 5,500 academic staff, while those from developed countries represent 71,000 students and 8,500 academic staff.[9] In most emerging economies, access to graduate education is restricted to the privileged few. Options for access to quality courses are rather limited and often include a long stay in the North. Some students from French-speaking Africa typically undertake graduate studies in France, Belgium or Canada, something that is not possible for many. As a result, there is a wide base of bright graduates (mainly Bachelors) who have entered professional life and for whom formal continuing education is either unaffordable or inaccessible. MOOCs represent a real opportunity for all those who have the educational background and intellect and are looking to further educate themselves (self-learning approach). For this to happen in Africa several challenges need to be overcome: first, improving Internet connectivity (access and bandwidth) in households and through wireless devices (3G and 4G); second, reducing costs of IT hardware (desktops, laptops, tablets) by favouring parallel imports to Africa so as to shake up the existing cartels that artificially inflate prices.

10 MOOCs as Instruments of Cooperation and Coordination

We have made use of the existence of the RESCIF network to develop and distribute MOOCs. In this model, universities from developed countries of the network, including EPFL, take the lead in developing a series of state-of-the-art undergraduate MOOCs in French, and help faculty from the South integrate them into local curricula. They also liaise with Southern partners to co-develop specialised courses for graduate or continuing education. In turn, universities in the network from developing countries take actions to optimise the dissemination of the MOOCs across their campuses, integrate MOOCs—in their original form, or adapted—into their curricula, and participate in the co-development of specialised courses and their local promotion.

Managing such a large-scale project within a network of 14 universities and several external partners requires tight coordination. Table 10.2 lists the internal and external stakeholders identified thus far and their fields of interest/action.

11 EPFL and MOOCs in Africa

Since the launch of the 'MOOCs for Africa and future emerging economies' initiative in Spring 2013, several milestones have been reached, and most importantly, several key stakeholders have confirmed their support by committing

9 See http://rescif.org (accessed on 7 May 2014).

TABLE 10.2 *Internal and external stakeholders of a MOOCs programme*

Stakeholders	Interest/Action	Project outcome
University management	Project promotion Provision of HR and funds Academic planning	MOOCs implemented as part of the educational offer
Faculty members	Development and use of MOOCs	High-quality educational content as MOOCs
Students	Use of MOOCs Feedback on educational experience	Improvement of skills and competencies
Ministries of Education Quality assurance and accreditation agencies	Legal and regulatory framework for the integration of MOOCs	MOOCs adopted as part of the instruction medium in HE
International funding and aid agencies International and regional academic networks	Financial and logistical support for the dissemination of MOOCs at the local level	Funding Internet access points Synergies and integration with complementary actions
Private and institutional donors	Financial support for the development and dissemination of MOOCs	Funding Promotion of the concept
NGOs with strong presence in Africa	Lobby telecom operators and IT hardware distributors	Access to high bandwidth fixed and mobile Internet Access to low-cost IT hardware
Telecom operators IT hardware distributors	Association with a high visibility, high impact project	Branding Marketing action User data
Citizens	Access to further/continuing education	Competencies with professional value

SOURCE: AUTHORS.

either financial, human or material resources. Early results are encouraging. In 2013, 8,573 African participants took part in six French-language MOOCs and while seven English-language MOOCs attracted 4,500 participants. Among these 13,073 participants, 22 per cent were active participants (who submitted assignments), 53 per cent were visitors (who watched videos) and 25 per cent were inactive.

Morocco is the country in Africa that features most connections to EPFL MOOCs (N=3,705 participants). In West, North and Middle Africa (N=11,325), most participants take French-language courses. In south and East Africa (N=1,748) participants follow English-language courses (see Figure 10.1). Since September 2013, five MOOCs produced by EPFL and delivered in French via Coursera have been followed and documented by African universities; three of those, *Initiation à la programmation JAVA, Comprendre les microcontrôleurs*

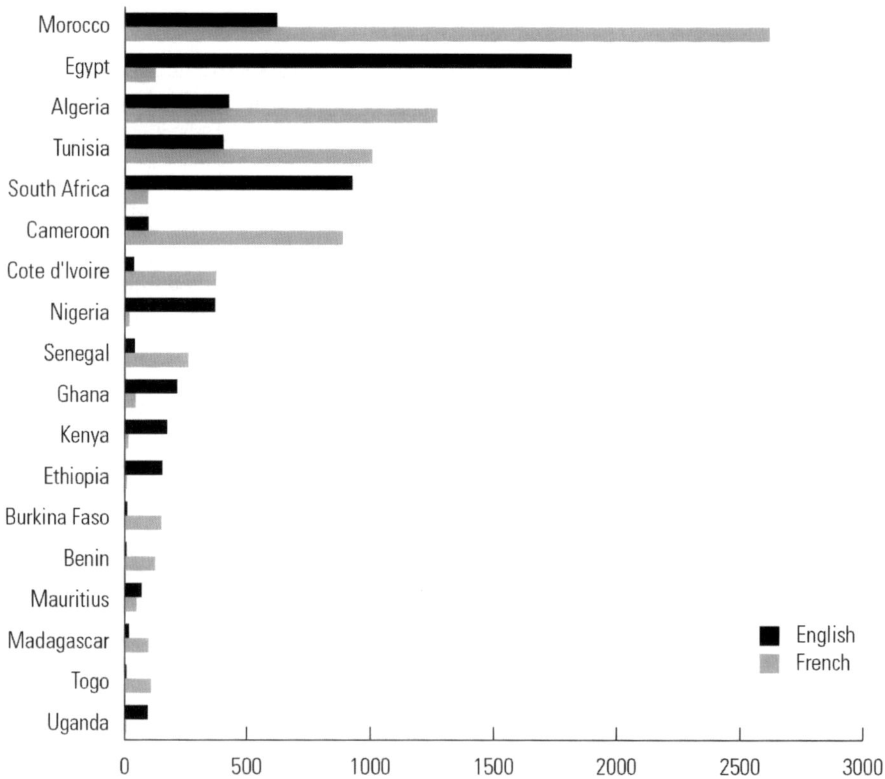

FIGURE 10.1 *Geographical distribution of MOOCs participants from African countries, by language of instruction.*
Note: Offering teaching in French has a positive impact on the number of participants in many countries of Francophone Africa.
SOURCE: AUTHORS.

and *La ville africaine: de la planification stratégique à l'aménagement urbain*, were integrated into local curricula, designed to run with a network of local correspondents and involving hands-on laboratories and fieldwork. The first educational outcomes are currently being analysed.

12 Conclusion

Science Policy Aspects: MOOCs are considered a significant lever for development by many nations. EPFL has teamed up with the Swiss Agency for Development and Cooperation (SDC); similarly, Coursera is teaming up with the US State Department to set up 'learning hubs' in developing countries to accompany the use of MOOCs. Recently the US State Department declared MOOCs to be a service and banned students from countries under economic sanctions (Iran, Cuba, Sudan) from Coursera. These difficulties paradoxically pave the way for European platforms unhindered by these political considerations.

More and better research is needed: MOOCs are clearly in their infancy. While we are witnessing a non-reversible evolution of educational practices, we also know that the MOOC format will evolve; the name 'MOOC' may even disappear. The diversity of online education will inevitably be as broad as the diversity of education/training needs, and good study design is essential in this high-throughput education. There is no magic recipe for education; an ambitious educational project always encounters difficulties, which should not be a barrier to implementation.

The end of school? The radical intellectual Ivan Illich wrote in *Deschooling Society* (1971), 'A good educational system should have three purposes: it should provide all who want to learn with access to available resources at any time in their lives; empower all who want to share what they know to find those who want to learn it from them; and, finally, furnish all who want to present an issue to the public with the opportunity to make their challenge known.' MOOCs are getting close to this ideal of student empowerment. According to mathematician blogger Jo Boaler, 'A high-quality, innovative MOOC by someone who really knows what they are talking about is going to be better than low-quality face-to-face teaching' (Stanford, 2013). MOOCs will contribute to blurring the boundaries between universities and other units of knowledge dissemination, and will in the end shift the focus from institutions to a 'learning ecosystem' (Harvard Magazine, 2013). This 'global classroom' (Koller, 2013) will give people the opportunity to learn without limitations imposed by physical or socio-economic constraints; and will offer schools and instructors around the world the ability to transcend boundaries to bring high-quality education to their students.

References

Aebischer, P. and G. Escher (2013) 'Can the IT revolution lead to a rebirth of world-class European universities?' in Weber, L.E. and J.J. Duderstadt (eds.) *Preparing Universities for an Era of Change*, Glion Colloquium Series No. 8 (London: Economica).

Bacon, J. (2013) 'MOOCs: Hyped, Humbled, Hardy', *Bacon's Rebellion*, 11 December, http://www.baconsrebellion.com/2013/12/moocs-hyped-humbled-hardy.html (accessed on 2 February 2014).

Bloom, D., D. Canning and K. Chan (2006) *Higher Education and Economic Development in Africa* (Washington, D.C.: World Bank).

Brabham, D.C. (2013) *Crowdsourcing* (Cambridge: The MIT Press).

British Council (2012) *The Shape of Things to Come: Higher Education Global Trends and Emerging Opportunities to 2020*, http://www.britishcouncil.org/sites/britishcouncil.uk2/files/the_shape_of_things_to_come_2.pdf (accessed on 7 May 2014).

Brossard, M. and B. Foko (2008) *Costs and Financing of Higher Education in Francophone Africa* (Washington, D.C.: World Bank), https://openknowledge.worldbank.org/handle/10986/6449 (accessed on 7 May 2014).

Christensen, G., A. Steinmetz, B. Alcorn, A. Bennett, D. Woods and E.J. Emanuel (2013) *The MOOC Phenomenon: Who Takes Massive Open Online Courses and Why?* (Rochester, NY: Social Science Research Network), http://papers.ssrn.com/sol3/papers.cfm?abstract_id=2350964 (accessed on 15 May 2014).

École polytechnique fédérale de Lausanne (EPFL) (2012) *Cours massifs en ligne en Afrique et dans les futurs pays émergents*, Résumé du projet préparé en vue du Sommet de la Francophonie de Kinshasa par le Département fédéral suisse des affaires étrangères et l'EPFL (Lausanne: EPFL).

Emanuel, E.J. (2013) 'Online Education: MOOCs Taken by Educated Few', *Nature*, 503, p. 342, DOI: 10.1038/503342a.

Haggard, S., W. Lawton, A. Katsomitros, T. Gore and T. Inkelaar (2013) *The Maturing of the MOOC: Literature Review of Massive Open Online Courses and Other Forms of Online Distance Learning*, Report for the UK Department for Business, Innovation and Skills, BIS Research Paper, No. 130, http://www.obhe.ac.uk/documents/download?id=933 (accessed on 4 February 2014).

Harvard Magazine (2013) 'What Modularity Means for MOOCs', *Havard Magazine*, 12 May, http://harvardmagazine.com/2013/12/harvard-mit-online-education-views-changing (accessed on 10 February 2014).

Illich, I. (1971) *Deschooling Society* (New York: Harper & Row), http://www.davidtinapple.com/illich/1970_deschooling.htm (accessed on 9 February 2014).

Kelly, R. (2014) 'Inside the First Year Data from MITx and HarvardX', *Campus Technology*, 27 January, http://campustechnology.com/articles/2014/01/27/inside-the-first-year-data-from-mitx-and-harvardx.aspx (accessed on 12 February 2014).

Kepler (2013) *Project description*, http://static.squarespace.com/static/51efe601e4b0a8f058512075/t/51f6c1f2e4b0d96d011b07f2/1375126002526/Kepler%20project%20description.pdf (accessed on 16 May 2014).

Koller, D. (2013) 'How Online Education Can Create a "Global Classroom"', *CNN*, 21 June, http://edition.cnn.com/2013/06/21/business/opinion-koller-education-petersburg-forum/?hpt=hp_c5 (accessed on 12 May 2014).

Lane, A. (2013) 'The Potential of MOOCs to Widen Access to, and Success in, Higher Education Study', *The Open and Flexible Higher Education Conference 2013* (Paris: EADTU), pp. 189–203.

Laurillard, D. (2014) 'Five Myths about MOOCs', *Times Higher Education*, 16 January, http://www.timeshighereducation.co.uk/comment/opinion/five-myths-about-moocs/2010480.article (accessed on 31 January 2014).

Lawton, W., M. Ahmed, T. Angulo, A. Axel-Berg, A. Burrows and A. Katsomitros (2013) *Horizon Scanning: What Will Higher Education Look Like in 2020?*, Observatory on Borderless Higher Education Research Series, 12, http://www.lfhe.ac.uk/en/news/index.cfm/horizonscanning (accessed on 4 February 2014).

Lawton, W. and A. Burrows (2013) *Is There a Technical Fix for sub-Saharan Universities*, Observatory on Borderless Higher Education, http://www.obhe.ac.uk/newsletters/borderless_report_june_2013/is_there_a_technical_fix_for_subsaharan_universities (accessed 2 February 2014).

Lawton, W. and A. Katsomitros (2012) *MOOCs and Disruptive Innovation: The Challenge to HE Business Models*, Observatory on Borderless Education, http://www.obhe.ac.uk/documents/download?id=929 (accessed on 10 February 2014).

Liyanagunawardena, T., S. Williams and A. Adams (2013) 'The Impact and Reach of MOOCs: A Developing Countries' Perspective', *Elearning Papers* (*33*), pp. 1–8, http://centaur.reading.ac.uk/32452/1/In-depth_33_1.pdf (accessed on 1 February 2014).

Mkandawire, T. (2005) *Targeting and Universalism in Poverty Reduction* (Geneva: UNRISD).

O'Neil, M. (2013) 'Rwandan Degree Program Aims for a "University in a Box"', *The Chronicle of Higher Education*, 16 September, http://chronicle.com/article/Rwandan-Degree-Program-Aims/141631/ (accessed on 1 February 2014).

President's Council of Advisors on Science and Technology (PCAST) (2013) *Education Technology*, Letter to the President on recommendations related to technology in higher education, http://www.whitehouse.gov/sites/default/files/microsites/ostp/PCAST/pcast_edit_dec-2013.pdf (accessed on 10 February 2014).

Samoff, J. and B. Caroll (2003) *From Manpower Planning to the Knowledge Era: World Bank Policies on Higher Education in Africa*, Forum on Higher Education, Research and Knowledge, Division of Higher Education (Paris: UNESCO).

Stanford, P. (2013) 'University Education: Maturing of the MOOC?', *The Telegraph*, 2 November, http://www.telegraph.co.uk/education/universityeducation/10414989/University-education-maturing-of-the-Mooc.html (accessed on 12 February 2014).

UNESCO (2013) *Introduction to MOOCs: Avalanche, Illusion or Augmentation?* (Paris: UNESCO), http://iite.unesco.org/pics/publications/en/files/3214722.pdf (accessed on 31 January 2014).

Varghese, N.V. (2004) *Higher Education in Africa* (Paris: UNESCO – IIEP), www.unesco.org/iiep/PDF/pubs/PrivatHEAfr.pdf (accessed on 1 February 2014).

We Are Social (2014) *Global Digital Statistics 2014*, http://www.slideshare.net/wearesocialsg/social-digital-mobile-around-the-world-january-2014 (accessed on 4 February 2014).

World Bank (2013) *10 Principles to Consider When Introducing ICTs into Remote, Low-income Educational Environment* (Washington, D.C.: World Bank).

——— (2010) *Financing Higher Education in Africa* (Washington, D.C.: World Bank), DOI: 10.1596/978-0-8213-8334-6.

——— (2008) *New Economy Skills for Africa Program-Information and Communication Technologies* (Washington, D.C.: World Bank), http://web.worldbank.org/WBSITE/EXTERNAL/TOPICS/EXTEDUCATION/0,,contentMDK:22335863~menuPK:617610~pagePK:148956~piPK:216618~theSitePK:282386,00.html (accessed on 7 May 2014).

Younous, A. (2012) 'Online Education for Developing Contexts', *XRDS: Crossroads*, 19(2), pp. 27–29, DOI: 10.1145/2382856.2382868.

Index